Solo Training 2

*The martial artist's guide to building the core for
stronger, faster and more effective grappling,
kicking and punching.*

Solo Training 2

The martial artist's guide to building the core for stronger, faster and more effective grappling, kicking and punching.

by
Loren W. Christensen

Turtle Press   Hartford

To contact the author or to order additional copies of this book:

>Turtle Press
>P.O. Box 290206
>Wethersfield, CT 06129-0206
>1-880-77-TURTL

ISBN 1-880336-88-X
LCCN
Printed in the United States of America

10 9 8 7 6 5 4 3 2 1

Library of Congress Cataloguing in Publication Data
Christensen, Loren W.
Solo training 2 / by Loren W. Christensen.
    p. cm.
1. Martial arts--Training. I. Title: Solo training two. II. Title.
GV1102.7.T7C456 2005
796.8--dc22
                                        2005006277

Acknowledgements

To my parents: Lester and Frances Christensen

And to Lisa Place: Thanks for your support, encouragement and patience with me. I love you.

Many thanks to the photographers:

Lisa Place
Amy Christensen

And to the patient models:

Lisa Place
Amy Christensen
Mark Whited
Wim Demeere
Martina Sprague
Barry Eisler

Special thanks

To my warrior friends Wim Demeere and Martina Sprague who contributed their writing, photos and who were always there to share their expertise and experience. Thanks to Michael Healy for sharing his knowledge of physical therapy.

Contents

Section Two: Sharpening the Warrior's blade   149

Section 3: 15-, 20- and 35-minute workouts 291

Using This Book

Throughout *Solo Training 2*, you will find icons that highlight important sections:

 Sometimes you need to take extra care during your training. The caution symbol calls your attention to these places in the text.

 Get the most out of every workout by paying special attention to these workout tips.

 Advice you don't want to miss. Discovering the reasons behind the drills is just as important as doing the reps.

 Although this is designed to be a book about training alone, some drills can be done with a partner. When you see this symbol, call up a friend!

 Streamline your training for maximum impact with these expert training tips.

Introduction

I want to thank the many readers who bought *Solo Training* (also published by Turtle Press), my first book on training alone, and helped propel it to bestseller status for well over two years, and where it continues to reign at this writing. Also, many thanks for your nice emails and the positive reviews on a host of web sites. I'm especially thrilled when readers tell me that my training tips completely changed their workouts for the better, that the book helped them to overcome plateaus, and that it even helped them to win tournaments. I've had several police officers tell me that a technique or a fighting concept "saved my bacon." As a martial arts teacher and a writer it's wonderful to hear these things. It's especially interesting to hear about a reader's success in a tournament since most of my writing is on street oriented martial arts. I'm glad that they were able to modify the exercises and drills to fit their needs in the ring.

While I always give myself a thumbs-up in the mirror when I get positive feedback, I also pay attention to those readers who have complaints and suggestions. Sometimes someone will just make an observation, like the guy from Japan who said that he really liked Fighter's Fact Book and he especially liked that I "looked like an average guy who drinks beer and loves his kids." That was really a review! Well, I'm not much of a beer drinker but I do love my kids. I especially pay attention to reviews that have valid and constructive suggestions. It was because of those that I penned this second volume on solo training.

Lots of readers said they liked my easy and sometimes amusing writing style, so I've continued to use it. I use a lot of humor in my classes, finding that laughter relaxes students and helps them learn faster. Readers have also said that my books always contain tons of information, sometimes beyond what the book is about, and always more than the cost of the book. For me, this happens because one idea begets another and another, and so on. That is just the way it goes when studying the martial arts and when writing about it. I've done that in this book, too.

A few readers said that while they liked *Solo Training*, they thought the material was basic and aimed at colored belts. Well, I would not agree that the material is basic, but I would agree that it's not complex. That is because I don't believe in being complex when it comes to defending yourself. Fighting should be simple, especially self-defense.

I own a few martial arts videos and books that contain complicated and intricate offensive and defensive movements. Some of them are so complex that they are laugh-out-loud funny. My educated guess is that these authors have never applied these techniques when their heart beat was machine gunning at 175 to 200 beats a minute from a combined surge of fear and boiling adrenaline. At that level, untrained people fight with wild arm swings and bear hugs. Trained people, that is, people who have been trained to function in high-adrenaline situations, fall back on their basics – reverse punches, backfists, front kicks and roundhouse kicks. This is a truth I learned from personal experience during my 29 years living the warrior life in the trenches as a cop and soldier, and learning from a host of martial artists, soldiers, cops, warrior trainers and warrior scholars. Therefore, I only write about the simple stuff and how you can make it stronger, faster and more ferocious.

I have worked hard to make this second volume about training alone meet the suggestions offered by readers of *Solo Training*. Additionally, I have included new research and training ideas that when implemented into your workout regimen will take your fighting techniques and understanding of fighting concepts and fighting principles, to a new level.

I took my first lesson in the martial arts in the summer of 1965 and I've been at it ever since. As has everyone who has reached my age, I have had my share of ups and downs and gains and losses. Through it all the martial arts have remained a constant in my life. They were there for me when I needed help to survive many dangerous moments in Vietnam and they were there for me as a cop working the mean streets in a big city. They have been there to help me maintain my sanity when all about me was insane, and they have been a means to help me stay physically fit and healthy (unless you count all the sprains and breaks).

Although I've trained in many schools under many fantastic instructors, I have always liked training by myself: just me and the pleasant looking fellow in the mirror. Actually, there are always three other forces present when training alone, and they can be far tougher than even the biggest, meanest outlaw biker.

THE THREE CONFLICTS

In Japanese, the word *sanchin* means "three conflicts," specifically, the body, mind and spirit. Every time you train, you face a body that wants to snooze on the sofa, a mind that wants to vegetate in front of the television, and a spirit that wants to take the easy way. Facing these three conflicts is indeed tough, some days tougher than others. Learning to fight them, learning to control them, and learning to conquer them is part of what being a martial arts warrior is about.

Can you learn to confront these three conflicts in class working with your training partners? Yes. Can you also learn to do it training by yourself? Yes, and I venture to say that you learn to do it faster by yourself. When you're in class, you train with concerns about being a good training partner, obeying the instructor, following school rules, being forced to train under your ability or over your ability, and having to work on material that you don't want to work on.

While having to deal with these issues is part of facing the three conflicts, I believe the battle is of greater intensity when facing them alone, when the only one you have to answer to is you. *You* have to confront and conquer that tired or lazy body. *You* have to battle a mind that rationalizes, is often distracted, and that frequently lies to you. And *you* have to forge an iron-hard spirit that instills in you the strength and will to endure when those who are weaker crash and burn by the side of the path. Yes, you derive some motivation by seeing your friends in class and not wanting to displease your teacher. But your primary motivation is to build yourself to your physical and mental best as an outgrowth of facing and conquering the three conflicts: your mind, body and spirit.

I hope this book inspires you and guides you to do just that.

Section One

Building a powerful foundation

There are a number of reasons to train in the martial arts: the enjoyment of social interaction with others, to study an Asian culture, to participate in a unique form of exercise, and to be the best you can be as a competitor or as an expert in self-defense (and as one of my comical students offered, to be the best subway mugger you can be). While possessing a powerful foundation is important in all of these motivations, it's absolutely mandatory for competition and street survival.

For our purposes, the word "foundation" refers to a powerful system of abdominals, back, legs, arms, and joints that have been developed to their optimum strength, power, speed and health. You might be able to do well in local competition without these attributes, but their optimum development is paramount when fighting in the big leagues. And you might fare well in a shoving match with the local bully without them, but should you have to defend your life or the life of a loved one, your core foundation had better be in top condition.

You have heard it said many times that the martial arts is all about the basics; that when you fight for real you're going to rely on your basic stances, basic body movement, basic punching, and basic kicking because the street is no place for fancy-smancy techniques best left for a Jackie Chan movie. However, should you want to do flowery, fancy-smancy techniques in modern forms competition or to participate in fun, over-the-top demonstrations, your basics must be solid, too. But before you can build them to their optimum, you must have a rock-solid, powerful foundation.

Most martial arts schools don't provide sufficient time to do the essential exercises needed to create this mighty trunk from which everything branches. No problem because that is why solo training was invented. When you spend quality time away from class working on building a solid foundation, you will find your progress moving forward by leaps and bounds.

11 Ways to Develop
Powerful Fighting Abs

Let's move from what has been called "your greatest weapon," your mind, down to the center of your body, your midsection, and look at some tough and highly effective abdominal exercises. These aren't the usual crunches, but rather intense warrior exercises specifically chosen to develop abs that will dynamically assist in the delivery of fast and powerful kicks and punches, fast avoidance movements, power at your core for ground grappling, and speed to get back up in a quick hurry.

While these exercises will give you a powerful midsection, to get a showy six-pack, you have to reduce your body fat to a low level. To learn how to do that using an intelligent eating plan and your martial arts training get a copy of *The Fighter's Body* by Wim Demeere and me, available through Turtle Press. That said, know that working for a six-pack isn't as important as is ridding yourself of unnecessary fat. A fighting warrior shouldn't have excess. Sorry, there is no argument to that.

So are you ready for some gut pain? Let's get started.

Abs-a-fire

Caution

This exercise looks weird, feels weird, but it attacks the front, sides and back of your midsection in areas normally not hit by a single ab exercise. And as a free-of-charge bonus, it strengthens your knees, too. Warning: Don't do too many of these at first because you will wake up the next day coughing up chunks of your stomach. Okay, that won't happen, but you will wake up super sore. One set is plenty for the first week or so, then add a second set, and after a couple more weeks, add a third. Here is how you do the (cue up echo chamber) Abs-of-fire, fire, fire, fire.

• Grip a dumbbell with your right hand, 5 or 10 pounds is plenty at first, and stand up straight with your feet about shoulder width apart, the dumbbell down at your side.
• Bend your right knee and lift your right foot a few inches off the floor.
• Bend down to your left and touch the dumbbell to the outside of your left foot.
• Stand up and lift the dumbbell, with a slightly bent elbow, straight up, over, and behind your right shoulder, bending your knee as you twist to your right.
• Pause for a moment – your body should be leaning back 45 degrees with your arm and leg in alignment - then lower the dumbbell back to the outside of your left foot. Do 9 more reps.
• Then do 10 reps with the dumbbell in your left hand, touching it to the outside of your right foot, then lifting it back over your left shoulder.

Do 1 set of 10 reps on each side 2 times a week for the first week. If you feel like adding a second set on both sides the following week, do so. If one set is still tough, do it one more week and then see if you're ready to add a second set on the third week. There is no hurry to add. Don't listen to that nagging internal clock that thinks you have been doing one set for too long. Let your muscles develop at their pace and add additional sets only when your body tells you it's time.

HIGH REPS OR LOW REPS?

No, high reps aren't going to slim you down and no, slow reps with weight resistance aren't going to give you a thick waist. Both are good for your midsection and ultimately for your martial arts.

High reps attack your smaller, endurance-oriented, slow-twitch muscle fibers, and low reps with heavy resistance stimulate the fast-twitch muscle fibers.

Do both.

Training Tip

Praying Mantis

This is a tough exercise that not only targets your abs most acutely, but also strengthens your shoulders, lats and pelvic area, all critical to optimum martial arts performance.

- Kneel before a Swiss ball and place your forearms on top of it, your elbows pointed outward. Place the tops of your toes on the floor with your knees together. Keep your back straight.
- Roll the ball forward, without moving your feet, and allow your hips, upper body and arms to move forward with it.
- Roll as far as you can without your back sagging.
- Hold for 5 seconds to enjoy the pain.
- Slowly pull back to the starting position.

Do 1 set of 10 reps 2 times a week for 1 week. Add another set the second week and a third set the third or fourth week. Anytime you're not ready to add a set, don't, and don't fret about it. Allow your muscles time to strengthen before you add another set.

Deep contractions

Training Tip

Just because you're not bending, crunching and twisting doesn't always mean you're not working your gut. Here is an exercise where all you do is lay there, sort of. It attacks those deep abdominal muscles that help stabilize your hips and lower back for power kicks, punches and throws.

• Put on your favorite music CD and lie on the floor, knees bent and feet flat.
• Place both your palms on your stomach, your thumbs touching your upper abs and your fingers spread over your lower abs.
• Blow out all your air, pull in your stomach as far as you can, and hold for 10 seconds *as you continue to breathe.*

- **Important difference:** This exercise is typically done by blowing out the air in your lungs, sucking in your gut, and holding it in until you have to take a breath. This variation is more effective. You blow out your air, suck your gut way in, and then breathe normally while still holding in your stomach. The struggle to breathe while holding the contraction is what makes this variation so intense and effective.
- Relax and do another rep.

Do 1 set of 10 reps on each side two times a week for 1 week. Add a second set the second week and a third set the third or fourth week.

Caution

Since this is one that will sneak up on you and give you some serious soreness the next day, consider contracting your abs only 80 to 90 percent the first few workouts. After two or three weeks, kick it up to 100 percent contractions. Don't say I didn't warn you.

BEST CRUNCHES: FLOOR OR BALL?

Important

So what is the answer to the often debated question: Is it better to do crunches on a Swiss ball or on the floor?

According to a study done at the University of Waterloo in Ontario, Canada, the Swiss ball wins. They found that the rectus adominis, AKA, the six-pack muscles, worked over twice as hard on the ball, and the obliques (those muscles under your love handles) worked four times as hard.

So get on the ball.

Backfist crunches

Here is a 2-in-1 exercise that benefits your abs and your backfist strike. I've written in the past as to how you can increase the impact of your backfist by suddenly tensing your abdominals when your fist is about 12 inches from the bag. This is still true, and when done repetitiously the technique also serves as an excellent ab exercise. Actually, you get three benefits from this drill: You work on delivering a strong backfist, you work your stomach muscles by flexing them hard as you strike, and you learn how to coordinate contracting your powerful midsection with your blows.

- Begin in your on-guard position, hands up.
- Launch your backfist at the bag (it doesn't matter if you're close enough to hit it or you have to step in). About a foot or so from impact, crunch your abs hard. You want to actually sink your upper body into them a couple of inches.
- It might take a few reps to get the timing, but when it's there, you will appreciate a greater degree of impact on the bag as well as the positive impact on your abs.

Workout Tip

- **Tip:** To feel this even more, do two or three of the other stomach exercises in this chapter first, and then finish your session with backfist crunches. You will feel every backfist in your stomach muscles, which is good because that means you're on target.

Do 3 sets of 10 reps crunching your abs with each backfist.

Brace

This is an intense exercise that will have you trembling like an autumn leaf, which is okay since that makes you stronger, especially your abs, obliques and lower back. After a couple of sets – sets that consist of only 1 little rep – you will be convinced that your stomach is flatter and tighter. For sure you will know that it hurts.

Caution

Warning: If you have a bad lower back, do this for only 5 or 10 seconds per single rep and progress slowly with additional seconds over the weeks. If you experience a lot of pain in your lower back, delete this exercise from your regimen until it feels better.

- Get into a push-up position, resting on your forearms rather than your hands.
- This is key: Your body must be absolutely straight from your ankles to your shoulders because your abs won't benefit if you raise your back or butt.
- Tighten your abs to help hold your body straight and stiff.
- Hold for 20 seconds then relax by lowering your knees to the floor.

Braces are sneaky little critters that can leave you with a painful stomach. In just a few workouts, however, you will be ready to bump up the intensity. Here is a good way to add on to this popular exercise:

- Do 1 set of 1, 20-second rep, say, Monday and Thursday the first week. Always rest two days between workouts.
- The second week increase the time to 1, 40-second rep each ab day.
- The third week increase the time to 1, 60-second rep.
- If you want to add a second rep the fourth week, do the second one for 20 seconds and then increase the seconds progressively as you did with the first rep.
- If you do several sets of other ab exercises and finish with this one, 1 set of 1 rep will probably be plenty.

Side brace

Training Tip

This is a great ab exercise to strengthen the sides of your abdomen as well as your lower back, muscles that assist in fast avoidance movements, kicking, getting up from the ground, and a host of other fighting applications.

- Lie on your side with your elbow directly under your shoulder, your forearm pointing outward to balance you.
- Lift your body until your top hip is in perfect alignment with the rest of your body: chin tucked, head and spine in a straight line, your top leg on top of the other.
- Slowly lower your hip until it lightly touches the floor, and then go back up again.
- Hold the top position of each rep for 2 seconds.

Perform 1 set of 10 reps, then flip over to the other side and do 1 set of 10 reps. If these are new to you, stick with 1 set for a week or two, then add a second set of 10 reps.

Rolling jackknifes

The big difference between this exercise and braces is that this one is more dynamic, especially in the way your hips and upper thighs are drawn toward your abdomen, similar to when you chamber a front kick. It's a great exercise that involves several pertinent muscles for fighting.

Important

- Get in a push-up position with your hands in line with your shoulders, but slightly wider for support.
- Place your shins on top of a Swiss ball with your back flat and your body - from your shoulders to your ankles - absolutely straight.
- Using the power of your abs, hips and thighs, pull the ball toward your hands as you raise your hips as high as you can.
- Hold for 2 or 3 seconds and then lower your hips as you push the ball slowly away until your body is once again straight.

Do 1 set of 6 reps for the first week, add 2 reps the second week and 2 more reps the third. One set of 10 reps should be plenty when the exercise is done in conjunction with other ab work. If you really want to torture yourself, begin a second, 6-reps set the fourth week, progressing by 2 reps for the next 2 weeks.

A jackknife variation

Important

This variation also duplicates the chambering motion of a front kick as well as a front knee strike. So not only are you zapping your abs, you're stimulating the very muscles that add power and speed to these specific leg strikes. The last exercise, the rolling jackknives, is fairly static, but this variation is done nonstop in a rhythmic motion. Don't think about sets and reps; think in terms of time.

- Get in a push-up position with your hands in line with your shoulders, but slightly wider for support.
- Place the tops of your feet on top of a Swiss ball, keeping your back flat and your body straight from shoulders to ankles.
- Using the power of your abs, hips and thighs, contract your gut and pull the ball as close to your chest as possible.
- Pause, then roll the ball back to the starting position, again using the power of your ab muscles.

Depending on the condition of your abs, do these nonstop for 40 to 60 seconds. Depending on your strength and endurance, you might do 1 rep per second or 1 rep every 3 seconds. It's all good as long as you keep pumping in a smooth tempo.

Caution

MUSCLE SORENESS

I've been warning you about taking it easy with many of these exercises because they are different than the usual crunch motion that you might be used to. Since many of them require that you contract your abs differently and more intensely than how they contract with regular ab exercises, you will likely be sore. With your ab muscles nestled in the middle of your body, major soreness there can ruin your day.

Start out slowly and progress wisely.

PS 1: There are no supplements at this writing that help prevent muscle soreness.

PS 2: Anti-inflammatories might ease the pain, but they limit post-exercise muscle growth.

Everything in moderation, Grasshopper.

Old fashion sit-ups with resistance

This is a good power developer that hits the abs and the hip flexors. Since you're using resistance, you don't have to do many, and you only have to do them once or twice a week. If you do other ab exercises, do these only once a week.

- Sit on the floor with your knees bent and your feet pinned under something.
- Pick up a barbell bar and cradle it in the crooks of your arms. Choose a weight you can handle for 3 sets of 10 to 15 reps.
- Slowly lift your upper body until it's *nearly* vertical, almost straight up and down. By stopping short of vertical you keep continuous tension on your abs.
- Pause for a 3-count and then lower your upper body back to the floor. Don't crash down, but lower yourself to the floor with control.

Do 3 sets of 10-to 15 reps.

WHEN A HARD GUT ISN'T A GOOD THING

Do you know someone who has a beer gut and is always trying to convince people that it's muscle?

"Just feel it," they say. "It's hard as a rock."

Indeed it is, but the bad news is that a big, hard gut is actually reason for alarm. In fact, some experts in the medical field say it's more dangerous than high cholesterol and smoking.

A big, hard belly is the result of an accumulation of visceral fat packed between organs in the abdominal cavity, lard jammed in so tightly that the belly can't jiggle. The other kind of big belly, one that jiggles, is a result of subcutaneous fat located close to the surface of the skin. Both types are dangerous.

To get rid of that visceral fat, you need to drop 5 to 10 percent of your body weight. So if you weigh 200 pounds and you have such a belly, trim off 10 percent, 20 pounds, and see how you look and feel at 180. For sure your martial arts will improve.

Russian twists

Caution

These are a favorite among boxers who recognize the necessity of having powerful midsection muscles for greater punching speed and power. Like other exercises in this chapter, Russian twists can aggravate existing back problems. So if you have one, approach this cautiously. You can do them empty handed, while holding a towel or belt, or you can add resistance by holding a medicine ball or weights in each hand.

- Lay on the floor with your knees bent and your feet pinned under a stationary object.
- Extend your arms above you to a point slightly below your chin. Touch your hands palm to palm or, if your ab muscles are especially strong, hold a single weight - 5 to 25 pounds - with both

hands.

- Lift your upper body off the floor 12 or 15 inches. Your straight arms move with you so that they extend in front of you at an upward angle.

- Rotate your shoulders to the right side until your arms are pointing 90 degrees to your side. Hold your hips rigid so that all the twisting is happening in your waist. Don't snap your upper body to each side, but twist at a medium pace.

- Now rotate your shoulders to the left side until your arms are pointing 90 degrees to that side.

- Return your arms to straight ahead and lower yourself to the floor. All of that counts as one 1 rep.

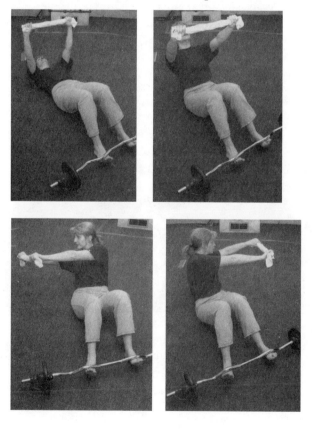

Do 2 sets of 20 reps, 10 to each side.

Arm-stretched, weighted sit-up

Caution

This works the entire midsection, strengthening all the muscles needed for fast body evasion, for whipping out hard kicks, and for driving in powerful punches. Know that this exercise requires strength. If your abs are weak, do this one first without resistance, or hold off doing it until you have built some power from the other exercises listed in this chapter. It's better to have enough strength to do the move properly than struggle awkwardly and hurt something.

- Lie on your back on a Swiss ball with your arms stretched out behind you and level with your upper body. Hold a weight in your hands.
- Lift your head, shoulders, arms, and upper body as one unit until you're sitting all the way upright.
- Pause for a couple of seconds and then descend slowly back to the starting position.

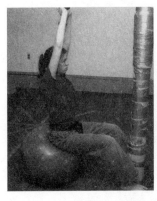

Workout Tip

Don't think about sets or reps, but think in terms of time. Depending on the condition of your abs, do these nonstop for 40 to 60 seconds. You might do 1 rep per second or 1 rep every 3 seconds. It's all good as long as you keep pumping in a smooth tempo.

Many of the ab exercises in this chapter are quite tough. Do they hurt? Yes. Will you develop a powerful midsection from them? Yes. Will that improve the overall quality of your martial arts techniques? YES.

Remember, while your ab muscles don't have to be ripped into a finely etched six-pack for the martial arts, they have to be strong. Like most people my abs fluctuate in their appearance. Sometimes if the bathroom light is juuust right, I can see the beginnings of a six-pack on my midsection. Other times – right after a vacation, right after the holidays, or right after a weekend chocolate binge – my gut begins to look like the Pillsbury Doughboy's. But no matter how it looks, it's always strong, because I stay consistent with the ab work.

So am I saying it's okay to look like the Pillsbury Dough-boy? No. I'm saying that it's okay to be human and relax a little and enjoy good chow from time to time. But stay consistent with your ab training as you do. Then when the fun time is over, trim off the extra weight so that you enjoy better mobility, better endurance, better health and a better appearance. In the end, you will have a strong gut no matter how it looks.

.

2

16 Innovative Push-Ups and 3 Ways to Bench Press

Push-ups. You love 'em and you hate 'em. Though you've been doing them forever, maybe you're not sure if they are doing anything for you. You can knock out 50 in a minute, but still your arms are the same size they were when you had to struggle to do 15. So what does this mean? Are push-ups doing anything for you? And most importantly, are they good for your martial arts?

The short answer: Yes. Now for the long answer.

YOU GOT TO BE CONSISTENT

Too many fighters do push-ups sporadically: They do them just one day this week in a burst of 50 reps, but then next week they do them every day for 20 reps. Not good. This does not progress make.

Push-ups are like any exercise in that they need to be done systematically, 2 to 3 times a week in sets and reps. Do them erratically and you stagnate. But do them consistently and progressively every week for three months and your punches and grappling power will take a giant leap forward.

Training Tip

Push-ups as punishment

Are there still instructors who punish their students for mistakes, especially kids, by making them to do push-ups? What in the world is up with that? We don't want students to perceive exercise as a negative, as punishment. We want them to enjoy it so they grow stronger and healthier, and so that it becomes a life-long habit.

Use positive reinforcement to encourage students to improve. Don't punish them so that they are turned off by the very thing that will make them better.

I devoted a chapter in *Fighter's Fact Book* to push-ups, in which I list a dozen or more variations, so I'm not going to repeat any of that information here. Instead, I'm presenting 16 new and unique push-ups and variations that build strength, speed and explosiveness, while you're having fun doing them. Okay, they aren't that fun to do, but when done two or three times a week, every week, you will see amazing results. And that's fun.

Push-up and row

Important

There appears to be a growing trend in weight training today to work multiple muscle groups at the same time. Don't worry, dumbbell concentration curls, chest flies and other specific-target exercises aren't going away, but more and more athletes are discovering the benefits of exercise that works many muscles simultaneously. After all, in most if not all sports activities, martial arts included, there are always multiple muscles in play in even the most simplistic movement. Push-up and row works both your thrusting muscles and pulling muscles. This two-exercises-in-one movement stimulates your triceps, biceps, chest, shoulders, upper back, and even your abs. It also helps your coordination and balance.

Choose a pair of dumbbells heavy enough to give your back a workout when doing the rowing portion. However, if you normally use, say, 50-pound dumbbells, you might find that you have to reduce the weight due to the unique position in which you're rowing. Don't fret about it. By the time you're able to use your original poundage, you know you have gotten stronger.

You're going to assume the push-up position on the dumbbells so you need to consider the surface they are resting on. The argument for setting them on a bare floor is that their instability makes your muscles work doubly hard to keep the dumbbells from rolling. But you don't want the dumbbell to roll when you're leaning most of your weight on it and lifting the other one. Therefore, place the dumbbells on a rug. Or, use dumbbells that are hexagon shaped.

Caution

- Align the dumbbells directly under your shoulders, lower yourself between them, and thrust back up until your arms are straight.
- Lean your bodyweight onto your right arm and row the left dumbbell up your left side. Your butt will lift a little and that is okay.

- Lower the weight, shift your bodyweight to your left side and row the right dumbbell up your side.
- Lower it and congratulate yourself on doing 1 rep. Now do 9 more.

Do 1 or 2 sets of 10 reps. Remember, 1 push-up and one row with each arm counts as 1 rep.

Variations

- Do the reps s-l-o-w-l-y. Lower yourself at a 2-count – one thousand-one, one thousand-two - and then push-up at a 4-count. When rowing, do 2-counts on the lift and 4-counts on the lowering phase.

   • Do the reps explosively. Don't lockout your elbows. Lower yourself quickly and then ram yourself up hard and fast. Pull the weight up forcefully but lower it more slowly.

   • Do only the push-up portion of the exercise, but do it with the dumbbells on a hard floor so that you have to concentrate to keep the bells from rolling away from you.

Dumbbells and Swiss Ball push-ups

Caution

Leave those dumbbells where they are and go get your Swiss ball. Find a hardwood floor or cement floor you won't mind falling on face-first. Hopefully that won't happen, but for sure your muscles are going to be working overtime to prevent it, which is exactly what you want. Don't cheat: Use *round* dumbbells, not the hexagon ones (thought you were getting away with something, didn't you?).

   • Grip the dumbbell handles and assume a push-up position over them.
   • Place your feet and lower shins on the ball.
   • Keep your back straight as you lower yourself and press back up for 1 rep.

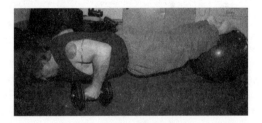

Between the ball and the dumbbells, your body is about as unstable as your weird uncle's mind. This is good because the instability recruits more muscle fibers in your chest, arms, shoulders and back, which is to say all of your punching muscles. The real good news is that you will see the fruits of your labor when you punch the heavy bag in a couple of months. Life is good, unless you do a hard kiss on the floor doing this exercise.

BUILD STRONGER BICEPS WITH PUSH-UPS?

It's true, according to Australian researchers who reviewed 13 studies that looked at how exercising one muscle affects its opposite muscle. They found that after 14 days of working one particular muscle, men and women increased strength in the opposite muscle by 8 percent. They don't know why it happens but it's good news for those times you tweak a muscle in training.

Say you hurt your biceps from tugging too hard on your opponent when grappling. The doctor and your common sense say to give the biceps a rest for a few weeks so you can recuperate. No sweat. Hit your triceps extra hard during this period with the many push-ups in this chapter so that by the time your biceps are healed, they will have gained 8 percent in strength - from doing nothing. Worse case scenario is that while you would normally lose strength in the injured muscles from lack of activity during the recuperation period, the stimulation they receive from your hard triceps work just might keep your biceps' strength at the level they were prior to the injury.

Do regular push-ups, but be ready for a new sensation and a good muscle pump.

Do 2 to 3 sets of 10 to 15 reps.

T push-up

Put away the round dumbbells and get out a set of hexagon ones, 5- or 10-pounders. I say again: *Use hexagon dumbbells*; you definitely don't want round ones rolling away on you when doing this one.

Training
Tip

This is another combination exercise where you attack two muscle groups, both of which are used in punching. The push-up portion develops the arm action of the punch and the twist develops your trunk area – abs, sides and lower back – muscles that add snap and whip to your hand techniques.

• Place the dumbbells shoulder-width apart on the floor and do a push-up.

• When your arms are straight, hold your right arm in a locked position as you lift your straight left arm out and up, rotating your body to the left, until the dumbbell is straight up over your shoulder and your body forms a T.

• Bring the dumbbell back to the floor, keeping your left arm straight all the way, and then do another push-up.

• When your arms are straight again, do the same motion with your right arm.

Do 2 sets of 8 to 10 reps on each side.

One-arm side push-up

I like this push-up because it really isolates the triceps muscle. Yes, this goes against what I said earlier about the value of exercises that work multiple muscles, but that isn't to say you should never isolate a muscle, especially one that is so instrumental in delivering powerful backfists. Additionally, one-arm side push-ups stimulate the muscles around your elbow joints that are so abused when executing arm techniques, especially snapping ones. Think of this as building protective armor around this all-important boney hinge.

• Lie on your right side and place your left palm on the floor in front of your shoulder.

• Wrap your right arm around your ribs so it doesn't get in the way or help you cheat.

- Push your upper body up with your left arm until your arm is straight.
- Then lower your upper body, but not all the way. Stop when your shoulder is about 1 or 2 inches from the floor.
- Push yourself back up again. By not letting your shoulder touch the floor, your triceps are under constant tension. Keep your body in a straight line with one leg on top of the other throughout the movement.

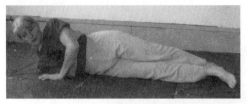

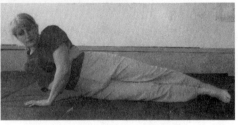

Do 1 to 2 sets of 10 to 15 reps.

Tip: If you have a light upper body and strong arms, consider doing this exercise last in your arm training. Your triceps, shoulders and chest will be pre-fatigued from the other triceps exercises, so this will be a nice finishing movement that isolates the triceps. If you have a fairly heavy upper body, you can do this exercise anywhere in your arm training because it will give you a tough workout.

Workout
Tip

Side-to-side push-ups

Maybe it's just me, but this is one of those variations where you go, "Doh! Why didn't I see this possibility before?" It's a nifty little variation of the classic push-up that puts a tremendous stress on only one arm at a time and gives you a dynamic sense of delivering a punch. When you can do 3 or 4 sets of 10 to 15 reps of these, you're on your way to possessing exceptional punching power. Then when you're able to do these in combination with some of the other more difficult variations noted in this chapter, your punching power will be progressing toward phenomenal.

- Assume a regular push-up position, hands under your shoulders or a tad wider, back straight and feet shoulder-width apart.
- Instead of lowering your upper body between your hands at an equal distance from each arm, lean over your right arm and lower yourself to your thumb.
- Push back up over that arm, then at the top shift over and above your left arm.
- Lower yourself to your left thumb and push back up.

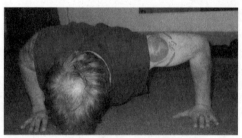

Do 1 to 3 sets of 10 to 15 minutes.

Variations:
- Do side-to-side push-ups with your feet on a Swiss Ball.
- Do side-by-side push-ups gripping hexagon dumbbells.

Bullet push-ups

Training Tip

It's the uniqueness of this exercise that builds strength, speed and endurance, all of which provides you with a well-rounded workout for your punch muscles.

- Drop into the push-up position, hands and feet shoulder-width apart or a tad wider.
- Lower yourself halfway and hold. This is your starting position.

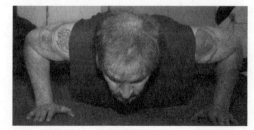

- Now, lower yourself 1 inch and then push back up 1 inch. That is all there is to it; it's all about 1 inch down and 1 inch up. Except that you pump out the reps fast, real fast. As fast as a speeding bullet.

    Do 3 sets of 10-15 reps

Variations:

- **Harder** From the push-up position, lower yourself until your chest is about 3 inches from the floor, then hold.
  - o Lower yourself 1 inch then press back up 1 inch.

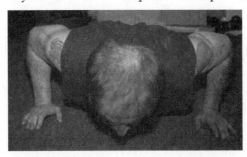

  - o Pump out the set as fast as you can, beginning at 3 inches from the floor, down to 2 inches from the floor then back to 3 inches from the floor. So its: 3-2-3-2-3-2.
  - o By using a position 3 inches up from the floor as your starting point, you place tremendous tension on your arms.

- **Easier** Lower yourself about 3 inches from the top of the push-up position, and hold. This is your starting position.
  - o Lower yourself 1 inch, to 4 inches from the top, then press up 1 inch.
  - o Now do the rest of the set as fast as a bullet: 3-4-3-4-3-4...
  - o This is easier because you're lowering yourself only a little from the top. Maybe use it as a beginner position or on days when you're tired.

Try alternating how you vary the sets, reps and positions each month. Remember, no matter the position, you only move 1 inch up and down.

Do this the first and third week:
Do 3 sets of 10 to 15 reps from the top position on Monday.

Do 3 sets of 10 to 15 reps from the middle on Wednesday.
Do 3 sets of 10 to 15 reps from the bottom range on Friday.

Do this the second and fourth week:
Do 1 set of 10 to 15 reps in all 3 ranges each time you train.
Since it's the easiest, do the top range last when your arms are the most fatigued.

"SURPRISE!" YOUR MUSCLES

Whenever you can make your muscles go, "What the heck is this?!" you're on your way to growth. Muscles adapt easily to a workout and "easy" isn't something you want in an exercise. You want to surprise them ever so often; some trainers say every third workout, others say every couple of weeks or so. Now, this doesn't mean you have to completely change your routine every three sessions. It's only necessary to make minor adjustments, such as changing the order of your exercises, set count, rep count, the poundage, or even the time of day you train. The idea is to keep your muscles surprised because it's the process of adapting that leads to growth.

Say you want to do "Push-up and row" and "One-arm side push-up" for one month.

Weeks one and three:
One-arm side push-up 3 sets of 10 reps
Push-up and row 3 sets of 10 reps

Weeks two and four:
Push-up and row 3 sets of 10 reps
One-arm side push-up 3 sets of 10 reps

Change to two new triceps exercises the next month and alternate as above.

Uneven push-ups

Speaking of surprising your muscles, uneven push-ups are a good alternative to regular ones. They feel weird because sometimes you can't quite decide which arm is doing the most work. Either way your punching muscles are surprised and stimulated. Also, the irregularity of it is closer to what you experience when doing mat work.

- Use a box, a punch pad, or a stair step for the high position of this push-up.
- Place one hand on the high object, the other on the floor and do your push-ups.
- Switch arms on the second set.

Do 2 to 4 sets of 10 to 15 reps.

Variation: As you lower your body, inhale and let your stomach relax. When you push back up exhale and suck in your stomach as far as you can. When you finish, you will have a nice upper arm pump and a tired and flat abdomen.

Bench press and push-ups superset for power

Here is a fantastic super-set of bench presses and push-ups. Not just any bench presses, heavy benches, and not just any push-ups, plyometric ones. Research has shown that some people develop tremendous power from a regimen of heavy benches followed by explosive push-ups. It's a tough session but you do it only once every two weeks.

Training Tip

- Warm-up with an easy set of benches and an easy set of regular push-ups.
- Load the bar with a weight that makes you struggle to squeeze out 8 reps.
- Rest no more than 10 to 15 seconds.
- Then drop to the floor and knock out 10 reps of non-stop plyometric push-ups.

o Lower your body then push up so forcefully that your hands lose contact with the floor.

o When you drop back down, allow your body to drop all the way to just barely touching the floor. That is one rep.

o Do all push-up reps nonstop.

- The benches and the push-ups make one super-set. Now rest for 60 seconds.
- Do another set of heavy benches for 8 hard reps.
- Rest no more than 10 to 15 seconds.
- Follow with 10 non-stop plyometric push-ups.

Two super-sets once every two weeks are plenty.

A great bench press variation

Important

I examined the benefits of benching in the books *Fighter's Fact Book, Solo Training* and *The Fighter's Body* so I'm not going to devote a chapter to it in this one. However, I do want to share this bench press variation that, like push-ups, builds your triceps and the many surrounding muscles that work together to make your punches powerful. I've been doing this one for a few months now and I've made huge progress in strength and punching power with it. I stole it from Ian Thorpe an Australian multiple-Olympic Gold winning swimmer who found that it helps his neuromuscular system recruit extra motor units in his pecs, shoulders and triceps to work as a team (in other words, his punching muscles).

Now, before you say, "Hey, he's a swimmer, not a fighter," give it a try. The movement is about as close to straight-line punching as you can get, and it will leave your punching muscles twitching and trembling.

To activate your fast-twitch muscle fibers, you need to go heavy, a poundage that lets you squeeze out 2 or 3 sets of 8 tough reps. First, let's look at the basic movement and then a variation.

- Grab a couple of dumbbells that weigh about 60 percent of what you normally use for dumbbell benches and lie on a bench, with your feet on the floor.
- Press both dumbbells overhead then lower the right one to your chest, while leaving the left one fully extended.
- Pump out seven more presses with your right arm without moving your straightened left.
- Thrust at a fairly fast pace, thinking "punch" on every rep, *never locking out your elbow joint.*
- Your right arm stays extended on the 8th rep, while your left arm punches out 8 reps.

Do 3 sets of 8 reps.

If you're an experienced lifter, feel free to change the weight for each new set. You can add weight or decrease it. Or you can use a medium weight on your first set, go heavy on your second, and return to medium on your 3rd. Let your experience be your guide but be sure to use a weight heavy enough to make you strain on the 8th reps.

Workout
Tip

All the muscles involved in extending your arm and holding the poundage in an isometric pose are taxed to the max. This helps develop your focusing power at the end of your punch, which is great for hitting the bag hard and great for developing a crisp snap to your punches in your forms. All the muscles in your thrusting arm – in particular your fast-twitch muscle fibers used for punching – are getting max taxed, too.

A variation
The benefit of this variation is that you can clearly mark your progress as you grow in strength. Say you usually use 50-pounders when doing flat dumbbell benches.

- Do a set as you usually do, then lower the dumbbells to the floor.
- Grab another pair that are 40 percent as heavy, a couple of 30 pounders.
- Push up the weight with your left arm and hold it up as you pump out 8 reps with your right.
- Hold your right extended on the 8th rep, and pump out 8 reps with your left.

That is one complete set. Do 2 sets.

- Once the 30s feel easy for you, maybe after 3 weeks of lifting 2 days a week, increase the weight of the one-arm presses to 35.
- When you can use 50-pound dumbbells for your two-arm sets *and* both sets of one-arm pressing, you're ready to add weight to your two-arm set.
- Move up to 55- or 60-pound dumbbells for your two-arm presses and do the one-arm presses with 50s. Monitor how the weight feels, and increase the poundage in the one-arm phase when you're ready.

Remember, this is about developing punching power and speed; it's not about seeing how much you can lift. Progress slowly and you stay injury free.

12 Ways to Develop Legs of Steel

Here is a bit of logic missed by a lot of fighters. With rare exception, a fighter who trains his legs with supplemental exercises is a stronger kicker and stronger grappler. Okay, nothing scholarly or terribly enlightening about that declaration, but again, many fighters haven't figured that out, or if they know it, they choose the easier path of simply not doing anything about it. If they aren't supplementing because their martial arts practice is just a fun recreation and a social outing for them, fine. But if they want to push themselves to progress, to be the best they can be, then supplement they must.

For a long time I didn't do supplemental exercises for my legs. I did tons of solo kicking drills along with my regular class training, thinking that the extra solo work was providing all that I needed, certainly more than what fighters who don't do the solo work get. While this belief has some validity, there was still more I could be doing, specifically, progressive exercises that build muscle. Not showy leg muscles to dazzle the beach crowd, but muscles that make the heavy bag buckle, that make a kick boxing partners' eyes tear up, and muscles that can squeeze the lunch out of a grappling partner. That kind of power comes from progressive exercises. Here are a few outstanding ones that helped me make huge gains in kicking power.

Squats, but not regular ones

Famed author Thomas Kurz – *Stretching Scientifically* and

several other books – wrote this in the July, 2002 issue of *Taekwondo Times* magazine:

Important

"People who can't put a barbell or a partner weighing at least as much as them on their shoulders and easily do a few squats are too weak to learn fighting techniques. The squat is a part of many fighting techniques. You squat to evade a punch or a high kick and to hit the opponent's knee or groin, to do a leg takedown, a shoulder throw, or a hip throw. When jumping, you squat (albeit not fully) on both legs or on one leg prior to takeoff. In the thrust front kick with the ball of the foot, the pattern of joint movements of the kicking leg is similar to that of the squat—simultaneous hip and knee extension, with ankle plantar flexion.

"Squats, in their various versions, are the most effective over-all strength exercises. Their benefits are not limited to developing lower body strength and endurance. Squats without additional resistance (weight), such as Hindu squats, strengthen knee ligaments, develop muscular endurance in the lower body, and improve lung function. Squats with weights increase muscle and bone mass of your whole body—not just of thighs and hips but of the trunk, chest, shoulders, and neck. This is because squats with weights put heavy stress on a majority of skeletal muscles and most of the bones. The greater muscle mass mobilized in an exercise, the greater are the releases of hormones promoting growth of muscles, bones, and other fibrous connective tissues (Conroy and Earle 1994; Kraemer 1994). Muscle mass grows much less in women who lift weights than in men, so ladies need not worry about becoming bulky."

While I can't say that I agree totally with Kurz when he says, "People who can't put a barbell or a partner weighing at least as much as them on their shoulders and easily do a few squats are too weak to learn fighting techniques," I do agree with all the rest. I've seen it in my progress and I've seen it happen to my students.

In *The Fighter's Body*, Belgium kick boxing champ Wim Demeere and I illustrate and talk about the importance of the basic barbell squat, so let's look at some other ways to incorporate the squatting motion, ways that are fun, different, and highly effective.

Sumo squats

I've written in other books about how the horse stance isn't as good of an exercise as it's cracked up to be. (Don't even get me ranting again on how some instructors use it as punishment, especially in their kids' classes. Refer to rant in the earlier sidebar "Push-ups as punishment." Don't do it!). The stationary horse is basically an isometric exercise and, as such, strengthens only in the one frozen position. To develop strength in another position, you have to sit static in it too. Wherever you want to be strong in your horse stance that is where you must sit isometrically. That hardly seems like the best use of your time.

Training Tip

Here is a simple alternative that not only saves you time but also develops functional strength and power in the full range of the horse stance. It helps your kicks and it provides you with tremendous strength for those deep horse stances in your forms. All that and it's fun to do, too. Since it looks like a sumo wrestling move, it's commonly called sumo squat.

- Place a dumbbell between your feet, a weight that allows you to do 8 to 10 reps.
- Assume a deep, wide horse stance over it while keeping your shins vertical.
- Squat low enough to pick up the end of the dumbbell with both hands.
- Straighten your back and push yourself up by straightening your legs.
- Lower yourself as far as you can go. It's important for the safety of your knees that they don't bend beyond your toes.

Do 2 to 3 sets of 8 to 10 reps. If you haven't squatted with weights in a while, you might want to do just one set for a couple weeks. Do too many of these at first and your inner thighs will be sore as they have never been before.

Hindu squats

These have been getting a lot of attention lately because they work, and work fast. I learned of them from several sources, many of whom referenced Matt Furey, a 1985 collegiate national wrestling champion and world Kung Fu Shuai-Chiao champion (Beijing, 1997). He swears by these squats and so do his many followers.

Some people say that Hindu's are easy on the knees when done right and others claim they actually help problem joints. Well, I don't know of any studies to prove any curing powers, but there are lots of people professing growth after doing them for just a short while. I have been pumping them out twice a week for several months now and I've found that my knees don't hurt after doing them as they do with weighted squats.

Training Tip

- Stand straight and tall with your feet shoulder-width apart. Point them forward or outward a little. Maybe point them forward one workout and outward the next.
- Extend your hands forward and then inhale as you withdraw your fists to your chest. Palm up or palm down, it doesn't matter.
- Exhale as you squat down, lowering your arms behind your hips for balance.
- Let your heels come off the floor and squat on the balls of your feet.
- Squat as low as you can but don't bounce at the bottom. Keep your back straight throughout the entire movement, though it's okay to lean forward a little.
- As you rise, reach forward with your arms and inhale. (Notice that the breathing pattern is opposite of how it's done in most squatting exercises.)

One of the characteristics that make Hindu squats unique is that they are performed in 1 single set of high reps. Your first objective is to do 100 reps in 3 minutes, 180 seconds. That means you get less than 2 seconds to do one rep.

So how many should you start with? Try 1 set of 25 to 50 reps twice a week. If, say, 30 are hard for you, stay at that count for a few workouts until you feel you're ready to add 5, 10 or 20 more. By then your legs will have gotten conditioned and you should be able to add reps every other workout or even every workout. When you can do 100 reps in 3 minutes, go have a pizza because you dun gud, son.

Workout Tip

Matt Furey says that when you can do 500 straight, you're on the road to greatness. His personal record is 2000. A guy named Karl Gotch did 9,001 non stop Hindu Squats in 4 ½ hours. He had to have his legs amputated afterwards, but at least he set a record. I'm kidding. He did do the 9001. I'm just kidding about hacking off his legs.

It's up to you how you format these into your training. Here are some ideas. I'm using your initial goal of 100 reps as an example. If you're not there yet, replace it with 25 reps, 50 reps, whatever.

- 100 reps 2 days a week
- 100 reps 3 days a week
- 100 reps 2 days a week and 300 reps on a 3ʳᵈ day
- 500 reps 1 day a week.
- 300 reps 2 days a week and 1 500-rep session every 10 days.

Experiment to find a training program that fits your recuperative powers and your martial arts training schedule. By the way, don't do Hindus *before* your training session. They are quite taxing and you will need a day or two to recover.

Caution

Remember, no bouncing. You want to strengthen your knees, not pop them off like buttons on a fat man's vest.

*Training
Tip*

ISN'T KICKING ENOUGH?

In a word: no. Of course doing lots of kicking is important. In fact it's critical. But most martial art trainers say that the best kickers, that is, those who can kick with flexibility, explosiveness, speed and destructive power, are those who supplement their leg training with weights and free-hand exercises to help develop these qualities.

Supplemental leg exercises that are martial arts specific, such as the ones presented in this chapter, will move your leg power to the next level, and beyond.

Plyometrics

Most fighters know about plyometrics and the controversy around them. Those that believe in them swear by the results, others feel that the inherent risk doing them isn't worth it. So is there a risk? Are they dangerous? Yes. But are they effective? Many believe so.

A plyometric is any exercise where the muscle is forcefully loaded before it's forcefully contracted. With the jump squat, for example, you forcefully load the muscles of your legs when dropping into the squat position then forcefully contract the muscles when you spring into the air. (In the previous chapter, we talked about doing heavy bench presses in a super-set with plyometric push-ups.)

Important

Power is similar to strength except for one factor: time. How fast can that muscle contract? A guy who can squat 800 pounds can squeeze you to death with his legs, but unless he practices exercises to develop explosive power, he will be a poor kicker (you tell him that, I'm not). Plyometrics are said to develop explosive power.

Why don't more people do them? Because they are dangerous. Even more so if you have an existing injury.

Rule 1: If you have a bad knee, a tweaked leg muscle, a sore ankle or any other condition, don't do these or any other plyometric leg exercise.

Rule 2: You must stay focused on the exercise. Lose your concentration – "Wow, who's the cute white belt?" – and that noise you hear is your shin bone flipping end over end across the room.

To repeat, when doing any plyometric exercise you must stay focused from the beginning to the end.

Plyometric jump squats

Note that there are two alternating jumps, one in which you touch your heels to your rear and one in which you draw your knees to your chest. The key element that makes this plyometric is that when you drop into the squat after each variation, you must leap into the air again *without hesitation.*

- Make sure your legs and knees are warmed up thoroughly.
- Stand straight with your feet parallel to each other, arms at your sides.
- Lower yourself into a deep squat.
- Jump and touch your heels to your rear and drop into a deep squat.
- Without hesitation jump and touch your knees to your chest, and drop into a deep squat
- Continue to alternate back and forth.

Do 1 set of 10 reps once a week. Choose a day when your legs are strong and have recuperated from your previous workout. Add a second set when you're ready but don't push yourself to do another too soon. Do these no more than once a week.

Note: Do I sound like your grandmother with all these precautions? Maybe. But with 40 years of martial arts training under my belt I've personally experienced and have seen others experience just about every kind of injury there is. Sure, you heal eventually (though not always), but that missed training time hurts. Train smart, listen to the warning signals your body is sending, and you too will train for many happy decades.

Leaping lunges

Caution

Here is an incredible power builder that is as risky to perform as it is productive. **Warning:** Don't get distracted in the middle of this exercise. Concentrate 110 percent on the precise form needed to execute this movement. Do it right and you will soon be kicking down trees in the park.

If you normally squat with 300 pounds, forget about it for this exercise. The dynamics, force, exertion, and the mandatory balance are entirely different here. I highly suggest that you grab a couple of 20-pound dumbbells to begin with and increase the poundage as your coordination improves. Okay, enough warnings; here is how you do leaping lunges:

• Stand with your feet shoulder-width apart and hold the dumbbells at shoulder level, your upper arms slanted downward about 45 degrees.

• Lunge forward with your left leg and drop your right knee an inch or two above the floor.

• As you begin to come out of the lunge, drive upward with both legs so that they both leave the floor.

• Simultaneously, drive the dumbbells upward as if executing a double punch at the sky.

• While airborne, move your right leg forward and your left leg back.

• Land in the lunge position with your right leg forward and your left knee an inch or two above the floor.

Do 1 set of 10 reps for a week or two, or until you feel ready to progress. Then do 2 sets of 10 reps. After a few more weeks, increase to 3 sets of 10 reps.

SQUAT JUST ONCE A WEEK

Say for whatever reason you can't lift more than once a week. First, stay calm and forget about lying down on a train trestle. Not all is lost. In fact, you won't lose anything.

Studies show that veteran lifters can maintain their hard-earned muscle by doing a total body workout once every seven days, in some cases, once every 10 days. This is definitely a case where one is better than nothing. Many lifters have found that their leg progress continued with only one day-a-week training and in some cases once every 14 days! Legs muscles are the largest in your body and therefore need time to recuperate after you give them a good trashing.

This is difficult to accept for many people because we have been conditioned to train two or three times a week. Will once a week work for you? Try it for three months and see. You won't lose a thing; most likely you will gain.

One-legged plyometric squat jumps

For this plyometric exercise you need a box, a step, or a strong, unmovable chair. Remember, it's not an option to do a warm-up when doing plyometrics, it's a rule. Warm-up well and live another day.

- Stand in front of your object, let's say it's a chair, and place your left foot on it. You want to start with your thigh horizontal with the floor, so you need to sink into your raised leg until it's positioned correctly. If your chair is quite high, your thigh might already be horizontal, and that is okay.
- Push off that leg and leap into the air as high as you can.
- Tuck your right leg under you.
- As you fall back to Earth, switch legs so that your right foot lands on the chair and your left foot on the floor. Your right thigh should be horizontal with the floor.

- *Without hesitation*, push off the chair with your right leg and leap as high as you can into the air, repeating the leg switch.

- Always sink upon landing until your thigh is even with the floor.

Do 1 set of 10 reps once a week. Choose a day when your legs are strong and have recuperated from your previous work-out. Add another set when you feel you're ready but don't push yourself to do it too soon. Do one-legged plyometric squat jumps only once a week.

Heavy squats combined with squat jumps

This exercise is based on the same power developing concept we examined in Chapter 2 when we combined heavy benches with plyometric push-ups into a super-set. With this exercise, you're going to super-set heavy squats with the good ol' squat jump. As with the benches and push-ups, do this routine once every 14 days. I'm betting that after the first time you do it you will wish it was once a month. But tough it out, so that in three or four months when you kick your heavy bag its seams will burst and shower the room with its stuffing. Expensive, but so cool.

- Place a barbell on a squat rack and load it with enough plates to make you groan and strain to get 8 reps.
- Rest 10 to 15 seconds then…
- Do 10 to 15 squat jumps. Stand with your feet about shoulder width apart and lower yourself until your thighs are parallel with the floor. That is your starting position. Jump straight up into the air explosively and then drop back down into the squatting start position. *Then without pause*, spring back up into the air and continue in this piston-like fashion for all 10 or 15 reps.
- Rest for 60 seconds
- Do another 8 reps of vein-bulging squats
- Rest 10 to 15 seconds and then do another 10 to 15 squat jumps.

Do 2 super-sets of 8 heavy squats followed immediately by 10 to 15 reps of plyometric squat jumps. Do once every two weeks.

Scooter squat

I got this unique exercise from veteran martial artist, author, and friend Martina Sprague. Martina is one of the toughest fighters I know, one who never settles into a routine but continuously strives to find new, innovative and productive ways to develop power, strength and speed. The scooter squat is one such example. Different? Yes. Result producing? Yes, as in "Oh my aching thighs!" Here is how it's done in Martina's words:

"The squat has been termed 'king of quad exercises,' and for good reason. The problem with the squat is that most people find it boring and, yes, painful, so they cheat, either by not doing squats at all, or by not going low enough. A horse stance is not a squat, folks! Your thighs are supposed to be horizontal, that is, parallel with the ground.

"Two years ago, when my job decided to move the employee parking lot three-quarters of a mile away from the airport terminal building where I work, I found a wonderful way to train the quads consistently, without ever getting bored. I bought a scooter!

"Here is a test: When on the scooter, which leg does the work? The one kicking or the one standing? After the first day, I knew beyond a doubt that the leg standing does it all. First, it must remain flexible, adjust to the forces, and help keep your balance. Second, in order to reach the ground with your kicking foot, you must bend your supporting leg slightly. Believe me when I say that a mile and a half roundtrip every day gives the untrained leg a good burn, especially if you're fortunate enough to have a headwind.

"But a tiny bend in the leg doesn't qualify as a squat, does it? So I toughened up and lowered the handlebars. Still not a full one-legged squat, but it's a start. Plus, it's consistent. In two years of going to and coming from work, I have only missed three days of scooter-squat practice due to ice and snow. I kick with my left leg on the way in, and kick with my right leg on the way out. It takes three and half minutes each way, for a total of seven minutes of one-legged squatting a day.

"The scooter weighs only a couple of pounds, folds up in a second, can be carried over your shoulder, and fits easily in the trunk of your car. So park the car on the neighbor's lot ten blocks away, and scoot in.

"And you thought they were just for kids!"

Use your imagination as to how you want to do this. If you're embarrassed to be seen on a scooter, do it at night, and wear your black ninja uniform. If it doesn't matter to you about being seen, take the scooter to a school quarter-mile track and do one lap crouching on your left leg and one lap crouching on your right. Get innovative and just have fun with this. Do it for six weeks and you will be just as amazed as was Martina Sprague as to how well it increases leg power.

Hamstrings

Hamstrings are the large muscles on the back of the legs, the ones most often neglected by fighters and weight trainees. Too many in the exercising world go by the philosophy that if they can't see the muscle why bother training it. Not good. In Chapter 6, "41 ways to relieve pain," we talk about the importance of muscle balance. In a word… make that six words: Unbalanced muscle development leads to injury.

WANT BIG ARMS? SQUAT.

Yes, you read that right. Squatting stimulates arm growth. Anytime you work large muscles, such as your legs, you release a large number of hormones that support muscle growth. While you're killing your legs with leaping lunges and Hindu squats, testosterone, growth hormones, and insulin-like growth are surging throughout your body, much more so than when you do, say, neck bridges.

Squats activate all your major muscle groups so they are forced to work together. Additionally, by working the largest muscles your body must create more capillaries, which translates to more blood flow throughout your system. Think of these as little paths on which growth-stimulating nutrients travel to your muscles.

Keep doing your curls to attack your biceps directly *and* keep working your legs hard to stimulate your arms indirectly. Not only will you develop kicks that can knock down pillars, but a couple of months from now when you're doing your nightly double biceps flex in the bathroom mirror, you're going to be one happy camper when you see what looks like baseballs straining to burst through your arms.

Your hamstrings need to be strong to deliver impact when throwing hook kicks, crescent kicks and mule kicks, and for returning your leg quickly after doing front, side and roundhouse kicks. When grappling, you need strong hams to pin, squeeze and sweep. Your legs need to be strong and the strength needs to be balanced.

Important

If you train with weights in a gym and regularly do leg curls on a machine, great. Keep at it. When it's time to change your routine, consider doing one of the hamstring exercises listed here for a few weeks. If you don't train with weights or you do but you don't have access to a leg curl machine, the following exercises are just what the doctor ordered to make your hamstrings strong and your kicks fast.

Swiss ball curl

One of the advantages of exercising on the Swiss ball, compared to a machine, is that besides the deep muscle contraction you get, the ball's instability forces lots of other muscles to come into play. In contrast, when exercising on a machine you're forced to follow a designated track, leaving those extra muscles to have nothing else to do but nap. But as a fighter you don't take the easy way because you know that sometimes the hard way gets the results.

• Lie on your back and place your calves on top of the ball, your head and shoulders on the floor, and stretch your arms out to the sides.
• Without moving the ball, lift your hips and lower back off the floor so that your body forms a straight line.
• Tighten your gut and use your legs to pull the ball toward your rear. Stop when the bottoms of your feet are flat on the ball.
• Pause to enjoy the contraction, and then push the ball away until your legs are once again straight.

Work up to 3 sets of 10 reps.

One-legged curl variation   Once your hams are iron tough, lift one leg straight up as you work the curls with just one leg. It's double the resistance and a fast path to possessing killer leg power. Is it hard? Ooooh yeah!

Work up to 3 sets of 10 reps.

One tough hamstring exercise

This one doesn't have a name so I call it "One tough hamstring exercise." It's important to progress slowly with this as too much of it too soon will have you cursing my name for a few days every time you take a step. But keep at because by the time you can do a couple sets of 10 reps, you will have developed enough hamstring strength to hook kick the hood off a Dodge pick-up.

- Begin by anchoring your lower legs under a barbell, sofa, or anything else that is low enough and heavy enough not to fall over on you.
- Slowly lower yourself without writhing, twisting your upper body, or twisting your hips (and without screaming curse words) until your chest touches the floor, with your hands on either side of your shoulders in the lowest position of a push-up.
  o If you find yourself crashing to the floor, you just have to keep working on it until you have the strength to lower yourself slowly and with control.
- Okay, lowering yourself was fun, but now you have to do the harder part: Lift your upper body back up to the vertical using only your tender hamstring muscles.
- Cheat a little by doing a thrust-like push-up to get you started, but as you progressively get stronger you want to use less and less help from your arms.
  o Start with a regular two-hand push-up and progress to pushing off with only three fingers of each hand.

o Eventually, don't use your hands at all. Your ultimate goal is to be able to lower yourself and curl back up without any assistance.

Want to impress your fellow training mates? Of course you do. Work on this exercise at home alone until you can whip out 2 sets of 10 reps of these bad boys. Then one day at class ask someone to lie across your calves because you want to try this *new* exercise you just heard about yesterday. Be sure to emphasize *yesterday*. "No way can you do that," the others will mock and scoff. Then you shock them by repping out a couple dozen. Some in the crowd will gasp, some will cry out in amazement. All will chorus, "Oooh" and "Ahhh" as they gather around to touch you. Try to act humble, and say, "Aw shucks. It weren't nothin'."

If you're a kicker, this exercise will give you an amazing hook kick. If you're a grappler, it will give you tremendous leg power, especially squeezing power.

Work up to 2 sets, 10 reps, all unassisted by your arms.

Calves

Calf and Ankle Plyometrics

Strong ankles and powerful calves are important to not only prevent injury, which often occurs from sudden and unexpected weight changes while sparring and doing drills, but also to develop explosive speed for thrusting your feet off the floor to kick, execute leg checks, and lunge. Here is a plyometric exercise that works fast to develop strong ankles and calves. Be sure to warm-up first.

- Stand tall with your arms hanging at your sides, your feet shoulder-width apart.
- Without bending your knees or moving your arms, use your calves and toes to thrust yourself 2 to 4 inches into the air.
- Upon landing *and without hesitation*, thrust yourself up again.

Do 1 or 2 sets of 10 to 15 reps once a week. Add a second set when you're ready.

Free mental trick: Put your head into that kick

We are discovering more and more about the power of the mind for developing warrior skills. I've written before about how my speed improved from just *thinking* I was getting faster. Others have reported the same findings. You think it, you become it. Your solo workouts are a perfect time to perfect this kind of thinking.

For example, when you whip your roundhouse or sidekick into a bag, don't limit your thinking to:

My leg is kicking the target.

My leg is hitting hard.

Such thinking is restrictive because you're limiting your potential by just focusing on your leg power. What about the rest of your body? There is a whole lot of muscle there not being involved. Many times I have simply talked a student into delivering more powerful punches and more powerful kicks by standing behind his shoulder and guiding him to mentally tell himself, his entire body, to deliver more powerful blows than ever before. There is

Workout Tip

nothing complicated about this and it's not supernatural, though the sudden power can seem freaky. It's just about learning to use your mind to communicate with your body and direct it as to what you want it to do.

The positive way to communicate is to believe that this will work. One more time: *Believe* that this will work. Believe it deeply in your gut and your mind will make the necessary adjustments so that your entire body gets into the act. Say to yourself:

I'm kicking with all my body

I'm putting all my being into the target through my leg.

I can feel the power in my hips; I can feel the power in my upper body; I can feel the power in my arms; My mind is directing all of my body, via my leg into the target.

Keep working at this and you will soon discover a whole new level of power

13 Ways to Improve Your Core Grappling Strength

If you have been weight training for a while you can probably squat all day with a 100-pound barbell. And bench press? Fuhgeddaboudit: You could bench 100 pounds until the cows come home (ever wonder what the heck that expression means?). But carry a 100-pound human a short distance and you're huffing and puffing like a hard rode yak. Human weight feels different than barbells, dumbbells and machines: It's awkward, it's uneven, and it shifts when you don't want it to. The question then is what can you use in training that approximates human weight?

Of course you might find an actual human to volunteer to let you do sets and reps with his body, but if someone is that weird you probably don't want to be lifting him, anyway. So that leaves a sandbag, a large bag of rice, or a large bag of flour. There are no handles on these bags and the weight isn't distributed as it is in dumbbells and barbells. One hundred pounds of so-called dead weight feels like 200. Without a doubt, training with bags is different, challenging and productive.

Use a weight that fits your strength and level of fitness. Acquire or build bags in increments of 25, 50, 75 and 100 pounds. Progress slowly and systematically and be prepared to be happily amazed at your new strength.

Here are four exercises that target your core.

Important

Core defined

Technically the word "core" means "the innermost part." Many fighters think of their core as only those muscles in their exact center: the abdominals, sides of the waist, and the lower back. Among fitness trainers, core means the deep muscles of the spine, pelvis, hip, and shoulders. I agree, and I also believe that the neck is equally important, so I've included strengthening exercises for it in this chapter. Refer to Chapter 1 for several abdominal exercises to build an iron-like midsection.

Clean and press

• Squat over a bag with your feet shoulder-width apart and grasp it by its sides.

• Shrug your shoulders as you come up on your toes and pull the bag to your chest.

• From here, bend your knees and rotate your forearms so that they are under the bag after you curl it to your shoulders.

o Be careful here because this action – the clean - forces you to snap your wrists and sort of catch the bag at the front of your shoulders.

• Straighten your knees and press the bag overhead.

• To return it to the floor, simply reverse the action.

o Lower it to your shoulders, rotate your arms and wrists back to the starting position and lower the bag to the floor.

Workout Tip

• **Tip**: Don't just drop your bag like Olympic lifters do with huge barbells. Bags burst and you will have a mess. Besides, lowering the bag is half the exercise.

Do 2 sets of 10 reps and increase to 3 sets of 10 when you feel ready. As your strength improves, get a bigger bag.

Lift a bag, turn and put it down

Be especially cognizant of moving smoothly with this exercise or your lower spine, which is getting the majority of the stress, is going to seek revenge on you.

Caution

- Stand with your feet about shoulder-width apart before a table or any other surface that is about hip high.
- The bag is on the floor next to your left foot. Twist to the left, bend down and pick it up by its ends.
- Lift the bag across your body as you straighten your legs to stand, and place it on the surface in front of you.
- Don't let go of it. Just pause for a two-count then reverse the motion and set the bag back down next to your left foot.
- Stand back up empty handed and congratulate yourself on doing 1 rep. Now do 9 more.
- After you have completed 10 reps on your left side, place the bag next to your right foot and do the same thing on that side for 10.

Begin with 2 sets of 10 reps on each side, increasing to 3 sets of 10 when you're ready. Increase the weight when your strength has improved enough to handle it.

MAKE A NOTE OF IT

The best way to create an instant visual of your progress over a month is to make notes on a calendar. Write down how you felt each workout, how many sets and reps you did each day and whether you increased the poundage or the degree of difficulty. At month's end, review the past weeks and feel good about the progress you made and let it inspire you to keep at it.

Uh oh, according to the calendar you didn't progress, or maybe you regressed. It might even show you why. Maybe you didn't do enough over the month. Maybe you skipped workouts. You can't progress if you don't do enough or you don't train at all.

The calendar might reveal you're doing too much. Many times that is the case.

Be sure to eat healthily to repair your tired muscles, and get plenty of rest, too. Be sure to note that information on your calendar, too.

Get a big calendar.

Hug and lunge

This exercise can also be added to the leg exercises discussed in Chapter 3 since the lunge phase attacks your upper leg muscles so intensely. I placed it here because it does such a good job conditioning you to physically and mentally handle an awkward, human-like weight. Use a heavy bag as shown or acquire a large sandbag which might be even more awkward. Awkward is good for this.

This is a rather unique exercise because each lunge advances you forward a step.

• Begin by cradling the bag in the crook of your arms and hugging it to your chest, your feet hip-width apart.
• Step forward with your right leg and lower your body until your thigh is parallel with the floor. Keep your upper body

straight and tall, and keep hugging that bag.

• Push back with your right foot until your leg is mostly straight, then step forward with your left foot and place it next to your right so that you're once again in the beginning position. This advances you forward a step.

• Now step forward with your left leg and repeat the above procedure (with opposite legs), again advancing forward a step.

Do 1 set of 10 reps with each leg, progressing over the weeks to 3 sets of 10 reps. When you feel you're ready to add weight, move up to the next heavier bag.

Hug and lift

Before I elaborate on this one, allow me to imprint this in your mind: *Use your legs to lift the bag.* A back problem caused by poor lifting form hurts. One second you're fine and the next instant you're 95 years old, bent, grimacing, and complaining about smart-alecky young whippersnappers. Been there, done that.

Caution

This tough exercise works all your major grappling muscles: arms, legs, back and shoulders as you lift and move a weight similar to a human's. This is a tremendous exercise that I got from my friend Mark Hatmaker's video *The Floor Bag Workout* published by Paladin Press. I'm using it here with his permission.

• Place the heavy bag on the floor between your legs.
• Bend over and squat down enough to reach the bag.
• Wrap your arms around its middle and lift it straight up in front of you as you straighten your legs.

- Continue to lift until the bag is on your right shoulder.
- Lower it back to the floor (bend your legs).
- Lift it up again, this time onto your left shoulder, and then place it back down between your legs.

• Add-on 1: When you get the bag to your shoulder press it overhead for one 1 rep.

• Add-on 2: Each time you place the bag onto a shoulder, shuffle step to the right a few steps and to the left a few steps. Then place it back on the floor.

Begin with 2 sets of 10 reps and increase to 3 sets of 10 when you're ready. Also increase the weight when you're ready for it.

Build a powerful neck with bridges

Arguably one of the most important muscles to strengthen is that column holding up your incredible face. A strong neck helps you to endure awkward ground positions and survive hard blows to the head. A muscular neck might even cause a bully to think twice about picking on you.

There are many neck exercises in which you push against your hands and there are health clubs with neck machines that provide resistance. While these work to a lesser or greater degree, I believe in exercises that duplicate the activity in which you want to be strong. For grappling, especially on the ground, the exercise of choice is the neck bridge.

Important

Wait. Don't even think about doing any neck exercises without first doing a warm-up. Here is a good one that gets the blood pumping throughout all your neck muscles and primes them for a tough training session.

A good, basic neck warm-up

Do 1 set of 8 – 10 reps of each warm-up exercise.

- Rapidly turn your head to the right.
- Rapidly turn your head to the left.
- Rapidly tilt your head down to the right, as if looking down
    the side of your shoulder.
- Rapidly tilt your head down to the left, as if looking down
    the side of your shoulder.
- Rapidly tilt your head back and forth (but not too far back).
- Rapidly circle your head in both directions.
- Left hand to the left side of head - push and resist.
- Right hand to the right side - push and resist.
- Both hands to the forehead - push and resist.
- Both hands to the back - push and resist.

I wrote a little in *Solo Training* about the bridge exercise and illustrated one version on my back and one on my stomach. If you have a copy, notice that I roll only part way. While that is still correct, know that you can roll even farther, as shown here by judo black belt and famed novelist, Barry Eisler. If you're new to bridging, I strongly suggest that you hold off on doing Barry's version until you have practiced bridging for at least three to five months. Hearing a loud *twang!* in your neck means two things: You were not ready to advance, and for the rest of your day you're going to be in a world of hurt.

Beginner bridges

Do these for the first few weeks to build strength and flexibility in your neck.

FACE-UP BRIDGES

Lie on your back with your head on the floor. Roll your head back and lift your hips off the floor so that your weight is supported by your feet, shoulder blades and neck. Roll back and forth slowly.

Do 2 sets of 10 to 15 reps.

FACE-DOWN BRIDGES

Get on your knees and place your forehead on the floor. The closer your knees are to your head the less resistance on your neck; the farther away they are the greater the resistance. Find a knee placement where you can roll back and forth without over engorging all the veins in your face. Place your hands on the ground in whatever placement seems most comfortable and where you can support some of the weight. This allows you to easily do the full range of motion since your arms are bearing as much of the load as needed. As your neck grows stronger, use your arms less and less until (in the advanced stage) you can clasp your hands behind your back and let your neck bear all the weight.

Do 2 sets of 10 to 15 reps.

Intermediate bridges

Don't consider doing these until you've been bridging for a month or longer. If you think you're ready but the exercise feels too strenuous – your neck feels strained or stiff afterwards – return to the beginner bridges for three or four more weeks, or until you build sufficient strength and flexibility to do the intermediate workout without suffering.

FACE-UP BRIDGES

Lie on your back with your head on the floor. Roll your head back and lift your hips and shoulders off the floor so that your weight is supported by your feet and the back of your head. Roll back and forth striving to roll from the base of your neck up onto the top of your head.

Do 2 sets of 10 to 15 reps.

FACE-DOWN BRIDGES

Get down on all fours and place your forehead on the floor. Come off your knees so that your weight is supported by your head and feet. Roll back and forth from your nose to nearly the top of your head.

Do 2 sets of 10 to 15 reps.

Advanced bridges

Caution

It's time to progress to the advanced stage when intermediate bridging is just too easy for you. However, if any part of the advanced hurts, stop and return to intermediate bridging. Why hurt yourself? You're doing this to build strength and flexibility. Do it progressively and intelligently, and you will achieve your goal, and do so injury free.

FACE-UP BRIDGES

Roll your head back and lift your hips and shoulders off the floor so that your weight is supported by your feet and the back of your head. Roll back and forth, striving to roll from the base of your neck up and over your head until you can touch your nose to the ground. After two or three months, try to roll to your mouth.

At this stage you're ready to roll from side to side to attack the muscles on the sides of your neck even more. Just roll an inch or two in either direction at first, increasing the range over the weeks as you get stronger.

Training
Tip

Consider experimenting with your foot placement. Barry Eisler says: "With the face up bridges, the placement of your feet in relation to your head, and whether you're on your toes or the soles of your feet, creates a lot of variation in the exercise. I'm always looking for slightly different ways to do the basics because I feel like the variations develop the muscles in different ways, building a fuller range of strength and resiliency."

Do 2 sets of 10 to 15 reps or rolling back and forth
Do 2 sets of 10 reps of rolling from side-to-side.

FACE-DOWN BRIDGES

Place your forehead on the floor and come off your knees so that your weight is supported by your head and feet. Roll from your nose to as far back on the top of your head as you can. Do your reps in a continuous back and forth motion.

As you did in the advanced face-up bridges, roll from side to side in this stage to attack the muscles on the sides of your neck even more. Just roll an inch or two in either direction at first, increasing the range as you get stronger.

Do 2 sets of 10 to 15 reps or rolling back and forth

Do 2 sets of 10 reps of rolling from side-to-side.

Warning: Whether you're new to neck exercises or a veteran, you should always do them with care and attention to good form. Sloppy form and over fatigue can cause short-term or permanent injury. One little error and you spend the rest of your life looking to your left and right the way Robocop does.

Caution

5

48 Ways to Build a
Bone Crushing Grip

I once attended a bodybuilding contest in which there were several strongman acts, including a guy who bent a railroad spike until the ends nearly met. He wrapped the heavy, thick spike in a handkerchief and then as the theme from *Rocky* blared in the auditorium, he bent it into a narrow U. While this was impressive, I was amazed that his forearms and wrists looked normal. Not huge and bulging with rope-like veins, just normal - and they could bend railroad spikes! Maybe there is hope for me and my wimpy forearms after all, though I can't think of any good reason to bend an innocent railroad spike.

Hands, wrists and forearms that can be trained to come even close to such incredible power would be a real boon in the fighting arts. Imagine grabbing an opponent's forearm and squeezing until he whimpers his mama's name. Or grabbing his neck with one hand and crushing until unpleasant things ooze from every opening. A powerful grip might make the difference between success and failure when applying a grappling hold from an awkward position. For sure, a strong grip is a definite plus when manipulating a weapon in training or competition, and it can make a difference when prying a weapon held fast in a mentally deranged person's steel grip (been there, done that a few times).

Here are 47 ways to develop tremendous power that can crush, rip, pull and punch. The exercises might or might not develop bodybuilder-like forearms, but when practiced consistently they will develop functional fighting power in just a few months.

Workout Tip

Here is a goal for you   At one time there were Japanese dentists who could pull teeth – with their fingers. They developed this tremendous finger power by pounding tooth-sized pieces of wood into the cracks of boards. Then, using only their thumb and index finger, they would move the small piece of wood back and forth until they had worked it free. Eventually, they developed enough strength to do that on humans with bad teeth.

> If you do regular exercises you will develop a regular grip.
> John Brookfield – *Mastery of Hand Strength*

IT'S NOT JUST FOR HITCHHIKING

Have you ever looked at your thumbs and thought, "What the heck are these things for, anyway?" The answer is this: Thumbs are for crushing your opponent.

If you have a weak grip it's probably because your thumbs are weak. While they need to be strengthened along with your other four fingers, many exercises typically fail to work them. This is unfortunate because for the hands to have true crushing power and for all the fingers to work in unison, all the muscles must be exercised.

Build the muscles in your thumbs and you will have crushing and pinching power that will bring strong men to their knees.

Pinch grip

Possessing a strong pinch grip helps you hold onto a grappling opponent. I used to co-teach a police defensive tactics class with an officer who had grown up working on a farm where he milked cows, carried milk buckets, and handled a variety of heavy tools. This guy had a pinch grip that could pop a car tire. Even when he applied a hold incorrectly, he could still make you whine just from the power of his grip. In fact, sometimes his crushing grip hurt more than a correctly applied hold.

To build pinching power you have to develop thumb power because without the thumb, you've got no pinch. It's as simple as that. Let's look at three exercises that develop powerful pinchers.

Important

Barbell plate pinching

Watch your toes with this one because you're going to be gripping two plates with one hand right over them. The poundage of the plates depends on your strength. You might have to start with two 10-pound plates or you might be able to begin with two 25-pounders. It doesn't matter what you start with because as with any exercise your objective is to progress. So if you have to start out with a couple of 2 ½ pound plates (or two dainty tea saucers), just lie to people about how much you lift. But don't exaggerate. Only a few men have been able to pinch 100 pounders.

Caution

Get two plates that are the same weight but without ridges. Ridges make gripping easy, while smooth plates force you to squeeze hard when you pick them up with only your thumb and four fingers. It's best to exercise just one hand at a time.

Now that you're holding two plates in your right hand you can:

- swing them forward about 45 degrees and back about 45 degrees for 10 reps.
- walk to a given point in your room, then back. Repeat for a set of 10 trips.
- pass the weights from hand to hand for 10 reps. Watch out for your toes!
- stand in place and hold them for 30 seconds, increasing the time and the poundage as your strength increases.

Repeat the exercise holding the plates in your left hand.

Softball holding

I like this exercise although I sometimes get a hand cramp from it. You need a large softball in which you drill a ½-inch in diameter hole all the way through. Insert a length of rope – I use clothesline – and tie it at the ball end with the strongest knot you learned in the Scouts and then insert the other end through the hole of a barbell plate(s), the size or number of the plates depends on your strength. The rope should be a length that allows you to hold the ball down at your side without the plates touching the floor. I'm nearly six feet tall so my rope is about 15 inches long.

Sometimes hold the ball with all five fingers, sometimes four, three and two fingers (you can try one but it's probably not going to work). Try these variations.

• Swing the ball forward about 45 degrees and back about 45 degrees for 10 reps.
• Walk to a given point in your room, then back. Repeat for a set of 10 trips.
• Pass the ball from hand to hand for 10 reps. Watch out for your toes.
• Stand in place and hold the ball for, say, 30 seconds, increasing the time and the poundage as your strength increases.

Play catch

This exercise has a built in plyometric. There is a potential risk to your hand, wrist and forearm muscles and, again, a whole lot of risk to your toes if you forget and do it over your feet. I keep mentioning the danger to your toes because I've had some close calls with these exercises. Concentrate on the exercise and know where your feet are.

Caution

Choose a barbell plate that doesn't have a ridge around its edge. As with "Barbell plate pinching," you don't want to make this easy.

• Sit on a bench, spread your feet and, using your thumb and four fingers, pick up a barbell plate - a 10-pounder, 25, 50 or 100. Your goal is to progress to using only your thumb and three fingers, your thumb and two fingers, and then your thumb and two fingers.

• Curl the plate up with your palm down, until your forearm is parallel with the floor.

• At the top of the curl let go of the plate and snatch with your other hand using the same number of fingers as the first hand.

• Allow the plate to drop from its own weight, but stop it before it hits the floor.

• Without stopping, curl the plate until your forearm is parallel with the floor, release the plate and catch it with your other hand.

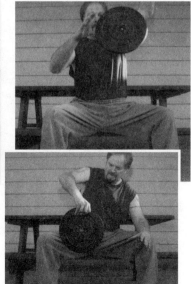

Do 2 to 3 sets of 20 reps, counting each catch as a rep.

Crushing force

Pinching force involves mostly the muscles of the fingers and a few in the hand, while crushing force involves the muscles of the entire hand and forearm. When working both, you ultimately develop powerful fingers, hands and forearms that assist in all grabbing techniques, holding, manipulating, punching and even blocking.

Crusher grip

I like this type of gripper because it provides a range that allows you to crush from an almost fully open hand all the way to a closed one. It also provides a way to measure your growing strength and a way to increase the resistance as you get stronger.

First, find a spring placement that allows you to squeeze out 8 to 10 reps and then experiment with these variations.

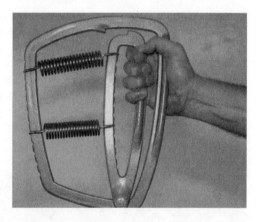

• Grip the handles at their widest and squeeze 10 reps at a moderate pace.
• Grip the handles at their narrowest and squeeze 10 reps at a moderate pace.
• Grip the handles at either place and squeeze 10 reps, holding the handles together for 5 seconds on the 1st, 5th and 10th rep.
• Grip the handles at either place and squeeze 10 reps, holding the handles together for 5 seconds on every even numbered rep: 2, 4, 6, 8, 10.
• Squeeze 10 reps as quickly as you can.
• Squeeze as many reps as you can and as fast as you can.
• Assume your fighting stance and hold the gripper in your rear hand. Launch a cross punch and squeeze the gripper as your arm reaches full extension.

Hand grippers

It seems like these hand grippers have been around forever. They look more modern than they did 40 years ago, and the
movement is smoother, but the same benefits are there if you work
them consistently. And there's the rub. Most people start using
them regularly then lose them. Papers get tossed on top of them or
they fall behind the sofa. The ol' "out of sight out of mind" kicks
in and soon they are forgotten. It's unfortunate because you really
can benefit from them. Here is what novelist and judo black belt
Barry Eisler told me.

"I used the hand grippers regularly when I was wrestling.
I got my hands so strong that I saved myself from many unfamiliar
or disadvantageous positions just by grabbing onto a wrist and
not letting go until I'd managed to improve the situation. I like the
grippers because they are small and light and you can take them
anywhere."

Agreed. Place them in the side pocket of your car door, to
the right of your computer monitor, next to your phone on your
desk at work, on the dash of your delivery truck, or in your lunch
bag for a noon workout. The idea is to place them somewhere vis-
ible in an area you frequent.

Workout Tip

Here are some ways to work the grippers to benefit your
martial arts.

Basic position   Grasp the gripper in the basic upside down
V position and do two or three of these variations

• Squeeze as fast as you can. Be sure to touch the handles on
each contraction.

• Squeeze the grips as slowly as you can. Touch the handles
on each contraction and release them s-l-o-w-l-y.

• Squeeze 10 reps as fast as you can, rest for 30 seconds, then
do 10 slow reps.

• At normal speed, squeeze one rep until the handles touch
and on the next rep squeeze the handles only half way. Continue
to alternate for 10 reps.

• At normal speed, squeeze one rep until the handles touch
and then release them only half way. From there, squeeze them
shut and then release them to their fully open position. So its: full
squeeze, release half way, squeeze shut, release all the way.

• At normal speed, squeeze the handles ½ an inch and release slowly. Then squeeze 1 inch and release slowly. Then 1 ½ inches and release slowly. Continue in this manner until you squeeze the handles all the way closed. This is great for a pump.

• At normal speed, begin with the handles touching. Release ½ inch then squeeze them shut. Release 1 inch then squeeze shut. Release 1 ½ inches then squeeze shut. Continue until you release the handles all the way open.

• Do 1 set of ½-inch squeezes beginning with the handles open followed immediately by 1 set of ½-inch squeezes beginning with the handles closed.

• Squeeze until the handles touch and hold. Hold it the first time for as long as you can: 30 seconds, 60 seconds, a day and a half. Try to increase the time by 15 seconds each workout or every other workout.

Upside down (normal V position)   Your thumbs and index fingers will be working harder now than they did in the inverted V position. This is good because they are critical when holding an opponent's arm or gripping his clothing.

Use the same variations as listed in the Basic position.

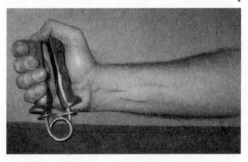

Two fingers   Hold the grippers upright or upside down. Squeeze the handles using only your thumbs and index fingers, or your thumbs, index fingers and middle fingers.

Use the same variations as listed in the Basic position.

Punch squeeze, punch squeeze

Here is a fun way to do single hand strikes, combinations, and forms while working the hand grippers. It might take you a minute to get the feel for coordinating the actions, but once you get comfortable you will enjoy the unique workout.

Single hand technique Assume your fighting stance and launch a backfist while holding a gripper in the attack hand. Go medium speed at first as you strike out with a backfist, squeezing the gripper at the point of impact.

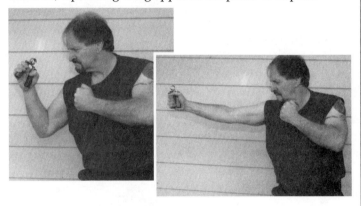

Do 2 sets of 10 reps with each hand.

Combination Assume your fighting stance holding a gripper in each hand. Throw a lead jab, right cross combination, squeezing each gripper at the point of impact.

Do 2 sets of 10 reps with each hand.

Forms Choose a form that is primarily hand techniques. Hold a gripper in each hand and squeeze the handles together on each strike and block.

Note: It's important to warm-up your hands and forearms with 1 or 2 sets of 10 reps before using the grippers with your hand techniques. As you get comfortable with the movements, you will find yourself squeezing the grippers forcefully, which is what you want to do. But if your arms and hand muscles aren't warmed up properly, you might tweak a muscle.

Pliers crush

This exercise is most beneficial when you have three or four sets of pliers of varying sizes so that your muscles are strengthened in different posi-  tions. The object is to pick up a weight by gripping the plate or the handle with the pliers and squeezing the handles. Once you have picked up the weight by the pliers, you can:

- Hold the weight at your side for 15 to 60 seconds.
- Hold the weight at your side for as long as you can.
- Hold the weight at your side and walk to a point in your room and back for reps.
- Grip the weight and curl it for 2 sets of 10 reps.
- Hold the weight in the pliers' grip as if holding a pan of water by one end.
  - o Hold at arm's length along your side for time.
  - o Hold with your arm at a 90-degree angle for time.
- Hold at arm's length or at a 90-degree angle and walk to a given point and back.

Thick-handled dumbbell exercises

This is an easy way to incorporate crushing strength exercises with those you normally do for your arms, chest, shoulders and back. All you need to do is wrap each dumbbell handle with a towel. This forces your hands and forearms to do more work because they have to crush the towel-wrapped handle to hold on.

Experiment with different thicknesses. Start with a standard-sized washcloth, and then progress to a dishtowel, and finally a regular-sized towel. The beauty of this is that it accomplishes two objectives: You work your crushing grip along with whatever body part you're targeting with the dumbbell exercise.

Workout Tip

Do your usual sets and reps of all exercises.

41 Ways to Prevent
and Relieve Pain

Pain and injury are part of the martial arts. We learn how to administer it, we feel it when our opponents hit us extra hard, and we experience self-inflicted injuries from over-training and incorrect training. While wisdom and knowledge go a long way toward prevention, stuff still happens – and pain comes-a-knockin' on the door.

We are going to examine ways to prevent injury and ways not to exasperate an existing injury in those three common trouble spots for martial artists - knees, shoulders and lower back. Let's begin by examining how cross training helps keep injuries at bay.

WHY BAD STUFF HAPPENS

Joint pain is often caused by poor technique or insufficient fitness: You don't have enough strength to properly align your limbs, but you do the difficult or awkward movement anyway; you don't have enough muscular endurance to continue training, but you do anyway; and you aren't flexibility enough to perform certain movements without overtaxing the joint, but you do anyway.

Cross training

I began training in the martial arts at the age of 19. I played a lot of softball prior to that and must brag that I was known for being able to throw a ball a mile, or close to it. I trained like a madman those first two years of karate, drilling endless hours on punches and kicks virtually every day of the week. While we did backfists, uppercuts and hammer blows, most of the training was on straight-line attacks: jabs and reverse punches.

After a couple of years of this, I could punch quickly and powerfully, but I couldn't throw a ball a fraction of the distance I could two years earlier. Or skip a flat rock across a lake as well as I used to. Not only had my ability to throw diminished, it hurt my shoulder a little to do it. Why?

Important

After two years of performing the same straight-line movements, my body had become conditioned to doing just those movements. My throwing muscles had been, relatively speaking, unused and had deteriorated. While my punching muscles were good for, well, punching, I had limited my fitness and conditioning. I had only improved in one area, and as such, I was at risk of injury.

Cross training means that you incorporate other forms of exercise along with your fighting art. Yes, you need to train hard on the martial arts for competition, rank promotion, and mastery, but most top athletes know that cross training is beneficial for maintaining a high level of overall fitness by working those muscles not exercised when kicking and punching. For example, bicycling, swimming or sprinting a couple days a week, hits your cardiovascular system and muscles in ways not usually worked.

CROSS TRAINING IN OTHER FIGHTING ARTS

This chapter isn't about the importance of cross training in those fighting arts that are different from your mother art. While learning other systems is of value to your overall development, this chapter is about benefiting your body by giving those muscles, tendons, ligaments and joints normally stressed in your martial arts some rest as you work to develop those that are underused in your training.

Cross training limits the stress you normally put on your martial arts muscles and cardiovascular system, while still benefiting them in other ways. For example, cross training:

- broadens your skill, agility and balance.
- gives you something else to do when you can't practice martial arts.
- reduces your injury potential.
- allows you to keep training while nursing a jammed finger or strained leg muscle.
- reduces training boredom.
- produces better overall conditioning.
- makes you a more rounded person. Your friends don't want to hear about the martial arts all the time.

Here are a few solo activities you can use for cross training.

CARDIOVASCULAR EXERCISE

- Sprinting
- Swimming fast laps
- Cycling
- Rowing
- Fast stair climbing
- Rope jumping
- Skiing (especially cross country)

Note: All of the cardio activities above are those that involve speed. The reason is simple: They stimulate your fast-twitch muscle fibers while they ignite your heart, lungs and the thousands of capillaries.

STRENGTH TRAINING

- Free-hand exercises: push-ups, crunches, weightless squats and pull-ups
- Free weights
- Machines

Note: I suggest that you do all the free-hand exercises fast (with good form), and go heavy when using the free weights and machines. Both stimulate the fast-twitch muscles.

FLEXIBILITY

- Stretching: seek out stretches from ballet or gymnastics
- o Yoga (tougher than you think and highly effective)
- o Pilates

Cross training is a dynamic and highly effective way to get stronger, more aerobically fit, more flexible, and mentally stimulated, all while reducing the risk of overtraining and injuring your martial arts muscles. It's just smart to do it.

Icing tricks

Before we get into preventative exercises and techniques to minimize pain, we have to look at the importance of icing injuries. Applying cold to injuries is still the number one recommendation for martial artists, and for a reason: It works wonderfully. Say that you're in a psyche zone slamming reverse punch after reverse punch into a hanging bag when your wrist abruptly bends all funny like. Oh yeah, that smarts! Mr. Pain screams up your forearm, past your shoulder, through your neck, and settles into your brain. In its wake, a wave of nausea and an overall sense of dread as you realize your hand is going to be out of commission for a while.

Give yourself a minute to whine, "Why me? Why me? Why couldn't it have happened to that six-year-old white belt over there?" and then retrieve the chemical ice pack you carry in your workout bag (you do, right?). Break it so the chemicals inside are activated and apply it to your wrist. Ahhh, relief.

Caution

Free tip: Always place something between the ice and your bare skin to prevent being burned, such as one layer of T-shirt, paper towel, or a couple of tissues. I've ignored this advice a couple of times to discover an irony: ice really can burn your skin.

Ice treatment is one of the most effective techniques for treating traumatized muscles, tendons, and joints. A simple application of ice decreases muscle spasms, acute pain and inflammation to bone and soft tissue. Apply it immediately after an injury, and continue to apply it in the later stages to help with rehabilitation.

During an initial injury, tissue damage might swell, sometimes a lot. Swelling can increase the damage of the initial injury and delay healing time. When you apply ice immediately, you reduce the swelling and decrease tissue damage, blood clot formation, inflammation, muscle spasms, and pain. Then it acts like a healing agent as it enhances the flow of nutrients into the troubled area, helps to remove waste products, increases your strength in that specific area, and promotes healing. Ice does all this and it doesn't care how old you are, whether you're a male or female, or how large the injured area.

Here are a few ways to enhance the icing.

• **Ice and drugs**   The ancient remedy of ice and the modern remedy of swallowing two anti-inflamatory ibuprophen tablets are wonderful bedfellows. Taken together, they have a dramatic positive effect on a host of martial arts injuries. First, be sure that your system is okay with ibuprophen. If it is, talk to your doctor about taking more than two at a time.

• **Tennis ball**   Cut a slit in a tennis ball and fill it with water. Stick the ball in the freezer until it's frozen. I used this on a strained forearm tendon and found that pressing down on the ball while rolling it over the injured surface penetrated far more deeply than just laying ice on my arm. When a student of mine tweaked a muscle in his lower back, he placed the frozen ball on the floor, laid on it, then rolled his body slowly around so that his weight pressed the cold deeply into his inflamed tissue.

• **Beer**   A cold beer can penetrate inflamed tissue as does the tennis ball, but it does one better: The metal transmits cold faster. Say you tweak the front of your shoulder and it's burning, throbbing and aching. You don't have an ice pack, but you do have a brew. Refrain from drinking it and slap it against your shoulder. Be sure to put a paper towel between the can and your skin, and secure the container in place by tying it down with a towel or T-shirt. Leave it there 20 to 30 minutes. Underage? Use a soda can or a can of frozen juice.

• **Elevate**   Position your injury above the level of your heart to minimize swelling.

FOUR STAGES OF ICING

Here is the progression of sensations when you slap ice onto an injury.
1. Cold
2. Burning or pricking sensation
3. Aching. Sometimes this hurts more than the injury. Eat the pain and keep the ice in place.
4. Numbness. This is the most important stage. Once you're numb, remove the ice.

How long the four stages takes depends on what you weigh. Generally 20 to 30 minutes should do it. If you want to reapply ice, which is permissible, let your skin return to your normal temperature first.

MY SUCCESS STORY

That forearm tendon I mentioned bothered me for years. At its worst it prevented me from picking up a cup, a bag of groceries, and no way could I throw a punch or snap a backfist. I'd ice it religiously after class and after doing physical work, but while that gave me relief, the problem persisted. One day a friend, who just happens to be a physical therapist, told me to ice my tendon several times a day, even when it wasn't hurting.

So I did. I iced it before class, after, at breakfast, lunch, dinner, and while watching TV. I even went to sleep with it on my arm a few times. Did it work?

Yes! Within a couple of months I was able to do normal things with my arm – pain free. A couple months after that, I was once again punching and backfisting just as I was several years earlier. The key to helping my injury was to ice the injury several times a day.

Will it work for you? Give it a try.

Let's begin by looking at ways to prevent injury to your knees and ways to reduce pain when you already have it.

Knees

I had been working lots of 14-hour shifts on the PD and not getting home until 3 and 4 a.m.. I would struggle groggily out of bed a short while later to get to my 9 o'clock beginner's karate class, then teach a 10 o'clock intermediate, and the advanced students at 11. I was beyond tired, and looking back on it now, I shouldn't have launched that spinning back kick. Because of fatigue, or whatever reason, my stationary foot didn't rotate with my body, though my knee did. It rotated and then rotated some more until it broke – excruciatingly.

There is nothing good to say about breaking your knee, tearing knee cartilage, or straining things around your knee. It all hurts, and in many cases it hurts so much you get to see your lunch again. Unless people have had knee problems, most don't give this very intricate mechanism much thought. But after they hurt it and a salivating surgeon slices into their flesh, these same people become expert on the subject. I'm one of them.

No, I'm not a doctor. I don't even like them very much because they always hurt me and I don't handle pain well (I have a tendency to whine and whimper like ice skater Nancy Kerrigan when she got her knee whacked). But because my knee hurts in cold weather and makes me limp if I over train, I've learned a couple things about pain relief.

IF IT HURTS, DON'T DO IT

Patient: "Oh doctor, my arm hurts when I move it like this."

Doctor: "Really? Then don't move it like that."

This advice is easier for veteran fighters to follow than for eager beaver newbies. Most veterans know that the old adage "Just work through the pain" is a bunch of hooey. Think about it for a second and it really is stupid advice, and it seldom works, anyway. Most often the problem gets more acute because the worst thing you can do is to continue the activity that is causing the grief.

But the other old adage "If it hurts, don't do it" is a tough one to take because it means you can't do your beloved art for a while. Or does it?

Let's say that the sidekick is killing your left knee. Every time you do a couple sets of 10 reps your leg hurts as if you slammed your kneecap into a table leg 20 times. Maybe it even swells. Whatever form the affliction takes, you need to cease doing the sidekick for a while. Now, before you get suicidal, know that there are still lots of things you can do to come out of the injury stronger than ever.

Stop kicking, sort of   Now, as your esteemed author my advice is that you see a doctor, but as a stinking coward I hate going to them unless I have an arrow in my back. If you're brave and smart, stop reading right now and go. To my fellow cowards: read on.

• Ice it often, more than often, even when it doesn't hurt. As I just mentioned, this helped me heal a tendon that plagued me for several years. The trick is to remember to do it when your leg isn't hurting. Create a schedule where you do it four or five times a day.

• Do slow sidekicks. Hold onto a chair and simply move your leg slowly through the track of a sidekick. At full extension, hold it there for a couple of seconds and tense the muscles around your knee joint. If tensing hurts, skip that phase and simply extend your leg slowly and then retract it slowly.

Do 2 or 3 sets of 10 reps.

• Stop doing whatever phase of the sidekick hurts. If all the other kicks in your arsenal don't hurt your knee, continue doing them, though you should eliminate all snapping kicks, and never ever lock your joint out at the end of a kick.

• Practice only the parts that don't hurt. Do the following with both legs.

o Practice quickly moving your rear foot to your lead foot. While many kickers have a fast leg thrust, they have slow footwork. Now is the time to get it up to speed, so to speak. Step as quickly as you can and lift your kicking foot a little as if you were going to kick.

Do 3 sets of 10 reps.

o Beginning where you just left off with your feet together, practice lifting your leg into the sidekick chamber. Thrust with your toes to launch your leg up as quickly as possible. Even if your fighting style doesn't use the pronounced sidekick chamber – maybe you fire it right from the floor – consider working the chamber anyway to enhance speed, flexibility and power in the hip and groin muscles.

Do 3 sets of 10 reps.

• Stretch. Recuperating from an injury is a good time to push your flexibility work. Do your normal stretches and add a couple new ones. You might even find that stretching relieves pain, as we discuss next. However, if a particular stretch hurts your injury, don't do that one.

Workout Tip

DO KNEE BRACES HELP?

Maybe. Consider these points.

• Companies that make knee braces claim that they work great, while scientific studies don't always agree.

• Scientists aren't even sure what knee braces actually do.

• It seems that functional braces – those that help you move - and rehabilitative braces are the most effective.

• Some people are helped more than others.

• Some doctors are concerned that knee braces might increase the number of knee injuries.

• In general, most people who wear them think they help.

Talk to your doctor about how you should wear a brace. Should you wear it only during training and not wear it all other times? Should you not wear it during weight training? Should you wear it constantly? Follow your doctor's orders.

Here are a couple of easy stretches that help to alleviate pain for a lot of people. Although you might have practiced these before in your regular training, for pain relief purposes you want *to do them on the hour*, or as close to it as possible. This keeps fresh, healing blood surging through the troubled area and keeps you stretched all day long. In so doing, you might find, as many others have, that it alleviates pain or at least reduces it. Do the following stretches with both legs.

Quadriceps stretch

- Stand straight and tall, and bend your left leg so that your foot is near your butt.
- Grasp your foot with your right hand and pull it up higher until you feel a nice stretch in the muscles in the front of your leg.
- You can rest your other hand on something for support or just place it on your hip to get in some balance practice at the same time.

Do 2 sets of 10 stretch reps, holding each for 30 seconds.

Figure - 4 stretch

While this stretch doesn't attack the knees directly, it stretches the surrounding muscles, specifically the glutes at the sides of your butt, an area often neglected. Remember, sometimes knee problems are a result of poorly balanced conditioning.

- Grab the back of a chair or a door facing for balance. Cross your right ankle over your left knee, and bend your left knee a little. Pull up on your ankle until you feel a nice stretch in the side of your rear.

Do 2 sets of 10 stretch reps, holding each for 30 seconds.

ARE LEG EXTENSIONS SAFER THAN SQUATS? NOPE

Research reported in *Medicine & Science in Sports & Exercise* found that open-chain exercise in which a single joint is activated, such as the leg extension, are potentially more dangerous than closed-chain moves in which multiple joints are engaged – such as the squat and leg press. The study's author, Anki Stensdotter, found that leg extensions activate your quadriceps muscles slightly independently of each other, and just a 5-millisecond difference in activation causes uneven compression between the kneecap and thighbone.

The knee joint is controlled by the quadriceps and the hamstrings," Stensdotter said. "Balanced muscle activity keeps the [patella] in place and appears to be more easily attained in close-chained exercise." Such as the squat and leg press.

Strengthening the knees

Any of the leg exercises listed in Chapter 3 are good for strengthening the muscles around the knees. If I had to choose two, I would select Hindu squats and one of the Swiss ball exercises for the hamstrings, the muscles on the back of the knees and legs. As I noted in Chapter 3, more and more people are finding that Hindu squats not only build tremendous power and endurance in the legs muscles and knees, but in many cases they relieve existing knee ailments. Will Hindus help every knee problem? No. The knee is far too complex for a one-size-fits-all fix. For sure, if your knees are healthy, the regular practice of Hindus will keep them that way and even make them stronger.

Refer to Chapter 3 and include Hindus once or twice a week to build strength, power, and endurance that will help keep the knee doctors away.

Most squat-type exercises are good as long as they are done correctly.

Important

- Don't allow your knees to go beyond your toes
- Work for balanced development.

- Keep your body straight and aligned.
- Don't use more pounds than you can safely handle.
- Always remember that you want to build your muscles, not tax them with overly strenuous and awkward exercises.

For women's knees only

Researchers are trying to find out why women tend to be more prone to knee injuries than men. They are looking at anatomical causes, such as looser joints caused by female sex hormones and their typically wider pelvises. Dr. Lisa R. Callahan, medical director of the Women's Sports Medicine Center at the Hospital for Special Surgery in New York says that while such factors play an important role, a more critical element might be that many women have not participated in sports training in their youth. Therefore, since their muscles, tendons and nerves are less trained, women might be less physically conditioned than men. So when women in their late teens and older participate in sports, martial arts in particular, their joints and tissues are more susceptible to breaking down.

Women are advised to strengthen their hamstrings, their butt muscles and their inner thighs. Hamstring weakness can also contribute to another knee problem that plagues women more than men: It's called patello-femoral syndrome, a problem that causes the underside of the kneecap to become swollen, sore and inflamed.

Dr. Callahan suggests that women make an extra effort to strengthen their hamstrings, gluteus muscles and the inner part of the thigh muscle. You might also want to cross train on a stationary bicycle, but be sure the seat is positioned so that your knee is bent slightly when your other leg is fully extended. Here are two exercises to strengthen these areas.

BIRTH CONTROL PILLS AND YOUR KNEES

A study conducted by McGill University in Canada and the McGill University Health Center researchers that was published in the *Clinical Journal of Sports Medicine*, showed that female athletes on the pill might have more stable knee joints than those not taking it.

Investigators evaluated the knee stability of 78 female athletes - 42 were taking the pill and 36 were not. An instrument called athrometer was used to measure the knee displacement of their knee joints. The women on the pill had significantly less than those not taking the pill.

The results suggest women on contraceptives have tighter knee joints and may be less susceptible to ligament tears or injuries.

Caution

Side leg raise   This is a common exercise found in women's exercise classes, one that strengthens the normally ignored area around the inside of your knees.

- Lie on your left side with your left leg slightly in front, the side of your foot resting on the floor.
- Keep your left leg straight as you lift it as high as you can.

This one will make you sore so start out conservatively. Do 1 set of 10 reps on each side for the first two or three workouts and progress over the next few weeks to 3 sets of 10 reps.

Wall squats This helps to balance out your leg strength by strengthening your inner thighs, your quads, and the muscles in your butt.

• Press your back against a wall and place a basketball between your knees and squeeze. Use a medicine ball to really tax your muscles.
• Your feet are shoulder width apart, about 24 inches out from the wall, and parallel to each other.
• Squeeze that ball as you slide down the wall until your thighs are sloped at a 45-degree angle.
• Hold for 15 seconds, and then push back up the wall.
• Do nine more and take a minute rest before you do a second set.
• If this is easy and painless on your knees, scoot your feet out a few inches more from the wall so that you can slide down until your thighs are parallel to the floor. Don't let your knees go past your toes and keep squeezing that ball.

Keep adding seconds to each rep over the weeks until you can do 2 sets of 10, 60-second reps.

Swiss ball curl
Refer to Chapter 3, "Swiss ball curl" for the particulars of doing this exercise to strengthen the muscles on the back of the legs and knees.
Do 2 sets of 10 reps.

Important

I have seen many martial artists as well as other athletes traumatized physically and emotionally from knee injuries. Such an injury can cause extraordinary pain that can affect every aspect of your life. Do all that you can to protect your knees and keep them healthy and strong. Train smart and your knees will keep working for you throughout your training years and into your senior years.

Shoulders

Shoulder injuries are a pain, literally and figuratively, affecting virtually everything you do, especially from your waist up. Most shoulder problems are a result of overtraining, high-risk training, and an imbalance in muscle development.

STRENGTHEN YOUR GUNS

Virtually every movement you do with your arms involves your shoulders. Just try to throw a punch without using them. If you have weak arms, your shoulders have to do extra work. Strong biceps, triceps and forearm muscles are critical for hitting hard, blocking fast, grappling with strength, and for reducing the chance of shoulder injury.

Lift weights twice a week and always do curls, triceps work and forearm exercises to get your strength up to par and to give your shoulders some relief. Free weights, as opposed to machines, are better for this purpose because machines don't work the synergistic and stabilizing muscles as well as dumbbells and barbells.

BENCH PRESS

We love to bench press. It feels good, it's good for punching power, and it strokes our egos when we slam up our best poundage. But if we aren't careful, or even if we are, it kills our shoulders. Bench presses are notorious for developing an imbalance between the muscles on the front of the shoulder and those on the back. Add to this all your punching reps, which also develop the front of the shoulders but do little for those at the rear of the shoulders, and you're at risk of tremendous imbalance in your development. An imbalance leads to injury when the weakest muscle is forced to do more than it can handle. For that reason, it's highly recommended that you follow the specialty shoulder exercises offered in this section.

Training Tip

Proper bench press form   Around 90 percent of all shoulder injuries incurred from the bench press happened just as the bar stopped at the chest then transitioned to move upward.

• When the bar is lowered quickly, or simply dropped as when doing plyometric bench pressing, there occurs great linear momentum forces that must be stopped by the shoulder muscles in order to thrust the bar upward.

o If the force is greater than what the shoulder joint or surrounding muscles can handle, the lifter gets a funny indentation in his chest and a ripping sound in his shoulder.

• The simple remedy is to always lower the bar with control.

o That doesn't mean you have to pause at the bottom, but rather allow the bar to touch the chest before you push it back up.

Pinch your shoulder blades together   Most benches are about 11 inches wide, which means your shoulder blades are left unsupported.

Training Tip

• To fix this, simply pinch your blades together and tighten your upper back muscles a moment before you lift the bar off the rack.

o This action keeps your shoulder blades supported on the bench and keeps excessive pressure off your shoulder joints.

Keep your feet on the floor   Many bench pressers lift their knees near their chest and cross their ankles, or they place their feet on the bench. I must admit that I've done this for years and have written in other books that it's okay. But new information shows that it isn't. Sorry.

• The problem is that in either of these positions your body is unstable, and instability when lifting is an invitation to injury. I've been lucky, but I'm not going to chance it any more.

• Place your feet on the floor about shoulder width apart.

o If you have to kick and squirm during the exercise, you have too much weight on the bar.

ROTATOR CUFF STRENGTHENERS

I mentioned earlier that I don't like doctors because, well, they frighten me. But with 40 years of martial arts training under my belt, I'm no stranger to them. Many of those doctor visits were for shoulder problems. On one occasion I separated a shoulder during a violent arrest of a guy who had just stabbed another guy in the temple with an ice pick. Most often I hurt my shoulders playing the bad guy to police recruits in training. Getting my arms jacked up hard behind my back a few thousand times by these young hotdogs strained my shoulders in more places than there are places.

Other times I developed problems from training too hard and resting too little. In other words, my shoulder problems have probably been no different than other martial artist with a long history of training, competing, and applying the fighting arts for real. And like other fighters, most of mine have been rotator cuff injuries, which are usually a result of overuse, improper development and lack of flexibility.

THE TECHNICAL STUFF MADE EASY

Your shoulder joint is surrounded by four muscles and their supporting tendons, all of which are referred to as the rotator cuff (not "cup" as many people say). This is surrounded by an empty sac, called bursa, which helps the tendons slide. The rotator cuff is susceptible to many problems that result in weakness, tenderness and pain, such as tendonitis, that dull ache you get when moving your arm this way or that way.

Punching, backfisting, blocking and other like movements can cause tendonitis. Sometimes a calcium deposit can form in the rotary cuff causing inflammation of the tendon and sac. As we get older, the cuff tendons tend to weaken and degenerate. A rotator cuff tear can occur as a result of all these problems, or when the weakened tendons are overstressed during hard martial arts training, including awkward takedowns to the floor. Most rotator cuff problems can be treated with ice, rest, medication and easy exercises. Pain lasting longer than two weeks should be checked out by your doctor.

Overuse and trauma from martial arts training and competing are hard on your rotator cuffs. Tendonitis is quite common, as are rips when the tendons are overloaded from lifting, throwing improperly, and not getting proper rest.

Your shoulder is capable of a large range of motion, requiring flexibility of the ligaments to allow for that range. When they become stretched or torn they become unstable. Even a little instability will allow your shoulder to slip part way out of its socket. This is called a subluxation and it hurts like the dickens. When your shoulder comes completely out of its socket it's called a dislocation and that hurts, too, maybe more.

There are many other types of painful injuries that can happen to your shoulder joint, but we don't need to list them all here. Just know that while your shoulder is vulnerable to many problems, you can take steps to reduce susceptibility. Specifically, you need to include rotary cuff exercises in your training regimen. Think of it this way: Prevention is much better and much easier than rehabilitation and cure. Hey, let's put those doctors out of business. Have I mentioned that I don't like them?

Like the martial arts, medical science is changing constantly and usually for the better. The four rotator cuff exercises listed here have been around for a while and have helped millions of athletes get stronger and injury resistant.

Important: These exercises are not to develop mass and they are not to impress onlookers as to the incredible poundage you can lift. They are designed to strengthen the internal workings of your shoulders. Maybe you can do 65-pound laterals (though no one has ever seen you do them) but with the rotator cuff exercises you're going to use 2-pound dumbbells, then 3-pounders, and max out at about 5 pounds. And you're going to do a lot of reps, 20 to 30 per set. If you can't do that many, you're using too much weight.

If you're doing these because you have an existing shoulder injury, be sure to slap a bag of ice on it afterwards for 20 minutes. That is all I'll say about that because you should be getting that information from your doctor or physical therapist.

Forward arm raise

- Lie on your stomach on a weight bench or the edge of your bed, your left arm hanging straight down, your hand grasping a dumbbell.
- Slowly raise your left hand, stopping when it's level with your shoulder. Your arm is now bent 90 degrees.
- Slowly lower your hand until your arm is once again straight.

Do 1 set of 20 to 30 reps with each arm.

Backhand raise

- Lie on your right side on a bench, bed or floor with a rolled-up towel under your right armpit.
- Extend your right arm out beyond your head and press the inside of your upper left arm against your left side, your arm bent, your forearm against your chest, palm facing inward.
- Roll your left shoulder out as you raise your left forearm until it's level with your shoulder, a motion similar to a partial backfist.
- Slowly lower the arm. Don't lift your elbow off your side.

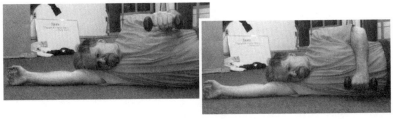

Do 1 set of 20 to 30 reps with each arm.

Shoulder curl

- Lie on a bench or the floor on your right side with your left arm extended along your left side.
- Bend your right arm 90 degrees with your forearm resting on the table.
- Roll your right shoulder in as you raise right forearm up to your chest. This is like a forehand swing for you tennis buffs.
- Slowly lower the forearm and repeat.

Do 1 set of 20 to 30 reps with each arm

Standing lateral raises   Do these one arm at a time, both arms at the same time, or alternate, right, left, right, left. Let's do it alternating.

- Begin in a standing position holding a weight in each hand half way between the front of your body and the side of your body.
- Rotate your wrists so that your thumbs are angled downward. If you had been holding two glasses of water, you just poured the water out.
- Raise your right arm until it's at a 45-degree angle, half

way between horizontal with the floor and hanging straight down. Lower it slowly.

- Lift your left arm and lower it in the same fashion.

Do 20 to 30 reps with each arm.

Your shoulder routine

Here is how you can include rotator cuff exercises with your workout. Remember, your objective, as always, is to not over train, which is arguably the leading cause of injuries in the martial arts, weight training, and every other sport except quilt making.

You lift weights and practice martial arts   Let's say you lift weights on Tuesday and Friday and you practice martial arts on Monday, Wednesday and Saturday. That is a lot of training without even doing rotator cuff exercises, so it's critical that you're cognizant about how your body feels, especially your shoulders. If they are tired and you haven't worked out, they are crying out for a day off. You owe it to them and your longevity in training to give them what they want. If it's a weight training day, skip your shoulder workout and work your other body parts. Don't worry, your shoulders aren't going to shrink and go away. They are still getting worked by virtue of helping with the other exercises. If it's a martial arts day, consider skipping class – where you have less control over what you do - and stay home to do several sets of solo kicking drills. Your shoulders will thank you. Your kicks, too.

Training Tip

- Do the above four rotator cuff exercises on your weight training day. Here are some ways to do that.

o If you have energy to burn, do them in conjunction with your regular shoulder exercises. Do the four exercises (remember, you're only using 2-to 5-pound weights) first, then proceed to your regular shoulder exercises.

o If you don't have energy to burn, do the rotator cuff exercises instead of your usual shoulder workout. Do them for two months then return to your regular shoulder routine for two months. Continue to go back and forth in this manner.

Training Tip

o If you're just itching to do a heavy shoulder exercise, do the four rotator cuff exercises first, then do one heavy set of your regular shoulder exercises, say, laterals for the side of your shoulders and bent over laterals for the back of them. You don't need to do anything for the front since your chest exercises and all your punching does a good job of it.

You don't lift weights but practice martial arts   First of all, shame on you. You need to lift weights to develop speed, power, bone density and to look good at the beach. The first three reasons are paramount.

- If you practice martial arts on Monday, Wednesday and Friday, do the rotator cuff exercises on two of the opposite days.

Caution

You have an on-going shoulder problem   How you incorporate these exercises with your other activities is up to your physical therapist. He might have you do them six days a week with one day to rest. If you have been told not to train for a few weeks or even a few months so that your shoulder can get better from rest and the rotator cuff exercises, follow that advice but talk to him about kicking and various other exercises. If he says yes, but warns you to be careful not to hurt your shoulder, great. You're going to come out of your shoulder recuperation period with awesome kicks. Check out *Solo Training* for lots of kicking drills you can do by yourself.

SHOULD YOU GO UNDER THE BLADE?

You're following a sensible exercise program but your arm still hurts or there is a glaring weakness in some arm motions. It's time to see a doctor, specifically, a surgeon, a guy with a great big glistening knife. Don't do what I do, but what I advise: See a doctor. I kid a lot about them, but I strongly advise you to go to yours when your gut tells you to.

Lower back

Logic dictates that possessing a strong, flexible lower back and well developed abdominals will ward off back pain. Not so. While having these qualities is better than not having them, you must still take care not to engage in activities that put your back at risk.

I like to think that I have a stronger than average lower back, a result of years of weight training, stretching exercises, and always following my mother's advice to "lift with your legs, not your back." Still, my back blows out about once every 18 months. A couple of those times it's sent me spiraling to the ground like a skid row drunk. I'm walking and talking and joking and *boing!* the lower back goes, and I'm whimpering and writhing on the ground. And talk about your pain!

Since coincidences are, well, coincidental, my back went out three days ago. Seriously. It's been about 18 months, and although this time it's not as bad as others, I haven't been able to train or do much of anything else. I'm guessing it was caused by a combination of trying new and especially strenuous exercises that involved the lower back and doing awkward yard work that required bending over while operating a heavy hedge trimmer.

Endurance might be more important than strength

It didn't matter that my back is quite strong and flexible, what mattered was that these new stressors – movements that were out of the norm of my usual training - were stacked one on top of the other, until my back had had enough and went out. It's possible that the cause of my problem was two fold: I have a muscle weakness in certain parts of my lower back, as well as a lack of endurance there. Many back specialists are now saying that it's often poor endurance that leads to lower back problems, not lack of strength and flexibility.

Important

FLEXIBILITY ISN'T ENOUGH

There is surprisingly little evidence to show that flexibility prevents pain and episodes of the back "going out." Even Olympic gymnasts, athletes whose flexibility is often without equal, suffer from back problems. So, does this mean you shouldn't stretch your lower back? No, as long as you have a healthy back. However, if you have a lower back injury, stretching it, though it might feel good, can lead to greater injury. I recommend you talk to your doctor about lower back flexibility exercises.

HOW A WARM-UP SAVES YOUR BACK

You sit in school or at work all day and then you sit in a car or bus to commute to your martial arts school. Now it's time to train. Know that when you have been inactive for a while your muscles tend to contract. Should you jump right into your workout, your resting (inactive) blood supply is inadequate to meet the needs of your muscles that are suddenly forced to work at or near full capacity. This makes you a target for one or more muscles going *boing!* and pain that grows more intense every passing minute.

A sufficient warm-up dilates the blood vessels so that the increased blood supply improves your performance in both aerobic and anaerobic activities. Be sure to include light stretching, too, so that your muscles reach their maximum length, making them less likely to become tweaked or torn.

Let's begin with three exercises that are often recommended for lower back strength and flexibility when you're suffering from lower back pain.

Caution

Note: It's highly recommended that you talk to your doctor first before doing any exercise, especially when you're injured or experiencing pain. Studies show that people with bad backs who design their own workout regimens did worse than those who sought advice from a physical therapist.

EXERCISES FOR LOW BACK PAIN

There are as many types of low back pain as there are low back exercises. The following are good strength, endurance and flexibility exercises that also relieve or reduce pain for many people. Ask your doctor if these are good ones for you.

Crunches Though you're probably familiar with these ab exercises,
just make sure you're including the
following elements.
• Cross your arms behind your
head, rest your hands on your chest, or
place the backs of your hands on your
forehead to work your neck at the same
time.

• Press your lower back into the floor and hold it there. This alone might give you some pain relief.
• Experiment with different leg positions to determine which ones don't cause additional back pain.
o For bad backs, it's often suggested that you bend your knees and keep your feet on the floor.

Do 2 or 3 sets of 10 to 15 reps two or three times a week.

Pelvic tilt This feels good and might provide relief.

• Lie on your back with your knees up and your feet flat on the floor.
• Tighten your butt and stomach muscles so they angle upward a little then press your lower back into the floor.
• Hold for a second as you breathe normally.

To progress over the weeks, add two seconds each workout until you can do it easily for 5 seconds. Then extend your legs forward a little every other workout until you can eventually do it with your legs straight. There is no hurry to get to this last position. Take your time and give your muscles time to strengthen.

Easy, feel-good stretches

Ask your doctor if these are okay for you.

STRETCH 1

- Lie on your back and draw your knees to your chest with your arms extended out to the sides.
- Slowly lower both legs, knees together, to your right as far as you can go comfortably while keeping both shoulders on the floor. Hold for 20 seconds.
- Roll your legs over to the left side and hold for 20.

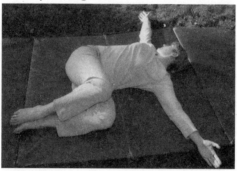

Repeat 5 times while breathing normally.

STRETCH 2

- Lie on your back with your legs extended on the floor.
- Draw one knee toward your chest, keeping the other leg where it was, and use your hands to pull your knee into your chest for a pleasurable stretch.
- Hold for 20 seconds and then do the same to the other leg.

Do 5 reps with each leg.

Stretch 3

- Get down on your hands and knees.
- Lift your right arm straight out horizontally as you lift your left leg.
- Reach as far forward as you can with your arm, and reach as far back as you can with your leg.
- Tense your abs and hold for 20 seconds.
- Repeat by lifting your left arm and your right leg and hold for 20 seconds.

Do 5 reps on both sides.

Carrying extra pounds?

Seventy percent of Americans are overweight. It's a shame that obesity needs to be discussed in a book for martial athletes. Although I'd guess there are fewer overweight people in the fighting arts, it's still an issue; indeed, being overweight is dangerous for fighters.

Excess bodyweight increases stress on the spine and pressure on the discs. A big gut tugs the spine forward and out of alignment and sets a person up for a back injury.

If this is you, get a copy of *The Fighter's Body* by yours truly and co-author Wim Demeere and get rid of those extra pounds that are hurting your back bones.

Your martial arts will improve, too.

Bow with weight

This is a great move to develop power for grappling, especially for muscling out of a hold.

- In a standing position, hold a barbell plate in the crooks of both arms, with your upper arms against your chest. If you suffer from lower back pain, do this exercise for a week or two without weights. When you do add weight, begin with a 5-pound plate, less if 5 aggravates your back.
- Your feet are shoulder-width apart with your knees slightly bent.
- Bend forward at your hips with your back straight until your upper body is about 45 degrees.
- Forcefully drive your hips forward to return to your starting position. If you're experiencing lower back pain, straighten slowly rather than forcefully.
- When returning to the upright position, stop at the vertical position. *Don't continue to bend backwards* because that will add stress to your lower back, and set you up for an injury.

Do 2 sets of 8 reps if you have a healthy lower back, and increase the poundage when you feel you're ready. If you suffer from lower back pain, do 1 set of 5 to 8 reps. Let your pain, or lack of it, determine when you add an additional set.

Cobra without cheating

The cobra exercise is a yoga favorite because it isolates the lower back so intensely that it doesn't require added resistance. The version presented here is tougher than most yoga cobras since you don't get to push yourself up with your arms and support your upper body weight on them. This one is all about your lower back with some additional work by your upper back.

- Lie face down on the floor with your arms along your sides and your chin on the floor.
- Keep looking downward as you lift your head and upper body, and then squeeze your shoulder blades together as you raise your stiff arms.
- Without lifting your legs and feet, rotate your hands so that your thumbs point upward, and lift your arms as high as you can as you continue to squeeze your shoulder blades together.
- Breathe normally as you hold that position and think about something pleasant.

One set consists of 1, 60-second rep. Do 2 or 3 sets if you have a healthy lower back. If you suffer from lower back pain, do 3 sets of a single 5- to 10-second rep per set. Let your pain, or lack of it, determine when you add additional seconds per set.

PROLONGED SITTING = BACK PAIN

If you're a school student perched on a chair all day or you ride a desk at work, you might already know that sitting for long periods hits the ol' back right where it hurts. It's even worse if you don't move around occasionally. When you're frozen in place trying to figure out a math problem in school, or you're at work trying to figure out why the Hensley account is all messed up, stress focuses in one area of your back. It's an intense pain that feels like Bruno, the black belt with the narrow forehead, just sidekicked you in the spine. The solution? Move around.

At least every 20 or 30 minutes get up. If you're in a school setting, make a trip to the wastepaper basket or pencil sharpener. At work, carry the file over to the window, or walk around the room as you close the deal on the phone.

Instant back stress relief   Stand with your feet about shoulder-width apart and reach up slowly toward the ceiling with both hands as your inhale deeply. Exhale as you lower your arms. Do about 5 reps and you will be going, "Aaahhh."

Nearly sixty million Americans suffer from back pain and they all want relief. They spend money on special mattresses, pillows, chairs, braces, and drugs in a desperate effort to rid themselves of pain. Now, if yours is caused by a lousy bed or a bad chair at work, then a new mattress and a different chair might do the trick. But if your back pain began with your martial arts training, or when you began a different phase of training, such as grappling or high kicks, the problem lies in how your body is responding to the new activity.

Begin by talking with your teacher about it. If he can't recommend a solution that works, make an appointment with a physical therapist (if you can find one with martial arts experience you're in luck). Talk to the therapist about your pain and your activities so that he can work out a course of action for you. It might be as simple as modifying how you do a movement, or a matter of assigning you supplemental exercises to strengthen a weakness in your back.

21 Ways to Develop a Powerful Mind-Set

Enthusiasm

"It is not what happens to you, but the way that you interpret the things that are happening to you that determines how you feel. It's your version of events that largely determines whether they motivate or de-motivate you, whether they energize or de-energize you."
- Brian Tracy – motivational speaker

I've had the pleasure of working with and being friends with two men who have the ability to electrify a room just by walking into it. Coincidentally, or maybe not, both have been commanding officers in the Army, one in an elite combat force in Vietnam and the other, my co-author of the book *On Combat*, Lt. Col. Dave Grossman, who recently retired as an Army ranger and a Professor of Military Science. Both of these guys could make a good living selling ice boxes in Antarctica, so contagious is their enthusiasm for everything, even unnecessary refrigeration in a land of ice.

The Vietnam veteran went on to climb through the ranks of the Portland (Oregon) Police Bureau where I served under him when he was captain of the gang unit. He had the ability to simply walk through a room full of gang enforcement officers, men and women who were laying it on the line every day on bloody, gang-infested streets, and leave in his wake officers pumped with enthusiasm to go out and do it again. His charms worked on me, too, even when I could see exactly what he was doing. One time he even convinced me to write a college course outline for a class he was teaching at a university. By the time he walked away I was excited for the opportunity to get to do extra work. Yes, he was a master of manipulating people, but a healthy part of his ability came from his enthusiasm for life in general, for the cops under his command, for police work, and on a personal level, for his career.

Lt. Col. Dave Grossman, who gives nearly 300 presentations a year around the country and overseas, is considered one of the most powerful speakers on the lecture circuit. The ex-West Point psychology professor paces a room like a panther, lecturing with passion and zeal for eight hours without referring to notes and with a contagious enthusiasm that more times than not has the crowd – whether it's cops, teachers, medics, Special Forces, pilots, or Marines - leaping to their feet as one body in thunderous ovation.

Co-authoring *On Combat* was one of those most grueling, painstaking and wonderfully inspiring experiences I've had as a writer, which was made all the more enjoyable by the Colonel's infectious enthusiasm for the project and the good that it will do for warriors everywhere. Not only is he a co-author but a friend whose zest for life makes him a joy to be around.

While these two men have never met, they share a commonality: an unbridled enthusiasm and optimism for all that they do. So intense is their enthusiasm that only a zombie would be immune. Everyone else is uplifted, inspired, and motivated by it.

STAY CHARGED

To stay enthusiastic and motivated, you must be optimistic. You must tell yourself ahead of time that you're going to respond positively no matter what is shoveled your way. Tell yourself that bad news, negative comments and rude actions will not drag you down. You're a martial arts warrior, driven to being the best you can be – no matter what. *No matter what.*

Say to yourself in your bathroom mirror, in the shower, and while driving in your car: "I'm a winner." "I can do it." "No matter what obstacles pop up in front of me, *I can do it.*"

In countless studies, psychologists have found that optimism and enthusiasm are powerful qualities needed for personal and professional success and happiness. Shrinks say that optimists share three personality traits, and I'm going to toss in a fourth.

Important

• Enthusiastic optimists aren't whiners but winners who seek solutions to problems.
- o The optimist martial artist doesn't blame his fighting style, teacher or classmates for his problems, but seeks solutions through study and training.
- o He asks for help, does research, and trains solo to focus on areas needing improvement.

• Enthusiastic optimists aren't set back by life's warts and thorns, but rather look for lessons in them that help them grow and become stronger.
- o When the optimist martial artist fails a belt test he analyzes what happened instead of throwing himself in front of a cement truck.
- o He talks to his teacher, other classmates and reflects honestly on his performance.
- o Then he does what he has to do to correct the problems.

• The enthusiastic optimists look for the good in every situation.
- o No matter what life throws the optimist martial artist – a broken toe, a tweaked wrist or a temporary change in work schedule that prevents going to class – he looks for the good.
- o A broken toe means he has more time to work on hand techniques; a tweaked wrist means he can work on elbow strikes; and a change in work schedule means he can have more solo sessions to work on techniques he wants to work on.

I believe goal setting is the fourth trait that optimists share.

Goals

The enthusiastic optimist isn't a rudderless ship sitting lazily in the water, but a battleship steaming ahead full throttle. He learns from past errors but he certainly doesn't dwell on negativity. Everything about him is positive, enthusiastic and oriented toward progressing – always progressing.

WHY GOALS?

Are you a procrastinator when it comes to training by yourself? Do you have trouble concentrating when training solo? Do you suffer from lack of motivation when it comes to being consistent in your regular martial arts class, let alone training solo? If you suffer from any of these, your goals are probably nonexistent or poorly planned.

Goal setting is a skill that needs to be worked at. Think of it like your biceps: to get them strong you have to exercise. Same is true with your goals. Without clearly thought out goals that are written down, you will only drift through your martial arts training, as well as your life.

Without a clear vision of what is important in your training, you will easily be distracted by whatever crosses your path. This isn't to say that you should not be intrigued and interested in things other than the fighting arts, but without focus, without knowing exactly where you want to go to keep you on track, you can easily drift off and risk never finding your way back.

I don't follow sports and rarely watch it on television. I do, however, love the Olympic Games and never miss watching a day of the two-week competition. Besides watching the events, I'm especially interested as to what these champions – these men and women who are arguably the greatest athletes on the planet – have to say about goal setting. Every competitor interviewed – whether the athlete is in gymnastics, judo, taekwondo, high jumping, or badminton (they really have badminton? Yup.) – talks about the critical importance of having training goals.

To sum up what they say: Without them you flounder; with them you progress.

WRITE THEM DOWN

There is power in writing. You think it, it has to bounce around inside your skull for a second, and then you have to think about how to put it into writing. There tends to be greater commitment when forming words and placing them on paper.

ESTABLISH A TIME SCALE

There are different ways to make a time scale depending on your goal. For example, if you're just beginning in the fighting arts, it's unrealistic to make a goal of achieving your black belt in one year. However, if you lack flexibility, it isn't unreasonable to set a goal of getting close to doing the splits at the 12-month mark.

With some goals your time scale might look like this:

• **Immediate goal** (this month, this week, this day) Example: Practice answering the oral questions this week for Saturday's belt test.
• **Short-term goal** (1 year) Example: Earn a blue belt by March, a green by August and compete in two tournaments, one in May and one in October.
• **Intermediate-term goal** (2 years) Example: Earn the brown belt.
• **Long-term goal** (3 years) Example: Earn the black belt.

The time scale might be shorter for other goals:

• **Immediate goal** (this month, this week, this day) Example: Do two kata workouts this week.
• **Short-term goal** (2 months) Example: Increase kata practice to three times a week. Kicks and punches in the kata must be fast, strong and crisp at the two-month mark.
• **Intermediate-term goal** (4 months) Example: Increase kata practice to 5 or 6 days a week. The form should be near competition ready. Work on flexibility and aerobic fitness.
• **Long-term goal** (6 months) Example: The kata will be flawless, flexibility will be optimum, and speed, power and crispness will be right on the money. I WILL be ready for the tournament this month.

In two months all the goals will move up one. For example, what is now listed as your Short-term goal will have progressed to your Immediate goal. The others will have moved up, too. That means you will have to establish a new Long-germ goal. It can be on the same subject or you can begin a new one as you continue to meet the first three timelines.

HIGH GOALS BUT REASONABLE

Your goals should force you to train consistently and progressively, but they shouldn't be so extreme that you can't possibly make the goal or injure yourself trying. Push beyond your comfort zone, but do so safely.

Be specific   Don't make your 6-month goal too broad, such as, "I want to be good." Make it specific: "I want my kata to be competition-ready;" "I want to sidekick head high;" "I want to increase my bench press by 30 pounds."

Write down *how* you will reach your goal   Say your 4-month intermediate goal is to be in good enough shape to practice your kata 5 days a week. Jot down underneath that goal how you plan to accomplish it. For example, you write:

- Check with my instructor that I'm doing the form correctly.
- Get the instructor's advice as to any particulars I need to work on.
- Do the kata 5 times by myself after my Monday, Wednesday and Friday classes.
- When my strength, aerobic capacity, endurance and recuperation are good, add a Tuesday session at home.
- When I've improved even more, add a Thursday session.

Find a way   As noted before, life has a way of interfering with your plans. Say your plan was to do your kata five times at this afternoon's workout, but your boss said you had to stay and work overtime. Instead of punching the wall (or your boss), spend five minutes before your morning shower working on, say, that difficult turn at the form's half way point. Move quickly and you can get in 10 or 15 reps of the movement before you have to get ready for work. You missed your planned workout, but your mini training session smoothed out a problem section in your form, even if just a little. You progressed a tad because you didn't overreact to the change in your schedule but instead made the best of it. Your optimism saved the day.

Goal setting is just another tool to help you on your journey. It's an important tool, one that is vital for success. But don't let it control you. Don't become so obsessive, so totally focused that you miss the joy and fun of the journey. Yes, you want to reach your goals, but don't let the objective make you miserable. Strive forward with the intent of progressing intelligently while enjoying all the other wonderful things life has to offer.

Mental toughness: fatigue training

I remember reading something karate great Joe Lewis wrote about a training regimen that he and his partner used. They would first thoroughly exhaust themselves with exercises, bag work, air reps, and so on. *Then* they would spar. They didn't spar when they were fresh, rested, high on sugar or caffeine. They sparred when their bodies were begging for a shower and sleep.

The idea was to see what they could and could not do when exhausted. They knew what they were capable of when fresh, but they wanted to know what worked physically when their bodies felt like road kill and their minds were crying to give up and get it over with. As competitors, this was important knowledge to have about themselves for those all-day, energy-depleting tournaments, and for tough matches that would go into overtime.

It's also important to know for the street, especially since the nature of a self-defense situation is sudden and explosive. One second you're thinking about buying a new athletic supporter and the next second you're thrashing around with a big, fat ape. Since there isn't time to warm-up and prepare your system for the battle, the suddenness of the attack taxes your cardiovascular system no matter how conditioned you are. To survive when your body and mind are enveloped in debilitating fatigue requires pre-established knowledge of what techniques to use and how best to draw deeply into your mental fortitude to keep fighting.

Let's look at two training methods that will help you to develop these qualities.

Warning: This is a tough regimen. Be especially cautious if you're out of shape, overweight, or you're nursing an injury. Check with your doc first.

MAXIMUM CARDIO, THEN LIFT WEIGHTS

Choose a cardio workout that you know drains your energy and strength. This is different for everyone. You can do:

- explosive sprints for 10 to 15 minutes.

- hard and fast shadow sparring for 10 to 15 minutes.
- fast rope jumping for 10 to 15 minutes.
- hard punches and kicks on the heavy bag for 10 to 15 minutes.
- hard and fast jumping jacks for 5 minutes, squat thrusts - squat and put your hands on the floor, kick your feet out behind you, kick your feet back up near your hands, and stand up - for 5 minutes, and jumping jacks again for another 5 minutes.

Partners

Tired? Good. Now, *without resting* and *without catching your breath*, pump out 3 sets of 10 reps of bench presses. You won't be able to use as much weight and you had better use a spotter. Focus on using good form and on keeping your mind zeroed in on the task.

Too easy, you say? What an animal! Okay, then the next time you pre-fatigue yourself with any of the above methods, follow with your entire weight workout. If it's chest, shoulders and triceps day, do that routine without resting after your aerobic session. Remember, your objective is to do the weight exercises carefully, with good form and with total mental concentration. This is a time to examine yourself to see how your muscles respond and how your mind works when you're tired, winded, and your heart rate is hammering at 175 beats a minute, just as when you're fighting in a tough bout or on the street.

MAXIMUM CARDIO, THEN WORK YOUR COMBINATIONS

Clearly this next exercise is best with a live partner responding to your techniques and making them difficult for you to do well. But you can still get a feel for the quality of your techniques and your mental condition when working on them by yourself.

- Choose any of the above pre-fatigue methods.
- Then without stopping, do as many Hindu squats (Chapter 3) as you can followed by as many fast regular push-ups as you can. To repeat, both of these should be done fast and to the burnout point.
- Then, without taking a moment's rest and without letting your heart rate and breathing return to normal, work your combination on the heavy bag.
  o Do it fast and do it hard, as if you were really trying to stop an assailant from hurting you and getting to your family.

As you huff and puff (and whine), check to see if you're doing any of the following.

- Are you telegraphing (winding up) to generate power?
- Are your techniques weak to the point of being ineffective?
- Are you excessively slow?
- Do you mentally just not care?
- Do you hate my guts for suggesting this training regimen?

These are common physical and mental responses to extreme fatigue that you want to understand and know how to respond to. For sure you want to use the best body mechanics to hit with optimum form and optimum power to the most vulnerable targets. When you're fresh, your reverse punch could normally drop a big bruiser of a guy when hitting him in the chest. But in your weakened condition, you're wiser to aim for highly vulnerable targets like the throat, groin and kidneys. If you're especially weak, use finger strikes to the eyes instead of your punch. If your roundhouse kick to the abdomen usually drops your opponents into a whimpering pile, you should now target the groin and peroneal nerve (a highly vulnerable nerve that runs the length of the thigh on the outside of the leg), targets that don't require as great an impact to do damage.

Training Tip

Know that when you train in this fashion on a regular basis (once a week is enough), your body will quickly adapt and, in a couple of months, your fitness level will be at an all-time high. That means you're going to have to work harder and longer during the aerobic session to get pre-fatigued. Some days it's going to be especially tough and you will wonder why and the heck you're putting yourself through this. So try to remember this: The value of this training is to experience physical and mental fatigue and then draw upon your mental toughness to execute quality combinations or lift heavy weights.

TRAIN TO KEEP GRAPPLING WHEN FATIGUED

After draining yourself of your energy and oxygen supply using one of the above listed aerobic exercises, choose one or all of the heavy bag exercises in Chapter 4 "13 Ways to Improve Your Core Grappling Strength." For example, clean and press a heavy bag for 1 or 2 sets of 10 reps. Or do a set of "Lift, rotate and put down" with the heavy bag.

It's tough enough doing a set of heavy benches when you're wiped out, but handling a bag is like manhandling a human being: awkward, heavier on one arm than the other, and difficult to move.

Find it within yourself to finish the bag-lifting sets no matter how your brain screams at you to lie down and rest.

Self-talk   During your quiet times alone or during your meditation, tell yourself that whether your fight is in the ring or in the street, you will keep fighting no matter how tired and winded you might be. Maybe you feel feint and you want to throw up, but you will keep fighting until the referee calls halt or the assailant gives up. *You will keep fighting. You will keep fighting.*

Your driving willpower, as well as your physical and mental exposure to the red zone of profound fatigue will teach you what you can and cannot do. Then when you encounter it in competition or in the street, you won't be shocked, frightened and debilitated. You will have experienced functioning in that place and, therefore, you will know what to expect and what to do.

8

Walking Meditation

Author's note: Not every meditation method works for everyone, so I encourage you to explore various ways to find one that works best for you. In my book The Mental Edge – available at www.lwcbooks.com – I offer several methods to bring on a deep state of relaxation for mediation and self-hypnosis practice. In Fighter's Fact Book and Solo Training – both published by Turtle Press – I discuss mediation as it relates to mental imagery practice. Since I cover several methods in depth in these books, I'm not going to repeat it here. Instead, I will focus on walking meditation.

In a nutshell, meditation is a powerful tool that works. Those who agree with that are Olympic champion athletes and other top sports competitors, top martial artists, elite warriors in law enforcement and the military, and a host of successful people in business and artistic endeavors. Would these people spend their precious time on something that wasn't critical to their performance? Of course not.

Why meditate?

Buddhists teach that meditation provides you with a way to quiet your mind so that you can be more aware of all the mental processes that lead to your greater fulfillment in life. Additionally, meditation gives you the tools to change your mental states so that you become happier, more productive and more successful.

Important

As a martial artist, meditation helps you find calmness and peacefulness. It also helps you develop a mind that is receptive to learning and perceptive to what is going on inside and around you. A conditioned body and a clear mind allow the two to work as one so that your martial movements are executed more smoothly, quickly, powerfully, and correctly. This is called harmony, and it will be yours through physical practice and the regular practice of meditation.

Although many religions incorporate meditation, the act doesn't have to be a religious one, or have nationality or politics. All it needs is you.

WALKING VS. SEATED

Perhaps one of the biggest differences that many people find between seated mediation and walking meditation is that when they are in motion it's easier to focus on their breathing and on de-cluttering their thinking. However, some purists believe that mediation can only be done while sitting in a lotus position and argue that any other method isn't meditation or, at best, is a watered down version.

Well, it's been my experience and the experience of many other people who practice walking meditation that that is an incorrect view. These particular purists are defining meditation by what is happening outwardly - sitting in a particular way in a dimly lit room with mellow music playing and incense burning - as opposed to what is going on inside one's mind. While this environment is nice, it's not necessary. Case in point: I've meditated while wearing a bullet-proof vest and several pounds of gear and weapons, while crammed in the back of a police van with several other cops, en route to raid a gang-infested apartment.

HOW TO MEDITATE MADE EASY

Walking meditation is active meditation. You use the physical, mental, and even emotional experience of walking as the basis of developing greater awareness of yourself, while at the same time instilling calm to your mind and a sense of control through awareness of your thoughts and breathing. For many, walking meditation is simply a more enjoyable way to engage in the process.

• You can walk outdoors or indoors, as long as you can walk without obstructions, pits, traffic, stairs, and so on.

   o It's best to have a quiet street, parking lot, empty room, some place that allows you to walk without having to turn.

   o That said, it's okay to turn, although at first you might find it a tad distracting.

• Your hands

   o You can hold your hands at your side.

   o You can place your palms together, finger tips up, in what is known as gassho.

   o You can make a fist and cover it with your other hand (a hand position used by many kung fu styles as their salute), then hold both against your navel.

   o You can clasp your hands behind your back.

• Your upper body is relaxed, though your back is straight and your head is held high. Your lower body is relaxed and natural.

• You can wear shoes or go barefoot.

• Before you begin walking, take a moment to center yourself with 4-count breathing.

   o Breathe in through your nose, filling your lower belly, and breathe out through your mouth.

   o Breathe in 2, 3, 4, hold 2, 3, 4. Exhale 2, 3, 4, hold 2, 3, 4. Repeat the cycle 2 or 3 more times.

Though there are several variations of how to walk and breathe, I think the following is the easiest.

• Breathe in as you take two or three slow steps.

   o If you want, say quietly "breathe in" as you step.

• Breathe out as you take two or three slow steps.

   o If you want, say quietly "breathe out" as you step.

   o Sometimes you take two steps, sometimes three or four. Sometimes there will be more steps on the out-breath than on the in-breath.

   o It's the concentration and awareness that is important, not whether you take two or three steps.

• Breathe normally and strive to find a natural rhythm with your steps.

• Walk and breathe at a slow pace, especially the first few times you do it.

• If you have to turn right or left or you have to turn completely around and head back in the direction from which you just came, do so smoothly and seamlessly while continuing to breathe.

• Walk for 15 to 20 minutes.

BREATH CONTROL

Every time you practice walking meditation you also practice breath control. For example, you control the frequency, allowing each inhalation and exhalation to calm your anxieties slowly and naturally. By controlling your breath, you control your mind.

When you're nervous, anxious and terrified, your breathing reflects these moods. Often, your accelerated breathing intensifies the moods in a never ending cycle. The control you learn from continuous meditation practice enables you to gain control of your breathing and help to regain control of your mental and physical faculties so you can function smoothly and appropriately.

Just as practicing martial arts strengthens and disciplines your body, meditation practice toughens and disciplines your mind.

WHERE ARE YOU GOING?

Your destination when practicing walking meditation is wherever you are at any given second in time. That's so deep! Like something you would hear from a white-bearded sage sitting in the lotus position before a high-mountain cave. Nonetheless, it's true. Walking meditation isn't about where you came from or where you're going. It's all about the moment: Your step, your breath and your perception of both. This simplicity of thought is what removes the clutter from your mind.

WHAT TO THINK ABOUT

You want to think about your breath coinciding with your steps. Not the last breath you took with your last steps or the one you're going to take with your next steps, but only the one you're doing now. This breath, these steps, right now.

• When distracted by things around you, look at the ground three feet ahead.
 o If a bird flies by, see it, then forget about it as you return mentally to your steps and breathing.
 o Should you hear a car honk somewhere (you're not walking in the street are you?), acknowledge that you heard it, and then return to your breathing and stepping.
 o Don't fret when you're distracted. Just recognize it and return to the moment.

Caution

• Should you get dizzy it could be because you're forcing your breathing.
 o Stop walking and take a few calm, controlled breaths, but blow out just a little more than you inhaled. This helps you get rid of excess CO_2, which occurs when the breathing phase is forced.

Understand that there is nothing mystical about walking meditation. It's simply a device to calm your mind and body to help you progress in your martial arts training. You're not going to clear your mind of all thoughts. Not only is it impossible, but the harder you try the more thoughts you put in. However, by being aware of your breathing, you delete, if you will, some of the mental clutter banging around in your head, which when gone leads to a sharper mind.

Don't expect to look into the mirror in a couple days and see a new, enlightened you. Meditation is a gradual process of becoming calm, collected and centered. Like doing your forms and your stretching routine, each time you do walking meditation, it feels a little different than the last time. And that is okay.

Keep at it and one day a friend will say to you, as a friend of mine said to me after I had been mediating for about five months, "What have you been doing? You seem calmer lately."

WHEN IT'S RAINING OUTSIDE

If it's raining outside, or it's a scorcher even in the shade, or you simply want to meditate differently, here is a simple method that works like a charm.

- Sit comfortably, quietly and with your eyes closed as you count your s-l-o-w breaths.
- Think "one" on the inhalation, think "two" on the exhalation, think "three" on the inhalation and think "four" on the exhalation.
  o Continue like this until you exhale on "ten." Then return to "one" and start over
- If your mind drifts off somewhere and when it returns you're thinking "twenty-three" or worse, "one hundred and nine"(what the heck were you thinking about, anyway?), simply start over at the beginning.

8 Ways to Create and Use Mental Triggers

I got the idea for this chapter after watching the Olympic Games and seeing the little rituals some of the competitors did before their events. In some cases, the ritual, or as it's called here, the "trigger," literally transformed the competitor from a mild mannered person into a hungry, blood thirsty beast.

My friend Wim Demeere used triggers during his competitive years so I thought he would be the best guy to present the process. Here are his thoughts in a piece called:

Mental Triggers

By Wim Demeere

Wim Demeere began training in the martial arts at the age of 14, studying the grappling arts of judo and jujitsu for several years before turning to the kick/punch arts of traditional kung fu and full-contact fighting. Over the years he has studied a broad range of other fighting styles, including muay Thai, kali, pentjak silat and shootfighting. Since the late 1990s he has studied combat tai chi chuan.

During Wim's competitive years he won four national titles and a bronze medal at the 1995 World Wushu Championships. In 2001, he became the national coach of the Belgian Wushu fighting team. A full-time personal trainer in his native country of Belgium, Wim instructs both business executives and athletes in nutrition, strength and endurance, and a variety of martial arts styles. He has managed a corporate wellness center and regularly gives lectures and workshops in the corporate world.

Wim was my co-author on The Fighter's Body: An Owner's Manual *and* Timing in the Fighting Arts *both published by Turtle Press. Wim Demeere can be reached through his website The Grinding Shop at www.grindingshop.com*

"On your mark... get set..." *Bang!* the sprinters explode out of their starting blocks.

A starter gun is commonly used in sporting events, as are whistles and buzzers, devices that ensure every athlete receives the same "go" cue. For our purposes here let's call this cue a trigger.

Trigger defined

A trigger is a psychological starting block that you program into your mind for a specific purpose. It's pulled mentally by a cue from your senses (you *see* a specific image, you *hear* a specific sound), or as a result of a physical ritual that you do. Most often the trigger is programmed to call up a specific mind-set for you to ignite into action - Attack! Explode! Concentrate! - as I'll illustrate in a moment with a glove tapping ritual. Other times the trigger is programmed to build to a climactic explosion, as you will see with a volcano metaphor I use. There are an infinite number of devices to serve as a trigger; the one you choose depends on your needs and what works best for you. Just because one trigger works for your friend doesn't mean it will work for you. It might, but it might not. As will be explained in a moment, you have to experiment. Here are a few examples of triggers that are used by other fighters for you to consider implementing:

- Banging your fists together before a sparring match.
- Bowing to the judges before you perform your kata.
- Stepping into your I-don't-want-to-fight stance when a street thug threatens you.
- Imagining that you're a samurai about to do battle. When you mentally draw your sword, you're ready to launch into your form (this is Loren's).

ACTIVATE YOUR PROGRAM

Think of a trigger as clicking an icon on your computer screen to start a program. If you don't click on the icon, though the program is installed in your PC, nothing happens. Clicking on it triggers your computer to do a specific action. It's the same with a mental trigger. However, as complicated as computers are, things can be even more complex in the human computer, and sometimes it takes more effort to get your program to do what you want it to do.

In point or full-contact fighting, there is the ritual where both fighters touch gloves or bow to each other before the referee shouts, "Fight!" In forms, the competitor bows to the judges, gets into his ready position, and then launches his opening move. Although the fighters' cue is an external one from the ref, and the forms competitors' cue is an internal one that he gives himself by bowing, both competitors are responding to triggers. Just as pulling the gun's trigger ignites the *bang!* and launches the sprinters, the mental trigger you use determines when you ignite physically and mentally.

Having a trigger at your disposal not only ignites you at the outset, it also helps you stay focused and thus be less distracted by your anxiety and the presence of a crowd.

DECIDING ON A TRIGGER

- Full-contact fighting, forms competition and street self-defense all require different triggers since each activity requires a specific mental and emotional state.
- Picking the wrong trigger can be counterproductive, even dangerous. You need to control which trigger you pull. For example, going into a street brawl with the mind-set that you're in a point fighting match isn't in your best interest. Conversely, inducing a mental state to "fight for your life" in a kickboxing match might cause you to forget the rules and get disqualified.

YOU EVEN NEED CONTROL IN THE STREET

Say you're being annoyed by a loud drunk as you walk home from class. Although he is obnoxious, there is no direct physical threat to you. Then, he touches your shoulder to annoy you a little more, an action that triggers in you a combat mind-set, a ruthless, kill-or-be-killed state that pushes you over the edge. You grab his arm and break his elbow in one fierce move, and without pause you slam a horizontal elbow into his neck. As he begins to drop to the floor, you spike a knee into his body and stomp his face once he hits the dirt.

The good news is that you defended yourself successfully. The bad news is that you're guilty of serious assault and might be looking at jail time and a lawsuit. All for using your combat trigger in the wrong situation.

TWO KINDS

There are two kinds of triggers - internal and external - though there is overlap.

• Internal triggers are formed within your mind and body; you're in control of them.
    o They usually require a specific ritual, or a repeated mantra or keyword.

• External triggers use an outside catalyst to set you into motion, usually a specific stimulus from your opponent or the referee.
    o In the street, the trigger might be a threatening movement from the assailant: He moves into your personal space or he touches you.
    o In competition or in class, the trigger is usually a command from a third person: "Fight!" or "Go!"
    o Some fighters react best to external triggers while other respond best to internal ones.
    o You have to experiment to find what works best for you.

STEP 1: GET DEEPLY RELAXED

• Sit in a comfortable chair in a quiet place. Don't lie down because you might fall asleep.

• Scoot around until you find a position where you're completely comfortable.

• Use the four-count breathing procedure discussed in this book to induce a wonderful sense of physical and mental relaxation.
  - o Breath in 2, 3 4, hold 2, 3, 4.
  - o Exhale 2, 3, 4, hold, 2, 3, 4.
  - o Repeat this sequence as many times as you need until you're deeply relaxed. Usually three of four cycles does the trick.

• Think of a specific scenario in which you want to program a trigger: forms, sparring, fight competition, or a street confrontation.
  - o At first, it's best to think of only one activity.
  - o Later, when you're more experienced at programming triggers you can work on several scenarios during one session.

• See and hear everything in the environment in which you will be acting: include sounds, the feel of your uniform, smells, the surge of energy in your muscles, and so on. The more detail the better.

• As you create this mental picture, pay attention to how you feel.
  - o Do you get an adrenaline boost or shaky knees when you imagine facing a street assailant?
  - o If you're imagining doing your form, do you feel a sense of exhilaration before you start?
  - o By acknowledging and recognizing your reactions to your mental imagery, it's easier to implement the triggers.

Deal with obstacles If there is an adjustment needed, do it at this stage. Say you're concerned about the intensity of the fear you feel when you visualize a street confrontation. While fear is reasonable and acceptable in a real situation, fear that paralyzes you isn't.

Important

Caution

• If you find that your fear is increasing as you visualize, then you need to take a different approach, one that helps to control it.
  o Many fighters find that thinking about technique helps them gain a sense of control: Would a groin kick work well here?
    An eye jab?
  o When you find a solution, your fear begins to dissipate, though not completely, which is okay since a little makes you strong and fast.

• Give yourself lots of positive self-talk.
  o Think about how hard you have trained for the tournament and feel good about that since most people don't train as hard as you do.
  o Think about how well you do your form and how fast and crisp your techniques are.
  o Remember how the other students went "ooh" and "ahhh."
  o Remember how your teacher praised you and meant it.

• Remember all those things and let that memory send a surge of energy through your muscles.

• Think and believe: *I am sooo ready for this competition.*

Once you have your debilitating fears and concerns under control, it's time to implement a trigger.

YOU GOTTA WORK AT IT

Finding your trigger requires hard work, so don't be alarmed if at first you fail or achieve only partial success. Developing a trigger requires changing your current reactions, ones that have been embedded in your mind for many years, then programming in new and more powerful ones. For most people this is a process of trial and error but keep at it because the rewards are fantastic.

STEP 2: CREATING A TRIGGER

Turn your mind's eye towards the scenario, your form competition, and your emotional and physical reactions to it. For example, say you get a positive energy surge and a strong sense of wanting to compete. Once you have a clear picture of the scenario and your reactions, you need to link one to the other. That is, you create a conscious mental association between the scenario and your positive reactions to it, so that in time each will call up the other in your mind. For example, picture yourself standing in front of the crowd and judges when you feel that energy and desire to perform. Conversely, when you see yourself standing before the crowd and judges, feel that powerful sense of exhilaration and desire to give your form all that you have.

Creating an interaction between the mental scenarios and your emotional and physical reactions is half the work. Now you need to implement a trigger (use one of the triggers I listed earlier or one that you devise after experimentation). Remember, this might take some trial and error.

Let's look at a few specific situations common to fighters, and look at triggers I use in each of them. Feel free to use mine or create ones that work well for you.

Training A typical training session lasts 60 to 90 minutes in which you warm up, stretch, do basic technique, combinations, forms, spar, and hit the pads. Many students have trouble switching from one type of mental concentration to another within one class. If this is you, here is a trigger to help.

When practicing visualization in your quiet room, you must address all aspects of a typical class and link each one to your internal reactions as discussed previously. To program in triggers and to help you transition smoothly between class activities, try this.

- Imagine a big dialing knob on an old radio.
  - o Mentally put marks on the dial that represents the components in your class: "sparring," "basic technique," "drills" and "forms."

- Mentally turn the dial to one of them.
    - o Turn the dial to "sparring" and spend 5 minutes visualizing a perfect session.
    - o Turn the dial to "drills" and spend 5 minutes visualizing a perfect session.
    - o Turn the dial to "forms" and spend 5 minutes visualizing a perfect session.
    - o Turn the dial to "hitting the pads" and spend 5 minutes visualizing a perfect session.

- Repeat as necessary until you can do this smoothly and effortlessly.

During class, make a mental *click* of the knob each time you change activities.

- Turn the knob anytime you like
    - o Do it as you walk to the bag, or do it as you assume your stance in front of it, or do it as you take a swig from your water bottle.
    - o A popular method is to stand still for a moment, inhale, and then as you exhale, "see" the knob turn in your mind's eye.

- When the knob clicks, you experience what many people call "a feeling," though more accurately it's the mind-set you programmed into yourself along with the trigger.
    - o For sparring, you might feel the anticipation and thrill of competition. You might feel a burst of energy. You might see techniques flash through your mind as you saw them in your visualization.

It will take a while to get proficient at mental knob turning, but once you have it, your martial skills will progress by leaps and bounds.

Forms competition   If you're an active forms competitor, a trigger isn't a luxury, it's a necessity. For the duration of your one- or two-minute performance, you must be at your absolute best while surrounded by noise, people, and rivals who want you to fail. All of this creates tremendous stress and anxiety that can affect your concentration. You need to install two triggers: One to pull a couple minutes before your event and one to pull as you begin. First, you need to program it into your mind in your quiet place.

A trigger to pull a few minutes before your event: As you sit in your easy chair, deeply relaxed and viewing the tournament setting in your mind, imagine that it's just a few minutes before your competition begins.

• See the crowd and your fellow competitors, hear the cheers, smell your sweat, and feel the uniform on your body.

• Take extra deep breaths to calm your mind against any restlessness or anxiety.

• Think of how well you prepared and how ready you are to show it.

• As the 4-count breathing and positive thoughts begin to dissipate your anxiety and replace it with a sense of inner peace, mentally link this feeling to the image you have of being at that tournament.

• Implementing the trigger
  o Gently rub your eyes, inhale deeply, then exhale as you slide your fingers down your face, a sensitive area that has the most nerve connections in one area of your entire body. The sensation of your fingers rubbing your eyes and then sliding down your face gives your nervous system something else to react to instead of those knots twisting in your stomach.
  o To program this action into your mind, repeat the motion several times while concentrating on feeling calm and relaxed.
  o When you're at the tournament and begin feeling nervous, perform the eye rubbing ritual. Don't wait too long because you want to catch the problem before it grows too intense. Do it several times as needed. You might even want to close your eyes and imagine that you're back in your quiet room where you implemented the trigger.
  o To the outside world, your actions look as if you're tired. When competitors see you do it several times, they might even get overconfident because they assume you spent the night partying.

Just before you begin: The second trigger is engaged right before the first move of your form. Again, you want to establish the trigger in your quiet room. Imagine a volcano rumbling and steaming on the verge of a powerful eruption. See it building in your mind and feel its energy build in your body. When you finally see that volcano explode, that is the internal trigger that sets you into motion. Here is how it happens in your mind just seconds before you perform.

• As you imagine walking towards the competition area, feel a restless energy starting to bubble in your body, like lava beginning to bubble inside a volcano.
• As you step into the performance area, feel the energy begin to race throughout your body.
• The only "leak" shows in the intensity of your gaze, which reveals to everyone, including the all-important judges, your determination.
• As you imagine assuming your ready stance, feel how completely focused you are, feel how charged you are, and feel how ready you are to explode.
• Visualize that volcano rumbling louder, just seconds from erupting.
• Imagine saluting and taking a deep breath
• Your volcano blows! and you explode into your first move. Your mountain of energy, emotion, and warrior spirit continues to erupt throughout your imaginary battle.
• As you conclude your form, imagine the volcano quieting and then going back to sleep, a cue for you to salute the judges and step out of the ring.

It will take time and effort to make these triggers work effectively in a tournament. But if you implement them every time you practice, they will soon become second nature, just another part of doing the form.

Competitive fighting: In your quiet place, you again link the mental images to your mind-set, and implement a trigger. During my full-contact competitive years I used a powerful one that worked every time. Here is a segment from my essay "Fear and warrior mind-set in the square circle" that appears in Loren Christensen's excellent book, Warriors: On Living With Courage, Discipline and Honor.

"The mind-set you want for tournament fighting is complex. In essence you need two seemingly contradictory components: Raw aggression with perfect control. On the one hand you want to consciously inflict pain on your opponent by attacking him. This requires an aggressive and violent mind-set. However, you need to abide by the rules of the game. You can't let the aggression take over and control you because you will be quickly disqualified for using prohibited techniques. To achieve this compromise, visualize yourself landing full power blows on your opponent, while maintaining perfect control of your techniques. See yourself dodge, parry or block all your opponent's techniques, seeing them before he even launches them, while landing every single technique in your arsenal on him. Feel the violent rage inside yourself, focusing it in your techniques instead of on the opponent. You don't have to hate the other guy. You just have to get yourself to hit him as hard as you can."

Throughout the years, I have experimented with several rituals to use as my trigger, eventually settling on one that is simple and not unlike what many fighters do instinctively before they start their match. I bang my gloves together, bang them against my forehead, and then thrust them toward my opponent.

To get to where I could implement this in a match, I first imprinted it in my mind during my meditation sessions. Then I incorporated it into my training. I would bang my gloves together and recall the fighting mind-set I had experienced during my visualizing. I did this every training session, and though it took a while to make the link, it was one of the most powerful triggers I ever implemented. Even today when I do it just before sparring, it brings up that powerful mind-set that helped me in my matches. It's still there, partly for having used it for so long and partly because of the specifics of the ritual.

- Banging your fists together is an act of aggression.
  - o It ignites you and it tells your opponent, the judges, and the crowd that you're ready, willing and able to get the party going.
  - o Banging your gloves together gives you tactile feedback, something you're about to start doing on your opponent's face.

- If you're feeling weak-legged because of the rush of adrenaline or you're growing anxious, smacking yourself in the head clears your mind for the task at hand.
  - o You're also showing that you aren't afraid to get hit.

- The final phase of the ritual is to thrust your fists towards your opponent.
  - o I think of this as taking aim or putting my opponent into my crosshairs.
  - o It's also a mental commitment that you're going to use violence. Not against just anyone - *him*.

You can do part of this ritual throughout the fight to stay psyched. Say you or your opponent gets knocked down and there is a break in the action as you resume your fighting stance. Take advantage of the moment to bang your fists together to retrigger  your fighting spirit and remind your opponent that you're just as dangerous as before.

Self-defense: When defending yourself in the street, a programmed trigger is one of the most important tools you have. It moves you from calm and peace to a mental state of determination, awareness and fortitude to do what needs to be done. As always, the specific trigger is your choice. Here is how to incorporate it into the I-don't-want-to-fight stance (Chapter 11).

- Use 4-count breathing to bring on a deep sense of relaxation in your quiet room.
- See yourself, say, walking to your car when a street punk steps out of the shadows and into your path.
- Mentally assume the I-don't-want-to-fight stance and feel the adrenaline race through your body. Any fear you feel helps you become focused. You're more aware of everything around you including nearby improvised weapons. Does the thug have a buddy? Most of all, it fortifies your ice-cold determination to get home in one piece. Feel how your sense of will gives you strength, speed and confidence to apply your technique, whether it's verbal deescalation, evading and blocking, or kicking him into the next state.

Once you have spent sufficient time linking the I-don't-want-to-fight stance with the physical and mental feelings, you need to practice pulling the trigger with your training partner. Every time you assume the stance, draw upon those feelings you placed into your mind during your visualization sessions. You have to practice with control with your training partner, but then you should always be fighting with control, anyway.

Partners

THE SHORT AND SWEET OF DEVELOPING A MENTAL TRIGGER

- Bring on deep relaxation in a quiet place.
- Visualize a specific situation and feel the physical and emotional reaction to it.
- Once you can easily turn on that feeling during your visualization session, practice ingraining a trigger.
- Once your trigger has been ingrained in your visualization sessions, practice pulling it in your training, in class, and when training solo.
- In the end, your trigger will provide you with a powerful edge in every phase of the martial arts.

Spend time working on this trigger (or any other one you prefer) and you will be amazed at how quickly it can take you from calm and collected to a mental and physical place where you're primed to do battle.

Triggers are powerful fighting tools. Adding them to your arsenal requires dedicated training and discipline. In the end, you will be rewarded with a mind and body that functions as one powerful fighting machine.

Section Two

Sharpening the Warrior's blade

If we were building a sword, Section One would be a blue print for creating a solid, strong grip and hilt, and forging steel of maximum strength. Sections Two and Three would be specific blue prints for the blade: ways to make it razor-death sharp and ways to make its slashes swift and true.

9 Ways to Practice the Art of Fighting Without Fighting

Remember that scene on the passenger boat in Bruce Lee's *Enter the Dragon* where Lee suggests to the man who had been bullying people to get into a small rowboat so they could go over to an island where they could fight? The dumb guy gets into the little boat and Lee releases the rope sending him adrift. Lee called this technique "the art of fighting without fighting."

What a great concept. You don't get winded, sweaty or sued. No torn clothes, no broken furniture, and no bleeding knuckles. As a grownup, you know that to avoid getting physical is the best way to settle disagreements, though you might be left with a powerful itch to mess up the other guys' face. That itch will pass eventually, leaving you with a sense of pride and a sense of feeling smarter than the other guy.

I got into a few fights during my 29 years in law enforcement, a few hundred, that is. Some of those I'm most proud of are those I won using the art of fighting without fighting. For example, several times I ended hostile confrontations with enraged suspects by making them laugh so hard that they would say something like,

"Okay, I'll go with you. You're fun." One time I was carrying a case of cookies in the trunk of my police car that I was taking to a grade school. I offered a volatile suspect two of them, but only if he went peacefully. He laughed, agreed, happily ate them, and then I slapped on the cuffs.

Sometimes after suspects had threatened me, I'd reason with them. "Look," I'd say. "You might be able to beat me up, but then you have to beat up my partner, and the next cop who is on his way here now. Then the next one after him. We got 1,200 cops on our department, and pretty soon you're going to get tired. And about the time you get tired might be the time you get a cranky cop, a big cranky cop. It's a whole heck of a lot easier to just go along with me peaceful-like."

That one worked almost every time.

There are no absolutes when kicking and punching and there no absolutes when applying the psychological art of fighting without fighting. Perception is in the eyes of the beholder, meaning that no matter how good you get at this, there are some people who aren't going to get it. Maybe they are high, drunk, enraged or just dumb as a houseplant. Whatever the reason, they fail to recognize your brilliant psychology and want to get physical.

I used to tell the police academies that 90 percent of the time their application of good voice tone, professional demeanor, the power of their gaze, and their strong aura of confidence will prevent a situation from becoming physical. However, it's because of that remaining 10 percent that they need to practice their physical defensive tactics skills.

To begin making the art of fighting without fighting work for you, let's look at some basic elements of that 90 percent to get you thinking about them and experimenting with them.

Demeanor

This is obvious but still missed by many people. A person standing slump shouldered with a concave chest, limp arms, and head tucked as if trying to escape the world is a person ripe for being a victim, ripe for getting pushed down in the dirt.

You want to stand with a straight spine, shoulders back, chin up, and your stomach in. Check out those recruitment posters for the Marine Corps and for West Point. The models on them convey with their erect, ready posture a message that they are fit, alert and ready to do what needs to be done. That is exactly what you want to convey in your posture.

Yoga I've found that yoga helps my posture, especially the back strengthening and stretching movements. When I practice consistently, three or four days a week, I'm more conscious about standing straighter and taller. Give it a try and see if it works for you.

A ballet move Here is a trick you can do right now as you're sitting there reading this, one that ballerinas use to keep their heads up high and alert. (If you're packing 200 pounds of rippling muscle it can be our little secret that you're practicing ballet. Wearing a tutu is optional.) Think about the crown of your head, that top part near the back that is usually the first place to bald. Sit up straight and tall in your chair and use your neck to push your head up higher, crown first. It actually feels good as your neck stretches and releases tension. While feeling good is a nice side benefit, your primary objective is to stand straighter so that you look a tad taller and appear alert and aware.

Now don't get carried away and stand so stiff and awkward that you look like a dweeb and thus become even more attractive to bullies. Strive to be comfortable and natural as you stand strong, tall, alert and ready.

IT'S NOT WHAT YOU SAY BUT HOW YOU SAY IT

When you talk with someone, a friend or a street thug trying to bait you into a fight, that person receives information from you in more ways than by just the words you use. In fact, your words are the least of it. The listener perceives your communication in three ways. He gets:

1. 7 to 10% from what you say.
2. 33 to 40% from your tone of voice.
3. 50 to 60% from your facial expressions, body language and gestures.

Voice

A strong and authoritative voice gets attention and respect, at least at first. If the speaker's words are idiotic or obnoxious, he might still get attention, but he won't hold the listener's respect for long. An unwavering and in-charge voice tone, imparting verbiage that is not threatening, overbearing or bullyish, will go a long way toward neutralizing a volatile situation.

Most veteran cops have mastered the strong, authoritative voice that gets people to do things without browbeating them into doing it, while many rookie cops will at first over or under compensate with their voice. Many times when I was a rookie, I probably came across as if I were taking it personally when a motorist ran a stop sign. My voice sounded angry and most likely some of my word choices conveyed that, too. With experience, I lost that negative and confrontational tone and was eventually able to conduct my job without my voice getting me into trouble.

As noted in the sidebar, up to 40 percent of how you're perceived is determined by the way in which you expressed it with your voice. Have you ever gotten into a fight with your spouse or significant other and she or he complained, "It wasn't *what* you said, but *how* you said it." Well - are you ready for the truth? – your spouse was probably right. It's hard to know when you're using a tone – whining, nagging, critical, boastful, and challenging – unless you're especially cognizant of it.

Listen to yourself as you speak. Strive to find a tone, cadence and volume that are natural to you but convey all the positive elements just mentioned. Ask a friend or significant other for feedback as to how you come across, and then work to make appropriate adjustments.

Rehearse   I know a policeman who had the unenviable experience of having a bad guy place a gun against his forehead. Although the cop was a veteran, he had not prepared for this experience, so what came out of his mouth was not some clever verbiage such as manly-man actors like Van Diesel or Bruce Willis would utter, but rather a guttural, whiney, "Aaagghheee."

Now, Willis and Diesel can say cool things under stress because other people write their words and the actors practice them over and over. They rehearse. Hmm, maybe they are onto something. Maybe that is what you should do, too. Rehearse in your car, in the shower, or out on a jog. Imagine a volatile situation and practice what you would say. For example, imagine that you pull up to a fast-food joint where there are a couple of guys slumped against the wall next to the door, all wearing low-slung pants, oversized sweatshirts and bandanas. They take an immediate dislike to you. One of them slurs, "You ain't getting' no burger, boy, but you gonna get a hurtin'." (Okay, that's a little corny, but bear with me.)

Practice right now what you would say in a clear, strong and authoritative voice. Choose your own words to convey that you don't want a problem and that you just want to pass by and get your order. Say it with conviction but without challenge. Choose your words carefully so as not to provoke. This is key, since under stress it's so easy to say the wrong thing (been there, done that). Make up as many scenarios as your imagination allows and practice what you would say and how you would say it. In the end, your rehearsal will better prepare you to choose the right words and speak them with authority. More on rehearsal in a moment.

So what happened to the policeman and the armed bad guy who got the drop on him? The officer never did find the right words, but he did find an opportunity to kill the guy.

The neutral face

Your face can get you into a lot of trouble. Remember, 50 to 60 percent of communication comes from facial expressions, body language and gestures. Say a bully woofs in your face and you sneer back at him. You curl your lip and shake your head to indicate that the guy isn't intimidating you in the least. Maybe he isn't, but your facial expression just might set him off so that suddenly you're in a fight that you inadvertently provoked. A neutral face is one that doesn't show emotion. Your eyes, nose and lips are all normal. You look back at him without expression, even if you're disgusted, enraged or frightened inside. There is real power in a neutral face, one that helps you control your emotions and one that is often perceived by others as strong, even dangerous.

Important

POWER OF THE EYES

My grandfather died when I was quite young so I barely remember him. I do know that he had had a hard life that brought him to America from Denmark, only to have to fight for survival during the tough, early years of the last century. One of the stories my dad told me was how my grandfather would punish my father when he was a child. Whenever my father or any of his brothers and sisters misbehaved, their father would call the errant one to stand before him for a minute or two. During that time, that torturous time, their father would look at them, glare at them, with eyes that could shred bark from trees. My father said that a spanking, a beating even, would have been preferable to that wilting stare.

I read of a kung fu student who had been caught goofing off in class when he thought the old Chinese master was looking in the other direction. In fact, he had been looking away, but still he knew instantly what the student had done. He turned and gestured for the errant one to come over to him. "He was clearly angry," the student said. "But his eyes... it was indescribable. There was a force there, a frightening force that made me lower my head immediately. I looked up for a second but again those eyes forced me to look away. They were the eyes of an animal."

During my years as a police officer and a soldier in Vietnam I had the displeasure of looking into eyes - those belonging to both good guys and bad - that were chilling, eyes that would not have surprised me at all if they could have shred bark from trees. I remember the cold eyes of a white supremacist I interviewed behind bars: stupid eyes, killing eyes. I remember the fiery intensity in the eyes of a Vietnamese combat soldier; old eyes in a young face. Eyes that had seen much death.

Can you train yourself to have such eyes? For sure, a penetrating gaze coupled with a powerful demeanor and a commanding voice would give pause to nine out of 10 people bent on starting trouble (remember, that one out of 10 is why you train so hard). Can you fake such a gaze? What if you practiced before a mirror: widening your eyes, narrowing them? Maybe lifting one eyebrow like pro wrestler turned actor, The Rock. Would such training just create a superficial stare?

At one time, KGB recruits were purportedly ordered to study the killing stares of tigers and panthers at a local zoo. Looking into the eyes of a 600-pound Siberian tiger will humble even the toughest mixed martial arts fighter (I tried this on Lexii, my kitty that sleeps all day on my desk next to my PC, but I didn't feel a thing). Giant cats are natural killers, and they do so instinctually, with finesse and without remorse. There may very well be something to learn from them. But again, mimicry of these creatures would be superficial and would likely fall apart under stress.

The frightening gaze of the aforementioned humans is something that develops from experience. It's a trait you get from hard training in which you mentally conjure your warrior spirit, that inner force that lies within you and comes to the surface when there is a dragon to slay. You can turn it on to some degree with mirror training, after all actors do it all the time, but you have to be careful not to come across looking foolish.

Lt. Col. Dave Grossman, author of the Pulitzer Prize nominated book *On Killing* and the book I co-authored with him, *On Combat: The Psychology and Physiology of Deadly Conflict in War and in Peace,* says this about the power of the eyes. It pertains to combat soldiers, so it's a tad brutal.

"I think you have to make the decision (even the desire) to kill, deep in your soul. They [the enemy] must look into your eyes and see the steely determination to turn their brains into a fine, pink mist. It's about having made the decision ahead of time.

"I think that one way to get the 'look' is to envision the enemy dead, to desire them dead with blood pouring from their throats. The warrior has to look at them in a way that says, 'I want you dead. I desire you dead. I want an excuse to make you dead. Please give me an excuse.' He must look at them as though they were nothing, as though they were already dead.

"The tiger looks at you and doesn't see a person; he sees meat and that shines through in his eyes to frighten you. That is what the warrior needs to communicate. You cannot fake it. It has to be in your heart then it will shine through your eyes."

Practice: Putting It All Together

This is one workout where you won't get sweaty and you don't have to wear a protective cup.

Mirror time   Stand before a full-length mirror (you can get an inexpensive one for $15 to $20 in most variety stores).

• Check your posture. Don't make it conspicuous and odd, but find one that looks natural while conveying alertness, awareness and strength. It should feel comfortable to you, though it might not be if you have been a habitual slumper for most of your life. Work now to replace the old habit with a new one and it will soon feel natural.

- Practice your neutral face in the mirror along with your good posture. See what it looks like and *feels* like so that you can do it without referring to a mirror. Do you look natural? Do you look relaxed?

- Hold your open hands in front of you, palms toward the threat in the I-don't-want-to-fight stance, which is discussed in the next chapter. It doesn't look threatening; in fact it looks like you don't want any problems, especially as you display your neutral face, your good posture, and your overall sense of calmness.

- Practice speaking in front of the mirror. Imagine various scenarios – a guy takes issue when you accidentally bumped into him; two thugs approach you in a parking lot; a person flirts with your spouse in your presence - and practice what you would say to calm the situation. Choose words that don't inflame the situation. As Wim Demeere and I wrote in *Timing in the Fighting Arts*, you can't go wrong when you say "sir," "ma'am" (make sure they fit the person) and "I'm sorry." These words have power and go a long way toward calming someone who is agitated. Check your tone to ensure that it's calm and confident, not too loud, not too soft, and your cadence is neither too fast or too slow.

By practicing once or twice a week for 5 to 10 minutes, it will become second nature to you. The physical elements of fighting without fighting aren't tough to master, but learning to say the right thing might take longer. That is okay. Practice your verbiage in front of the mirror, in your car, or the first thing when you wake up. The more you practice, the better you get at talking and the better you will do when you're angry or frightened.

9 Ways to Attack & Defend From the I-Don't-Want-to-Fight Stance

This stance is sometimes called the deescalation stance. While deescalation is part of its purpose, I think of it as doing more, and therefore call it the "I-don't-want-to-fight stance." Think of it as conveying to the bully and to everyone watching that you don't want things to get physical; you want to talk about it. Then as you present this appearance, strive to deescalate the situation by using your body language and the verbal skills discussed in the last chapter. Should the situation turn physical, onlookers will tell the police that you didn't want to fight and that the bully attacked you.

The reality is that you're in a fighting stance. Close your hands into fists and bend your knees a little more, and you're in a classic fighting posture. That said, not all fighting postures need to be classic ones, as we shall examine in Chapter 12, "5 Everyday Fighting Stances."

Two positions

There are actually two variations of the I-don't-want-to-fight stance: "The Wall" and the "The Classic." Though somewhat similar, each has a slightly different function and slightly different visual impact on the bully.

The Wall   In this position, your feet, upper body, and head are positioned the same as in The Classic, but your hand position is such that it indeed looks like a wall, a physical and psychological one.

- If you're right handed you probably lead with your left side. If you normally train to lead with your strongest side forward, and that is your right side, then you would assume the I-don't-want-to-fight stance with your right side forward.
- Your arms are bent about 90 degrees and your palms face straight forward about as high as your upper chest. Your hands are straight across from each other creating a psychological and physical wall.
- Your arms, hands, and entire body appear relaxed though you're ready and willing to explode should The Wall not work.
- As you talk to the bully, move your hands in barely perceptible "holding back" motions by moving your open palms forward and then backwards an inch or two in each direction.
- Should the situation deteriorate and the bully indicates that he is about to use violence, you can easily shift from The Wall position to The Classic. If the situation calls for subtlety, change as you talk and he might not notice.

I've used The Wall when I've felt that an antagonist was still at a place in his mind where he could be influenced to stop moving toward me. As the name implies, the position acts as a wall - a shield – that stops the bully from advancing physically. As mentioned, you can still execute your blocks and punches from The Wall position, though The Classic is a tad closer to an on-guard fighting position. So it's your choice whether you want to make the change at all. If you do, practice the transition in the mirror so that you can do it easily and smoothly.

The Classic   This position is closer to your fighting stance, though your hands are open, your body is relaxed and your demeanor is one of trying to defuse the situation.

- Your arms are held in the standard on-guard position with your lead-side arm in front and your rear arm held near your solar plexus to protect your lower body. If you normally train to lead with your strongest side forward, and that is your right side, then you would assume the I-don't-want-to-fight stance with right side forward.
- If you usually hold your fisted hands along each side of your face, you have to modify that and position them a little lower. Should the situation suddenly turn physical, simply raise your arms higher and clench your hands.
- If you like to hold your arms near or at centerline, you can do so without it looking unnatural.
- Your hands are open, palms toward the threat.
- Make small, subtle circles with your hands, moving no more than an inch in any direction. Psychologists say that the open, nonthreatening position of the hands and the small massaging motions can have a soothing effect on some people. Keep in mind that *some* doesn't mean everyone.
- Your body is angled away from the threat and your feet are staggered as they are in most basic fighting stances.

The Classic I-don't-want-to-fight stance offers you all the offense and defense capabilities of a regular fighting stance without looking threatening.

How to Create Witnesses

You bumped the guy accidentally and now he is trying to make something of it. "You got a problem, man?" he asks, straight out of a *Bullying for Dummies* book. "If you're lookin' for a problem," he growls with a curled up lip," you've come to the right man."

"I'm sorry, sir," you say, assuming the I-don't-want-to-fight stance. "My fault." Talk loud enough for those around you to hear. "I'm having a clumsy day. I'm sorry."

With these simple words, spoken loudly enough for others to hear, and in a stance that clearly indicates that you don't want a problem, you have just made everyone around you, except for the bully's friends, a witness in your behalf.

"The good looking one [that's you]," the witnesses say to the police, "didn't want to fight. He said it was his fault and he apologized. He had his hands up indicating he didn't want a problem. It was the ugly one's fault."

Let's look at five ways you can attack from both The Wall and The Classic I-don't-want-to-fight stance, and five ways you can defend and counter (only The Classic stance is used in the photos). As with anything new in the fighting arts, the more you practice from this stance, the more natural it will be and the more fluid your movements. Practice it during your solo training and in your regular class. If your teacher doesn't allow it, and sadly some won't, practice it even more on your own.

Grabbing: hair

Important

I like grabbing and twisting hair. It hurts, it gives clear direction, it doesn't cause injury, and it stops hurting when you stop pulling. I used hair techniques often as a cop, though appearance-wise they were not good for public relations. I used them anyway. I wasn't running for office; I just wanted to get home safely at the end of the shift.

Whenever I teach hair techniques I always get the following question, so I'll address it right away. "What if my attacker doesn't have hair?" Answer: Then you can't do hair techniques on him. Hope that settles that.

- When your assailant has a shock of hair on his forehead, try to resist going, "Yesss!" Stay cool, lift your hands in the I-don't-want-to-fight stance, positioning your lead hand about as high as his forehead.
- When the moment is right, snap out your lead hand without telegraphing your intentions and grab a fist full of his hair.
- Snap your arm as if you were doing a downward elbow strike and lower your body a little at the same time. You're much stronger when you drive your elbow downward, as opposed to snapping only your hand downward.
- Step back to give him room to fall to the floor.

Variation Should the opportunity present itself, you can also grab the sides or the back of his head. If you can, grab deeply into his hair at the roots. This provides you with greater control and hurts him a lot more. I like to scrape his scalp as I close my fingers. Always make a tight fist around whatever hair you grab.

Simulate 1 or 2 sets of 10 reps with your lead hand on each side. Be sure to step out of the way so your invisible opponent has somewhere to fall.

Raking, poking, gouging: Eye attacks

Eye attacks are simple and quick because your hands are already open, loose and close to the target. When they appear unassuming, more people are apt to move into your range or allow you to move into theirs as opposed to when your hands are fisted and dangerous looking. Should the situation warrant such a level of force as striking the eyes, it's just a matter of a quick thrust with your four fingers to make your attacker scream in agony, and cry, "Where'd he go? Where'd he go?" Don't wind up or draw your hand back to build power. Just snap it straight in. You can rake it from right to left, left to right, downward, or upward. Which angle you use depends on where your hand is in relation to an open path to his peepers.

• To simulate a target, draw eyes on a wall, place eye-sized pieces of tape on a heavy bag, or use a mannequin-type dummy that comes with a nice set of eyes.
• Assume the I-don't-want-to-fight stance and practice different angles of attack. Think of a large asterisk (*) superimposed over the face. After you have practiced thrusting straight into the eyes, use the lines of the asterisk to work angles. Strike both ways on the line. For example, if you can rake from upper left to lower right, you can rake from lower right to upper left. This is true on all the lines, which gives you six angles, seven counting the straight in thrust.

The rear hand   Since we have been focusing on speed, we have been talking about the closest hand, the lead one. When practicing with your rear hand, remember that it takes a hair (an eyelash) of a second longer for it to reach the eyes.

• The best time to use your rear hand is when the bully has been distracted.
• The second best time is when your hands are straight across from each other and the same distance to the target, as in The Wall stance.

Practice 1 or 2 sets of 10 reps of each angle with each hand.

Punch, palm-heel: Nose attacks

Tap your nose with the palm of your hand and notice how it smarts a little. Whack it harder and notice how your eyes water and your nose hurts (and how someone called the police to report a crazy person hitting his nose). Always keep in mind that there are people out there who shrug off a nose hit and keep on fighting. Many full-contact fighters can go another 10 rounds with a broken snoz. Nonetheless, go ahead and hit the bully's nose when a path of opportunity presents itself, but always follow with other hits just in case he can tolerate the pain. For now, just practice the nose hit without follow-up blows.

- Assume the I-don't-want-to-fight stance and stand before whatever target you have that serves as an opponent's nose.
- Your basic angles of attack are straight in, downward and upward.
- No telegraphing. You're not going to hit it as hard when you don't draw your hand back first, especially your lead, but that is why you always follow with other blows. A nice quick smack to the nose makes most people vulnerable to whatever you do afterwards.
- When practicing straight-in thrusts, hold your lead, open hand about the level of the assailant's nose. Hold it lower if you want to strike on an upward angle, higher if you want to strike downward. I particularly like downward strikes because I like the nice wrist snap that adds to the impact.

Training Tip

Do 1 or 2 sets of 10 reps with both hands. As before, when the moment requires great speed, use your lead hand. Use your rear hand when he is distracted to give you an extra half second to deliver extra power.

Slapping: Stunning versatility

The I-don't-want-to-fight stance is an excellent position from which to deliver a distracting slap, a set-up slap, or a knock-him-senseless slap. Conveniently, your adversary's highly vulnerable head is virtually straight across from your hands. His cheeks, for example, contain many close-to-the-surface nerves that are easily shocked when hit. There are his vulnerable eardrums on both sides of his head, and a tender nose that can be made even tenderer after a solid slap. The back of his head dislikes even a mild slap, as do all four sides of his neck. Indeed, his head is a target rich environment for your nasty slaps.

Stand before a mannequin-type bag, a hanging double-end bag, or a regular heavy bag on which you have applied pieces of tape to indicate head targets. Let's begin by slapping the face, the imaginary lad's rosy cheeks.

Face   You can slap with your lead hand or rear hand. Since the rear hand is farther away it needs an extra half second to get there, but when you have the opportunity, the extra impact is so very worth the extra time.

• Spread your arms a little and subtly position your lead hand on a direct line with your assailant's face, as you talk about not wanting to fight.

• Without telegraphing, launch your open hand a split second before you twist/snap your hips, and whip your palm into his face.

o Don't think in terms of just impacting his, say, left cheek, but think about impacting his right cheek because your hand ripped all the way through from his left side.

• When you practice with your rear hand, imagine that the assailant looks away for a moment, perhaps to his friends to see if they are enjoying his bullying antics.

o That distraction gives you a moment of opportunity to use your powerful rear hand to whip in a devastating slap.

• How about a double whammy? Use your lead, left hand to slap his right cheek and follow immediately with a powerful right-hand slap against his left one.

o Do it fast so your first slap knocks his head into your second slap.

Practice 1 or 2 sets of 10 reps on both sides of all face slaps.

Nose   Most often when we think nose we think palm-heel strike, a blow typically delivered in a straight thrust. While you do hit with your palm, the impact is executed with a slap, which determines how it can be delivered.

Important

• When you're standing face-to-face with the threat and he looks to his right for some reason, his nose is in line for your left, whipping slap. Should he look to his left, his nose is ripe for your right slap.
o When using a mannequin bag, turn it so that its nose is facing to your left. Pretend that the adversary had been looking straight at you, and then suddenly looked away.

• Another method is to stand in front of the bag's face and lunge quickly to the left or right so that the bag's nose is off to the side, and aligned with your slap.

Practice 1 or 2 sets of 10 reps of both methods.

Ears   When slapping an ear, you have to be a couple of inches closer than when slapping the face.

• This means you have to lunge into range to slap an ear.
• Or hit when the threat steps into range.
• Also practice slapping both ears at the same time
o Stand in your staggered I-don't-want-to-fight stance, palms forward and straight across from each other, and your upper body toward the bag.
o Without telegraphing, whip both palms against the bag's ears, impacting with slightly cupped hands.

Do 1 or 2 sets on both sides.

Back of the head   Although slapping someone hard on the back of the head makes your palm sting like the dickens, it hurts him more. A hard slap jars the brain and can cause momentary stunning, thus providing you with a moment to escape or follow with additional blows. As is the case when striking the nose, you have to wait until the threat turns his head to the side, or you have to take measures to get sideways to him.

• Set up your bag just as you did when training to slap the nose.

o Assume your I-don't-want-to-fight stance to the side of the bag, pretending that the bully has just turned his head to the side, and slap the back of the skull.

o Or stand facing the bag, and lunge diagonally forward, turn and slap the back of its head.

• To clear a path to lunge diagonally forward, execute a left backhand block against an imaginary punch, and then whip your right slap against the back of the head.

Do 1 or 2 sets of 10 reps on both sides of all methods. When practicing in the air, strive to see your imaginary opponent's actions.

Here are three devastating combinations.

• Stand at the side of your bag pretending your opponent just turned his head or that you have moved there after blocking his attack.

• Slap the nose and follow immediately with a slap to the back of the head.

• Slap the back of the head first and follow immediately with a slap to the nose.

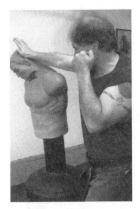 

Keep in mind that whichever side you slap first the other side is probably going to tilt downward from the force. This means that your second slap will have to be angled upward slightly. It's not that big of a deal, but you should practice that way occasionally so that it doesn't surprise you in a real situation.

Workout Tip

Do 1 or 2 sets of 10 reps on both sides of all methods.

Neck A hard slap to the back of the neck and to either side of it can cause immediate stunning. However, a hard slap to the front of the neck can be debilitating and possibly cause serious injury or even death. Be justified to use this level of force.

• Set up your bag as you did in "Ears" and "Nose" so you can imagine that the adversary has just turned his head or that you have just blocked his attack and have scooted to his side.
o Both actions allow you to reach the front and back of the neck.

Do 1 or 2 sets of 10 reps on both sides.

If a real bully has a short neck you might not be able to slap it since your hand won't fit between the shoulder and head. Not all is lost, as you can still slap the front by setting up an opportunity. Here is how to practice on a mannequin dummy.

- Stand in your I-don't-want-to-fight stance with your left side forward.
- See your attacker launch a right cross at your face.
- Sweep block it with your left hand, just enough to knock the punch off track, and then slap the palm of the same hand against his forehead as you step along side.
- Push against his forehead until his head leans back to expose his neck, and then whip your right slap into his throat.

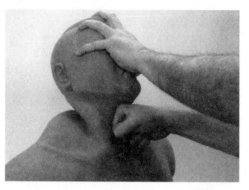

Caution

- Shoot a lead hand straight slap to his forehead and follow with a reverse punch to his throat (as pictured).

Practice 1 or 2 sets of 10 reps on both sides.

Warning: Be justified before using this dangerous technique in a real situation.

SLAP THE DOOR OPEN

While a slap hurts and can be debilitating, sometimes you might want to think of it as a way to open the door and enter with more offensive moves. Do the following on the bag or in the air as you visualize a live threat:

- Slap his ear with your left and follow with a hard right reverse punch to his chest.
- Slap his nose with your left when he looks to his right and follow with a right palm-heel thrust to his left ear.
- Slap the side of his neck and follow with a lead-leg shin kick to the groin.
- Slap his right ear, then his left, then head butt him.
- Create as many others as you can

Do 1 to 2 sets of 10 reps on both sides of all combinations.

Kicks

Kicks from the I-don't-want-to-fight stance are done just as they are from your regular fighting posture, though you have a slight advantage since your hands make you seem so unassuming.

- Raise your open hands and practice a little deescalation, such as: "Let's talk about this." "I'm sorry if I offended you." "My fault."
- Pretend that the bully isn't affected by your verbiage and is about to attack you, and then execute a kick of your choice.

Do 1 to 2 sets of 10 reps of each kick you practice.

Create an illusion of distance   Make him think you're too far away to be a threat.

- Hold your hands closer to your upper body than you have in previous scenarios. When the fight is inevitable, you can either keep your hands in the I-don't-want-to-fight stance or fist them as pictured below.
- Lean back, but not so far that you're off balance should he suddenly rush you.
- Though the lean of your upper body and the position of your arms make it appear that you're too far away to hit, your lead foot is within range and can be easily snapped into your opponent's groin.

Do 1 to 2 sets of 10 reps of groin kicks with each leg.

More on creating an illusion of distance in Chapter 14, "16 Ways to Cheat Speed."

Defenses

Creating a solid defense from your I-don't-want-to-fight stance isn't much different than a defense from your regular fighting stance, except that the former begins from a position that *appears* to the bully to be one that is nonthreatening. Well, too bad for him because you're ready for whatever he has up his sleeve.

CENTERLINE

In our book *Timing in the Fighting Arts*, co-author Wim Demeere and I devoted a chapter to the all-important centerline principle. Allow me to reduce the concept here to one sentence: By holding your open hands at the center of your body, the bully has to attack on either your right side or your left. Yes, some people will punch your arms, but the majority will go around them, which makes deflecting their attacks easier for you. You either sweep to the right or to the left with your palm or the back of either hand.

To work on precise timing and to develop sharp reflexes, you need to work with a live partner. You work solo to enhance your speed, to understand relaxation, to know how far or how little to move your hands, and to know how to counter simultaneous with your block, or counter right after you block. A mirror is helpful to ensure that your arms are on centerline and that your blocks are moving just enough to accomplish the task.

Workout Tip

RELAXATION

You want to *appear* nonchalant and *appear* completely relaxed when you're standing with your arms on centerline and your palms facing the threat, though you're neither. If you were totally relaxed, your arms would drop limply at your sides, your legs would buckle, and you would crumple to the floor in a heap. Although we use the words "completely relaxed," we don't mean it literally. We really mean "sort of relaxed."

Sort of relaxed   Stand in your I-don't-want-to-fight stance and relax your arms just short of dropping them limply at your sides. Let's call this 95 percent relaxed. Should someone throw a jab at you, you have to contract 95 percent of your muscle fibers to backhand-block the blow off course. We aren't talking about a lot of time here, but maybe it's still too much. So give 90 percent relaxation a try. It sounds like a small difference, but when you begin examining it you will find it a significant one. Try this experiment:

- Lift your arms and relax them until they begin to drop.
- Ever so slightly, add just enough tension to keep them up. This is 5 percent tension, or 95 percent relaxation.
- Pop out a few blocks of your choice at that percentage.
- Then increase the tension another 5 percent, so that now your muscles are around 90 percent relaxed. It's an ever so subtle difference, but it's indeed a difference.
- Now try your blocks at that tension.

Better? Most people find they are a little faster when beginning at 10 percent tension.

Hand/arm blocks

As in all aspects of fighting, blocking needs to be simple, fast and effective. The sweep and backhand blocks are found in most fighting styles because they are effective and easy to do. They are especially easy to do from the I-don't-want-to-fight stance. In the event you aren't familiar with them, here is how they are done.

Important

Sweep block   This block is most effective against blows ranging from your forehead to your belt.

    • Use your lead or rear palm to sweep the attack off course just to the outside edge of your body.

    o To sweep it any farther leaves you vulnerable to your opponent's counter.

    • You can sweep horizontally, diagonally upward and diagonally downward.

    • You can sweep without moving your upper body or you can simultaneously rotate it as you block.

    o While it's arguably best to rotate your body, sometimes an attack happens so suddenly you don't always have the opportunity.

Backhand block   This is a simple, quick and effective block to move an attack off course.

    • Snap your arm outward so that the backhand side – anywhere from the back of your hand to your elbow – connects with the attack and moves it off course.

    • Move it only to the edge of your body.

    o To go any farther risks leaving you open for your opponent's counter.

Head-shield block

    This is used by lots of full-contact fighters. It's basically a shield, or what I like to term a "sacrifice block." You sacrifice getting hit on a limb to protect something more vital. For example, a foot explodes toward your groin so quickly that you don't have time to block with your arms or take evasive action, so you simply jerk your lead leg across the attack line and your shin eats the kick. You sacrificed a bruised shin to avoid crushed… (it's too ugly to even say). With the head shield block, you sacrifice a forearm bruise for an indentation in your temple.

Full-contact fighters who wear padded gloves use it a lot because their forearms aren't getting crushed by bare-knuckled fists. While it's more painful to use in a street confrontation, a sore forearm is better than your head getting struck with a set of knuckles. The backhand and sweep blocks work marvelously to deflect a head attack, but sometimes when you're having a slow-perception day, you might not notice an opponent's fist until it's only a few inches away.

• Since your hands are already up, simply hunch your shoulder and snap the appropriate arm against the side of your head, and you save the side of your skull.
• To make the blow less painful, tuck your chin in and keep your arm tight against your head.

Do 1 or 2 sets of 10 reps on each side. Practice in front of a mirror to ensure that your block is covering the side of your head.

Blocking kicks

Blocking an attacker's kick is done the same way from the I-don't-want-to-fight stance as from your regular stance. Still, you want to practice them so that you know they will be there for you when you need them. Practice blocking high and low kicks.

Stimulus and speed

Solo training is an excellent opportunity for you to make sure you're executing your block properly without having the pressure of getting hit by a live opponent.

• Only after you feel that your form is correct should you begin increasing the speed of execution.

- As you push the speed, watch in the mirror to ensure you're maintaining your good form:
  - o You aren't extending your block past your body.
  - o You're not blocking so little that you could still get hit.
- Since you don't have a partner to provide you with a punch or kick stimulus, use an audible one to ignite your reflexes. For example, block on each pronounced beat of your favorite music. If you have a talk show on the radio or television, choose two or three common words – "the," "a," "and" - and block every time you hear them.
- Once your form is polished and you're blocking correctly, move away from the mirror and stand before a television to use a visual image to spark your reflexes. .
  - o Example: Block every time the camera angle changes.

Of course the threat level when hearing "the" or when seeing the picture change on television is hardly the same as when seeing a fist moving like a bullet toward your face. Still, your reflexes benefit. We will revisit this in Chapter 14 "16 Ways to Cheat Speed."

AFTER YOU BLOCK

There are three things you can do after you block: run, assume your combat stance, or counter attack. Now, the smartest thing would be to always run, but for guys like me who write for a living, that would make for a pretty short martial arts book. Let's just say that you should always take the avenue of escape, but when circumstances prevent it, you have to do one of the other two options.

After blocking, you can return to the I-don't-want-to-fight stance, you can assume your regular, closed-hand fighting stance, or you can counter, just as you would from your regular on-guard stance. Keep in mind that the I-don't-want-to-fight stance *is* a fighting stance, and whatever you can do from your traditional one, you can do from it.

In the next chapter we will look at even more positions that with an open mind and with practice you will soon consider as just another fighting stance.

12

5 Everyday Fighting "Stances"

In every instructional martial arts book or magazine you find the sentence "Assume your fighting stance" followed by instruction on how to do a technique. No doubt your instructor tells your class several times a night to get into their fighting stance so everyone can work on a drill. The assumption in these requests is that readers and students are going to form the usual free-fighting stance: hands up, feet staggered, and body turned at an angle. This is fine, but the question begs to be asked: Is this position, let's call it the "classic on-guard stance," the only fighting stance?

The answer is a big, fat no. Still, the classic on-guard stance is what most of us think of when we hear or read the term fighting stance and, as such, it's the position from which we mostly train our punches and kicks. The irony is that it's arguably the one position you're *least* likely to assume in a real fight. Now, don't take that statement to the extreme to believe that you will never use your classic fighting stance in self-defense. Sometimes you will. But I'll go out on a limb here and say that the odds are high that you're going to begin the fight from another position: sitting, lying, leaning against something, standing casually, or sitting in a bus, car, train, or movie theater.

If in your regular martial arts class you rarely or never get to practice fighting from positions other than your classic on-guard stance, your solo training is the perfect opportunity to learn how to adapt everyday positions for combat.

Begin by thinking about your typical day.

- Do you stand or sit in a subway or bus?
o Do you often lean your shoulder or back against a building as you wait for the transportation to arrive?
- Do you sit behind a desk at work?
- Do you work behind a machine in a manufacturing plant?
- Do you ever lie in the grass at the park?
- Do you ever sit on a park bench?
- Do you like to sit in a coffee bar in college or at a Starbucks?
- Do you ever wait for your significant other while seated in your car?

These are typical places where people frequent every day and night, places where as a police officer most of my victims were assaulted, robbed, sexually assaulted, and intimidated in various ways. On those occasions when the victim had a chance to fight back, never once was I told by one of them, "Well, I assumed a fighting stance and began moving around in a sparring mode." Those who fought back were forced to fight from whatever position they were in when their day suddenly took a turn for the worse.

Let's look at five typical postures from which people get assaulted to see what you can do in your solo practice to make it a fighting stance. If you practice these hard enough, in a few months when you're told by your instructor to assume a fighting stance, you will have to ask, "Which one?"

Casual leaning

For our purposes, casual leaning means you're relaxed and laid-back with a shoulder propped against a wall, pole, bus stop shelter, side of a car, whatever. Your arms might be folded across your chest or hanging loosely at your sides, and your feet might be crossed or both might be flat on the floor.

Martial artists are often "attacked" from these positions when fellow classmates or friends outside the martial arts throw a surprise controlled punch at them just for fun. Sometimes the "attackers" are successful and the defender takes solace amidst all the teasing that he could have blocked it if it had been real and he had been in his fighting stance. Well, he *was* in a fighting stance; that is, if he thought of it as such and regularly practiced offense and defense movements from it. Let's examine this position to see what you can do defensively and offensively.

Even if you're not a habitual wall leaner, practice this anyway. You could get knocked against one and attacked with follow-up blows before you can move away from it. Besides, the more positions in which you can practice, the greater your understanding of your ability and the techniques.

OFFENSE WITH KICKS

The photo here shows a typical way of leaning lazily against a wall. It doesn't matter if you place your outside leg in front or behind your support leg. What is important is to place it where it provides *you* with the most versatility. One method is to keep most of your weight on the leg closest to the wall so that you can easily launch sidekicks, crescents, back kicks and even front kicks with the other one. Your objective is to be able to kick easily in any direction. Experiment to find a position that works best for you and make it a habit to always lean that way, or if you don't want to have to think about where to put your foot, practice from both positions.

- Experiment with your front kick.
- o   With your shoulder touching the wall, experiment to see how far you can kick out from the wall without moving your shoulder.

- Experiment with the sidekick.
- o With your shoulder against the wall, you're limited as to how far you can lean. How does that affect your kick?
- Experiment with the roundhouse kick.

o With your shoulder against the wall, you're limited as to how far you can lean. How does that affect your roundhouse?

• Experiment with the back kick.
o The wall doesn't prevent you from leaning when kicking along the wall, but is there a limit as to how far away from it you can kick?

• Experiment with the crescent kick.
o With your shoulder against the wall, how far out from it can you kick?

Workout Tip

You won't be able to kick as hard when you're leaning against something as you can when standing in the middle of the room, so good target selection is critical. Instead of aiming for your imaginary opponent's chest, think knee and groin.

Do 2 sets of 10 reps with all kicks on each side.

OFFENSE WITH HANDS

I have my arms folded but my top hand isn't tucked in under my arm or in some other way "locked in." Instead, it's resting casually on top of my other forearm, in a ready-to-fire position. You're also in a ready-to-fire position when you have your outside hand resting on your hip, your elbow pointing out to the side.

The easiest motion from either position is the backfist, though you're not limited to hitting with just your fist. Since the motion comes from your elbow hinge, you can configure your hand into a:

• backfist
• backhand slap
• claw
• hammer fist
• chop
• forearm strike
• bent wrist strike →
• side elbow

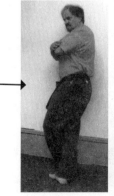

Play with these hand configurations along with the arm motion to learn in which directions you can hit and in which directions you can't. Sure, if you move your body away from the wall you can strike in any direction, but we are talking here about an instantaneous response to a threat, one in which there is no time to move your body.

Once you have figured it out, train repetitiously to develop the ability to explode with little or no telegraphing.

Do 2 sets of 10 reps of all hand techniques on both sides.

DEFENSE AGAINST A SURPRISE PUNCH

Lean against the wall and experiment with your basic blocks to see which ones are a sure thing and which are iffy.

Next, practice the head shield block I described earlier. It's a good defense when you can't do your regular blocks because of your body position, or you have been caught off guard, or because of the assailant's overwhelming speed. Think of it as an "eeek! block": Suddenly there is a punch racing toward your head and you have only enough time to squeal, "Eeek!" and cover up with your arm.

Now, muay Thai people might argue that the head shield is a regular block, to which I argue that it's regular only when you're wearing soft gloves, thus making those repetitious blows to your forearm muscles less traumatic on your bones and sinews. In my mind, it's an emergency, sacrifice block.

• While leaning against a wall, practice the head shield from both the arms-folded position and from the hand-on-your-hip position. Snap your arm up to the side of your head and lift your shoulder.

• Notice that you can twist your body back and forward a little to accommodate any direction of attack.

Do 2 sets of 10 reps on both sides from the folded arm position and the hand-on-hip position.

Defense Against a Kick

When an attacker launches a surprise kick and your position is too awkward to use regular blocks, create a shield with your lower leg, with your arm braced on top of your knee. There are other blocks that work well from this position, but give this a try first and see what you think. Notice that it does a good job of deflecting most kicks aimed anywhere from your shins to your head.

- Lift your outside knee and place your outside elbow on it so that your forearm is perpendicular to the floor.
    o Support your forearm with your other hand. Your leg can either absorb the impact of the kick, saving your groin, or it can sweep the attack aside with a subtle move in either direction.
    o Sweeping is done easily against straight-in kicks, such as front and side.
    o Absorbing a blow with your shin is usually reserved for circular kicks, such as the roundhouse.

- Variations: Do the following with your elbow on your knee:
    o Snap up your leg to jam an imaginary straight or circular kick launched at you from your front.
    o Snap up your leg to jam an imaginary straight or circular kick launched at you from your side. ⟶
    o Snap up your leg to sweep an imaginary straight or circular kick launched at you from slightly behind.
    o Snap up your leg to jam an imaginary straight or circular kick launched at you from behind.

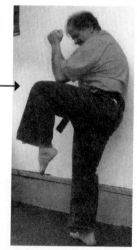

Do 2 or 3 sets of 10 reps of all variations on both sides

MOVING AWAY FROM THE WALL

No matter how skilled you become at defending yourself when leaning against a wall, you still want to move into a more typical and more strategic posture as quickly as you can after the initial exchange. For example, if your block, crescent kick, or backfist doesn't stop the assailant, and you have an ever-so-brief moment to move away from the wall, you want to do it smoothly. Solo practice is a good time to polish that move.

Lean your right shoulder against a wall with your ankles crossed. Practice moving into whatever stance you want - your regular fighting stance, forward stance, or transition into an attack.

- Step straight out from the wall with your left foot into your regular fighting stance or a forward stance. ————————————➤
- Step out diagonally to your left.
- Step out diagonally to your right.
- Spin to your right past the wall and step forward with your right foot (as if the threat were coming up from behind you along the wall).
- Use any of the above stepping methods as you execute a hand technique.
- Use any of the above stepping methods as you kick.

Whether you use the above techniques or develop your own, your objective is to move smoothly and quickly, which is to say, your objective isn't to stumble or fall. With practice, you will easily respond to an attack while leaning against a wall with your arms folded, or your hands on your hips and your feet crossed. Then without missing a beat, you will be able to step smoothly in the appropriate direction and either flee or follow with additional techniques.

Other standing postures

Refer back to the beginning of this chapter and look at the many postures noted there, or just think about situations typical to your lifestyle while at – work, school, the grocery store or the health club. Spend your solo training time studying the strengths and weaknesses of all them. You never know where you might be attacked. Remember, few assailants telegraph their intentions with a "Here I come!"

Sitting position

Important

As a cop, I investigated many assaults where the victim was seated in a restaurant or bar. Sitting on a park bench wasn't always safe for people either, nor was sitting at a bus stop or at a desk. These victims lost and lost badly, partly because they were not trained fighters and partly because their seated positions at the moment of attack put them at a significant disadvantage. But you have an advantage: You're a trained fighter and you have devoted solo training time to function in a seated position.

KICKING FROM THE CHAIR

Even if your instructor teaches self-defense from a chair, his methods might not be best for you, or maybe one technique is but two others are not. Solo training is a great time to explore what works for your body type. You can also spend extra time on polishing any of your instructor's techniques that you had trouble with in class. If all you needed was extra training time to improve them, you win. But if after considerable training you still can't do them justice, then that is good to know, too, so you can find replacement techniques.

I think of chair techniques as those you can do while seated in the chair and those that you can do as you stand. Notice it's *as* you stand, as opposed to after you stand. If you do them after you get all the way up they really aren't chair techniques. That seems obvious but lots of folks miss that point.

Let's begin by looking at a nifty way to get up, one in which you can do so smoothly, almost effortlessly, and one from which you can fire off a kick as you ascend.

GETTING UP STRATEGICALLY

Most people get up from a chair by placing both feet parallel to each other and then stand as if coming up out of a squat, which is exactly what they are doing. This is too slow, and should the attacker hit at that precise moment, it's also too unstable to withstand a push or hit. Here is a better way.

Caution

- Place one foot forward and the other back, about a stride-width apart.
- Lean your upper body forward as you push off with your rear foot.
- The push and lean propels you forward and upward smoothly and effortlessly into a fighting stance, a forward stance, or into a punch or kick.

Let's look at a few ways you can practice kicking while seated and while getting up.

SEATED WITH HANDS UP

- Sit with your hands up in your on-guard position as if an attacker has just rushed up and threatened you or attacked you in some manner.

• Experiment to see which kicks you can do and which ones are difficult given your seated, on-guard position. For sure you can do a:

o front thrust kick (impact with ball of foot).

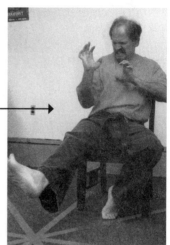

o snap kick (impact with the top of your foot or shin, usually to the groin).

o toe-out kick (impact the arch of your foot to the knee). ⎯⎯⎯⎯⎯➤

o crescent kick (impact with the little toe or big toe side of your foot).

• One other option is to keep one hand up for protection and use your other hand to lean on the seat or hold onto the chair back as you kick. Experiment to see if this:

o allows for other kicks, such as a roundhouse.

o increases your power since you can lean a little more.

Depending on your flexibility and hip structure, there might be other kicks available to you no matter how you're sitting, but you won't know until you spend solo training time learning what you can and cannot do.

Do 2 to 3 sets of 10 to 15 reps of all the kicks you can do from this position.

SEATED WITH BOTH HANDS DOWN

• Depending on the situation and the position and distance of the assailant, you might have time to support yourself by holding on to the chair's seat or back with both hands.

o With additional support, you can maneuver your body into better positions that allow for a greater variety of kicks than those listed above, thus increasing their overall speed and power.

- With a maneuver of your body, you can:
o grab the seat on each side of your hips.
o grab the chair seat between your legs with one hand and anywhere on the seat with your other.
o grab the back of your chair with one hand and the chair seat with your other.

- Your task is to explore all that you can do while still seated.

Do 2 to 3 sets of 10 to 15 reps of all the kicks you can do from this position.

WORK ON YOUR SEATED BLOCKS, TOO

It's easy to forget when having so much fun executing cool kicks from a seated position that you might have to first block the assailant's attack. To not practice blocking attacks means you're practicing only preemptive strikes, which isn't realistic.

- Imagine that the attacker is somewhere in your 360-degree space and that you must first deflect or absorb his attack before you can kick.
- Imagine that he hits and scoots back, thus providing you with more space to launch your kicks.
- Imagine that he punches and remains close in, forcing you to modify your kick, i.e., kicking with your lower shin, upper shin, and knee.

KICKING AS YOU GET UP FROM THE CHAIR:

As mentioned earlier, the key word here is *as:* As you spring up from the chair.

- Use the two previous methods – sitting with your hands up in an on-guard position and supporting yourself on the seat or on the chair back with one or both hands, to launch yourself
  o forward
  o to either side
  o diagonally forward or diagonally backward.
- Know the purpose of your kick.
  o If it's for a tournament demonstration, have fun with it and come up with all kinds of crazy variations from the chair.
  o If it's for real-world survival, you want your launch to be tactically sound without unnecessary bells and whistles.
- How many kicks can you deliver before you're standing all the way up?
- Does each kick move you toward standing up? For example:
  o Launch one kick while seated, one as you get up, and one more just before you're all the way up.
  o Launch two kicks while seated, one as you get up, and one more just before you're all the way up.

Do 2 to 3 sets of 10 to 15 reps of all the kicks you can do as you get up.

Free tip: Hit with the chair. If the chair is light enough, practice grabbing the seat, the chair back, or the legs as you stand. Practice swinging it seamlessly at the threat as you stand and assume a strong combat stance.

Training Tip

PUNCHING WHILE SEATED

It's much easier to punch and block from a seated position than it is to kick, though you still want to experiment to see how you need to adjust and use your body to maximize speed, power and reach. Consider these easy-to-execute possibilities from a seated position:

GET CREATIVE IN YOUR TRAINING SPACE

When you're training alone in your basement or garage, position some of the junk to create an aisle, such as in a grocery store. You want your practice in a cramped and narrow space to get a better idea of what you can and cannot do.

Say that you're particularly interested in sitting techniques since you ride the bus several days a week. For your solo practice, create an environment that is as cramped as a bus seat. A stack of boxes represents the window wall to the side and a stack of tires represents the seat to your immediate front. Your task is to determine how you're going to defend yourself in this tight space. If kicks are no longer an option, which hand techniques work best?

- Backfist *motion*
  o Impact with the knuckles in the usual backfist strike.
  o Impact with the heel in the usual bottom fist strike.
  o Impact with the edge of the hand in the usual chop strike.
  o Use the same motion to reach out and grab and squeeze the assailant's inner thigh or groin. (as pictured)
  o Use the motion to claw the assailant's eyes
- Straight punch with either hand while seated.
  o Sit and look straight ahead to 12 o'clock (3 o'clock is to your right and 9 o'clock is to your left).
  o Determine what you have to do to punch hard to your left with your left fist and what you have to do to punch hard to your right with your right fist. Once you get that figured out, it's easy to

throw punches to 2 o'clock, 10 o'clock, 1 o'clock and 11 o'clock.

o Create an image of an assailant moving in on you while you're seated. See his vital targets and practice hitting them.

• Experiment with other hand and arm blows.

o Forearms: Strike in various directions – upward into the groin, downward across the assailant's neck; and sideways into his ribs.

o Elbows: Strike in various directions – upward into his groin or chin; horizontal strike into the side of his head, ribs or thigh; and downward onto his grabbing arm or back of his neck.

USING HAND AND ARM TECHNIQUES AS YOU GET UP FROM THE CHAIR

Caution

Whenever there is a transitional move there is a potential for a weak moment. For example, you apply an arm lock on someone and then flow into (transition) another arm lock. Transitions can be weaknesses if you don't distract your opponent with your verbiage or give him a shot of pain elsewhere, like a quick kick to his ankle bone.

It can be especially dangerous getting up when you're distracted or caught in an awkward position. Don't attempt it when the assailant is close unless you can:

• kick him so he stumbles away from you.
• push or punch him so that he stumbles away from you.

While the above two techniques are ideal, you might have to hit multiple times to overwhelm him and to keep him busy while you make the transition.

• The assailant throws a punch at you as you sit minding your own business.

o Block it and counter with a punch or two from your seated position.

o Then hit again as you lean forward and draw one foot back under you, and hit again as you begin to ascend.

o Hit him when you're half way up.

o Hit once more for good measure when you're almost up, and a final shot as you stand straight and tall.

You want to fill every half beat of time with a hand technique, a barrage of them so that he doesn't have a chance to hit back as you transition from sitting down to getting up.

Do 1 to 2 sets of 10 reps on both sides

It's fun and a real eye opener to practice kicking and punching while seated in a chair and while getting up from it. Considering the large number of assaults that occur to people sitting in subways, on park benches, and in bars, this training is critically important to your self-defense knowledge.

Kneeling and squatting

Kneeling is defined as having one or both knees on the floor. A squatting position is anywhere between your rear sitting on your heels to where your thighs are parallel with the floor. While in any of these positions, you could get attacked:

- when you're kneeling on your job.
- when you're changing a tire at the side of the road.
- when you're picking up a dropped object.
- when you have fallen to one knee in the course of a fight.
- when you start to get back up.

These are all seen as moments of weakness by your assailant, perfect opportunities to strike. Your goal is to prove to him that they aren't moments of weakness and prove it with extreme prejudice. But you can only do that if you consider them fighting positions and you have practiced them regularly.

Important

PUNCHING

Does your fighting style contain one or more punching sets, a series of offensive and defensive hand techniques? Working on something with which you're already familiar is a good way to begin your training in these positions. If you don't have a punching set, simply organize a list of basic punches in your mind: jab, cross, backfist, uppercut, hammer, elbows and claws.

• Proceed through your set or list of hand techniques in the kneeling position.

o On both knees.

o On your right knee.

o On your left knee.

• Experiment to see what you need to do to maintain your stability as you punch and strike, and how you have to adjust your body to get the most out of each blow.

• For now, simply hit at an imaginary target directly in front of you. We will examine other targets and multiple hitting in a moment.

Do 2 to 3 sets of 10 to 15 reps.

Next, do the same thing from the squatting position.

• Squat as low as you can and execute your techniques from there.

• Then come up half way and do them from that position.

• Lastly come up just a few inches short of completely standing, and work everything from there.

• Be sure to do the same techniques and same quantity with both arms.

Do 2 to 3 sets of 10 to 15 reps.

KICKING

Does your fighting style have a kicking set with front, round, side and hook kicks? Mine, for example, has a set where we kick to the chest, groin, knee and ankles. A kick to the chest while kneeling or squatting is probably out of the question (unless your assailant chooses that moment to bend down and tie his shoe), but the other targets are all viable options.

Kicking from a kneeling or squatting position is tough. My suggestion is that in a real fight you use hand techniques before trying to kick. Hitting with your hands allows you to maintain good balance and to throw more blows as you ascend to a level where you can launch a solid kick. But of course it's not a perfect world. The situation might be such where you have no choice but to kick from a kneeling or squatting position. Maybe the attacker threw a chair, or some other object large enough to momentarily tie up your hands, then moved into your range. The window is open to hit him but your hands are busy dealing with the chair. It would be nice to have a few trained kicks at your disposal.

SQUATTING

Probably the only position from which most fighters can't kick is when squatting with their rear on their heels. There are some, however, who can kick when they are half way up, in a position where their upper legs are parallel with the floor. Their hip structure is such that they can lean a little in whatever direction makes possible a particular kick. If you're one of these fighters, experiment to determine your capabilities. If you find that you can do two different kicks, work them in sets and reps to make them as fast and powerful as possible. However, if your hip structure prevents you from kicking in this position, then work on your hand techniques from it.

Important

KNEELING

This position offers many more options.

KNEEL ON ONE OR BOTH KNEES WITH YOUR HANDS IN AN ON-GUARD POSITION

- You can execute a low front kick, say, to the attackers shin, thigh and groin.
- You might be able to execute an angle roundhouse kick or a low sidekick.

Do 1 to 2 sets of 10 reps of all the kicks you can do.

The above kicks are typical ones that most people can do with their hands up. Does your hip structure allow you to do others? Solo training is a good time to experiment without concerns of being embarrassed in front of others when you fall to the floor.

Say you try an angle back kick, one that is half way between a sidekick and a straight back kick. For sure it's awkward from this position and might cause you problems. But just because it's weak and barely gets off the ground is no reason to discard it.

Training Tip

Make a routine of 3 to 4 sets of 10 reps with each leg, 2 to 3 times a week. If after two months it's still lousy, work it hard for one more month. By then your consistent training most likely will have turned that once feeble kick into one that is fast and strong, and definitely a surprise attack from that position. If on the other hand it's still weak and ineffective, at least you learned something about that kick.

KNEELING WHEN YOUR HANDS CAN TOUCH THE FLOOR

You have an opportunity for greater stability, speed and power when the situation allows you to support yourself on the floor – one hand, two hands, or by dropping to the floor onto your side or back. While there is an inherent risk doing this, it might be your only option. Therefore, it's in your best interest to know how to drop and kick, and how to get up quickly afterwards.

WITH BOTH KNEES ON THE FLOOR

One hand
• Practice kicking when you're on both knees and leaning on one hand.
• Practice kicking *as* you drop to the floor.
• Practice dropping to your left side, right side, forward and back.
    o Practice kicking from these positions.

Two hands
• Practice kicking when you're on both knees and leaning on two hands.
• Practice kicking *as* you drop to the floor.
• Practice dropping to your left side, right side, forward and back.
    o Practice kicking from these positions.

Do 1 to 2 sets of 10 reps of all positions and kicks.

WITH ONE KNEE ON THE FLOOR

One hand
• Practice kicking when you're on one knee and leaning on one hand.
• Practice kicking *as* you drop.
• Practice dropping to your left side, right, forward and back.
o Practice kicking from these positions.

Two hands
• Practice kicking when you're on one knee and leaning on two hands.
• Practice kicking *as* you drop.
• Practice dropping to your left side, right, forward and back.
o Practice kicking from these positions.

Now practice on your other knee

Note: While the above one- and two-hand variations might seem similar, the feel is different enough that you should devote practice time to both.

See Section 3 for a killer calorie burning and aerobic workout using the above positions with kicks.

Mental imagery

You would get arrested for disturbing the peace if you were to practice 2 sets of 10 reps of crescent kicks in the breakfast cereal aisle of your local grocery, in a crowded subway, or in a line at the movies, though these are the very places where you might one day have to defend yourself. To avoid going to jail, you need to imagine these environments when you're solo training.

The next time you're in the grocery, take a moment to look around the aisle. See that guy over there reading the label on a can of soup? Crush him in your mind. First imagine that he confronts you in the aisle and threatens you in some way. Before you can back away, he launches an arcing punch at your nose. See yourself block and counter him, then flee down the aisle in the opposite direction.

In reality, you're pretending to look at soup along with the guy next to you who is innocently doing the same thing. By using your imagination, you benefit from looking at a real live person standing in the precise environment in which you want to prepare for. In the course of a 20-minute shopping excursion, you can mentally fight five more shoppers in the aisles.

Do the same thing when you're sitting in the bus, in the park, standing in a movie line, or at a fast food place, all places where in my experience as a police officer trouble can happen quickly. Use your imagination to see a confrontation unfold while you're in these places, and use it again when you practice physically during your solo time.

Your objective is to look upon any sitting, kneeling, squatting or standing position as just another fighting stance. To reach this point in your thinking, you must be consistent in your analysis, your mental imagery, and your physical practice, both solo and with training partners.

13

20 Ways to Practice Solo Grappling

For some reason training alone in the kick/punch arts is more acceptable than training in jujitsu by yourself. Probably a big part of it is that it looks a little odd, as if the one doing it were mentally ill and fighting off unseen demons. Well, that was the opinion of a lot of people 40 years ago when they first saw karate and taekwondo fighters practicing forms. In fact, when I was working a police car in the early 1970s, I got a radio call on a mentally deranged guy "flipping out" in a park. But when I got there I found a very sane karate man doing kata. I'm betting that just as seeing someone doing a form today is no longer freaky, soon the same will be true of solo grappling, especially with the arrival of grappling dummies and a growing volume of information on how to do it.

How I prepared for a belt test

A few years ago when I was preparing for my second-degree black belt test in jujitsu, my life was so crazy that I was having trouble finding training time. I trained a little with my students during classes, but mostly I did it alone. That wasn't a problem for me since I've always liked solo workouts, but I didn't have experience doing it with grappling techniques. So first I had to figure out a plan of attack.

The test required that I demonstrate 201 techniques (actually, it was 200 but I added one for extra credit). Besides technical skill, and the ingraining of that technical skill, I needed tremendous aerobic conditioning, partly because of the volume of material I had to demonstrate and partly because the last phase of the test involved a long sparring session against multiple attackers.

TECHNICAL SKILL

By having previously worked with my instructor and with knowledgeable students, I felt confident that I was good to go technically. But I needed to entrench the techniques more, get them imbedded in my head so that they would be there for me when I was stressed and fatigued. Also, the better I understood the techniques the more easily I could adapt them to the subtle differences in my partners' attacks.

About three months out I established a training regimen of high reps done in 90-minute sessions. I would go nonstop at slow to medium speed concentrating on executing the movements perfectly against my imaginary opponent. The second month I began executing the techniques faster in workouts that sometimes went two hours. The last month I incorporated anaerobic training and concentrated on techniques needing extra polish.

I found that when working on technical grappling skills by yourself that these points need to be emphasized:

Important

- Practice slowly in the early stages to ensure that you're doing all of the elements of the technique.
- When there is a breakdown in concentration, there is a tendency to "smudge" parts of the movement. For example:
  o When executing an arm bar, you might not "see" your opponent's wrist when you pretend to grab it.
  o You might place your forearm somewhere near where his elbow would be instead of seeing the point clearly in your mind's eye.
  o You might step only partially in the direction of the takedown, cutting short an important part of the technique.
- Because your practice lacked clarity of footwork and precise hand and arm placement, you wasted your time on something that isn't going to help you.

• To grow from your solo practice, you must "see" your hands, legs and entire body in relation to your imaginary opponent's hands, legs and body. You must execute the complete movement. For example:

o If you're doing an armbar takedown followed by a lock-up on the floor, don't stop in the standing position. Get down on the floor and simulate the lock-up, and then scramble back on your feet.

• If you're having problems with, say, the ground phase, drop down and do 10 reps of just that part of it. Then stand up and do the entire technique – the standing phase and the ground phase - five times. That makes a total of 15 reps on the ground and five reps standing.

"What if" variations When you feel you have good mastery of the techniques, practice a few "what if" variations. What if your opponent steps a little to the left as he punches at you? What if he pushes your face instead of your chest? What if a real attacker is taller or shorter than the height of your imagined attacker? You don't want to add variations to the attack that are so great that you are no longer doing the same technique, but it's important to examine subtle ones that alter the way you apply the movement.

Training Tip

ATTENTION TO DETAIL

I can't overemphasize the importance of including detail in your technique. It's so important that if you're unsure of all the elements, you shouldn't practice it solo until you have learned every facet of it and performed it on a live partner. It just makes sense: You can't solo practice with missing elements and expect the technique you skipped to be there for you when you do it on a live opponent. It isn't going to happen.

Pay attention to detail.

AEROBIC AND ANAEROBIC CONDITIONING

You're getting good aerobic work just by practicing several grappling techniques repetitiously and nonstop. Increase the speed and you get a tremendous cardio workout. Explode on some of the techniques and you get tough anaerobic work, the same as you experience in a real fight. Here is how I did it for my test.

Three months out   While I hammered out the technical aspects of all the techniques, I was able to get quite a lot of cardio training by virtue of practicing so many without stopping. That aspect of my training just happened on its own. My primary concern at this stage was polishing techniques and getting them entrenched in my mind through repetition so that I could perform them without having to think about the steps of each technique. Still, I was huffing and puffing since so many of them began in a standing position and then went to the ground where I applied a restraint hold on my imaginary opponent. I would then disengage and quickly get to my feet. Doing that repetitiously burned some serious calories and made my heart and lungs work overtime.

Two months out   With eight weeks to go, I felt good about the technical execution of the movements so I started doing them faster, half to three-quarter speed. Some were so easy for me that I felt it was okay to do them only once or twice. Those that I were not doing as well were given an additional 10 reps.

Due to the increased speed and my usual nonstop format, my aerobic conditioning improved tremendously; I even I dropped a few pounds.

It should be noted that I practiced with real people whenever I could during this three-month period. It's important to apply the techniques on humans because you need to understand how to make minor adjustments for bodyweight, height differences, awkward attacks, and a host of other little things that only a real person can give you. Still, because of other things going on in my life, most of my training – probably 80 percent - was solo.

One month out   At this point I felt that my aerobic conditioning was in good shape so I wanted to maintain it during the time left, even improve it a little. Also, I felt it important to include anaerobic conditioning, so very critical to survive those all-out 30- to 60-second bursts. I knew from having been in dozens of all-out brawls with resisting suspects that those times can be exhausting and even debilitating. It would not impress the testers if I were hacking up phlegm after a 40-second burst of techniques. By the way, good aerobic conditioning helps you recover quickly from anaerobic moments.

There are many ways to incorporate anaerobic training into one's program; this is how I did it.

- I did 5 to 10 reps of each technique at medium to fast speed.
- Once every 3 minutes, I'd execute a lengthy combination (I underlined about 10 of them on my list of 201) that required going to the floor with my invisible opponent to finish the technique, then scrambling back up on my feet again.

o I'd execute these all-out, as if my life depended on how hard and fast I did them.

- I'd then "rest" 3 minutes by doing 5 to 10 reps of however many technique I could do before it was time to execute another lengthy combination at an all-out intensity for 30 to 40 seconds.
- I'd follow this regimen for the entire 90-minute solo session. Tough? Oh yes.

o If I found myself dying at about the 45-minute point, I'd space out the anaerobic bursts to once every 5 or 6 minutes.

I did this tough regimen twice a week. To have done it three or four times a week would not only have risked injury but it would have retarded growth. On those training days in between the two anaerobic ones, I performed the techniques at medium speed to ingrain them solidly into my mind.

In the end, I was in outstanding aerobic and anaerobic shape and my techniques were as good as I could get them at that point. If you read my book *Crouching Tiger: Taming the Warrior Within*, you know that I caught the flu right before test day. I managed to pass but I was so sick at one point I wanted to throw myself into one of the big room fans. That said, if I had not trained as I had, there would have been no way I could have lasted the entire test, let alone have passed it.

Techniques

Let's look at a few specific grappling moves you can practice by your lonesome.

Wrist Twist Takedown

Important

I love this technique and have considered it a basic one for a long time. I used it several times on the street as a cop and never had it fail. As is the case with many techniques, there are several variations. In my opinion aikido has some of the prettiest and jujitsu's variations are a close second. I do a streamlined one that isn't as pretty as either of these, but it still makes my opponent smooch the ground really, really hard.

- When the opponent pushes your chest, rotate your upper body and reach for his wrist with the same-side hand.
- Slide your hand down to the back of his hand, your forearm in alignment with his.

- Rotate your upper body back as you grasp his hand with your other hand and begin to apply the twist. Continue to rotate your hips and twist his hand – his forearm is angled at about 45 degrees – until he begins to lean toward the outside of your body.

  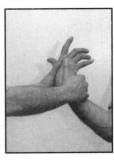

- Just before your hip reaches full rotation, snap it the rest of the way and turn your lead foot outward. This action transfers energy into his wrist. Down he goes. From here you can punch, kick or lock him up with another grappling technique.

 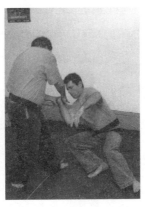

Do 2 sets of 10 reps.

LEG REAP

This is the classic osoto geri takedown but I like to add a little extreme agony to it. Hey, he started it!

• Your invisible opponent launches a swinging right punch that you block with your left arm.

• Grasp his punching arm and begin pulling it downward at an angle behind him.

Step out diagonally to your left on the same angle as his arm, placing your left heel on the same line as his heel. This by itself places him off balance. With your right hand, ram your fingers into his eyes. This snaps his head back (and makes him go "Ow!")

- Continue to pull downward on his arm and continue to grind your fingers into his eyes as you sweep his leg back with your leg.

- Dump him on the floor.

HEAD TWIST TAKEDOWN

This is a dangerous technique for your live opponent. Done without caution it could be fatal. As you practice solo, keep in mind that the function of the twist and tug is to take the person down, not to turn his head around in the opposite direction. You can reach his head by lunging in to grab it after you have blocked his attack, or by first hitting him and grabbing it. Let's hit him, shall we?

Caution

- Slam your left scoop kick into your imaginary opponent's right knee to buckle him forward slightly.

• Set your left foot down at 11 o'clock. Cup his chin with your right hand and cup the back of his head with your left.

• Pull the back of his head as you push his chin. Think of twisting a large jar lid. It's critical to tuck your left elbow into your side as you pull his head down.

- As his head nears your solar plexus, you will feel a need to move your left leg out of the way to maintain your balance. Slide it to a position between 8 and 9 o'clock as your opponent lands on the floor.

- Do any finishing techniques you want.
Do 2 sets of 10 reps.

FOOT SWEEP

Foot sweeps can either take your opponent all the way to the floor or just momentarily upset his balance so you can blast him with a punch. If your intent is to take your opponent down, you should still be ready with a quick follow-up punch in the event the sweep doesn't work. Here judo black belt Barry Eisler shows how to do a simple foot sweep by yourself.

- Clinch with your imaginary opponent by hooking his neck with your left hand and holding his left elbow with your right.

• Sweep your right foot so that it impacts with the arch area. Simultaneously with the impact of your foot, pull his left elbow down and push with your left hand.

• If he falls, execute whatever finishing techniques you want. If he doesn't fall, hit him before he recovers his balance.

• Unlike humans, trees don't complain when you sweep their ankles over and over.

Do 2 sets of 10 reps.

DEFENSE AGAINST DOUBLE WRIST GRAB

This is a slick defense. Though it's more likely that a woman would be grabbed this way than a man, both should practice this.

• Your invisible opponent grabs both of your wrists.

- Imagine energy streaming out of your hand in a downward 45-degree angle past your opponent as you slide your foot diagonally to his side. Use a low stance.

- Your right arm is relaxed as you move your elbow in front of your abdomen, with your hand pointing upward.
- Several things are happening simultaneously here. Step forward with your right foot until it's behind and between your opponent's feet. At the same time drive your right hand and forearm along the side of his neck and over and down the other side as you continue to move his right arm downward.

- He falls to the floor where you can do whatever finishing techniques you want.

Do 2 sets of 10 reps

ARMBAR STANDING AND PRONE

Caution

The second armbar in this technique can be executed as a deliberate follow-up move or as a quick way to recover should you fall when taking your opponent down. It's so powerful that you could easily break a live opponent's arm. So be careful.

- Your imaginary opponent tries to push you out of the way with his right arm.
- Grab his right wrist with your right hand and press your left forearm an inch above his elbow.

- Pull up slightly on his wrist and press down on his elbow, then spin him in a circle.

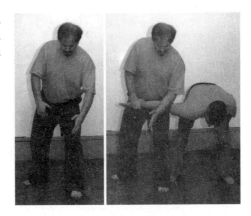

- As he lands on his belly, drop your left elbow over his upper arm so that you pin his arm in your armpit. Drop onto your left hip and shoot your legs out in a splayed position.

- Push up with your left hand and pull up with your right as you lean back to lock his elbow.

Do 2 sets
of 10 reps

BRACE AND CAROTID CONSTRICTION

Important

I used this often when I was a cop. I don't remember if I every put someone to sleep with it (I did with other neck restraints), but then that was never my intention. Most often I applied it to give a troublemaker a sense of helplessness and force him to think about himself instead of me. The hold prevented him from getting up from a chair or from scooting off a barstool where he would be in a stronger position to cause more problems. You can also use the technique as a momentary restraint hold until you get help to control the person.

- Approach from behind a seated invisible opponent
- From his left side, reach under his chin to the right side of his head with your left hand and grab a fist full of collar.
- Press your knuckles against his head in the area of his ear and then execute a fast and painful knuckle scrape down his face.

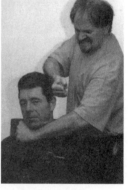

- Your right forearm acts as a brace to prevent him from turning when you pull on his collar. The blood supply to his brain is slowed when the collar tightens against his carotid artery.

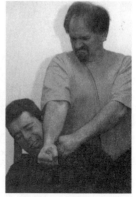

CHAIR DEFENSE

Since you got the chair at the ready, here is a nifty defense against someone attacking you while you're seated.

- Your invisible opponent attempts to push your face with his right hand which you catch with your right hand.

- Slam your left forearm into the crook of his arm and push his wrist back toward his shoulder.

- Grab your right wrist to make a figure-4.

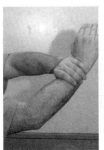 

- Apply pressure with your arms in a circular fashion to your left as you twist in the chair to your left.
- And take him down to the floor.

HAIR TAKEDOWN

There are hair techniques that are executed just to inflict pain and there are some that primarily give direction, usually to the floor. I rely on hair pulling and twisting as both a singular technique and as a supplement to help another grappling technique that isn't working too well. If your training partner hates having hair techniques done on him, convince him that getting it yanked and twisted stimulates his scalp into producing healthy follicles. Happily, a make believe opponent never complains.

- Your invisible opponent pushes at you but you brush his arms aside with both hands.

• Step along the outside of his arm. Move behind him as you reach for the hair on the back of his head with your left hand, and grab his shoulder with your right.

• Jerk both elbows downward as you yank downward with both hands.

• Step out of the way so your opponent has room to fall.
• Follow-up with punches and kicks, or a grappling lock

DEFENSE AGAINST TOP MOUNT CHOKE

Important

Clearly the assailant is in a dominant position to do you harm (if you're a seasoned grappler you won't agree that he is the dominant one, but I'm talking about in the eyes of the law). A prudent person (a juror) would assume that this person has bad intentions for you and therefore you have a legal right to raise the level of force in your defense. Here we go with attacking the eyes again.

- Imagine an invisible opponent sitting on you and choking you with both hands.
- Clasp your hands and smash both of them down into the crook of his right arm, forcing his head down.

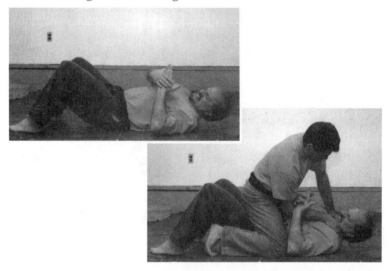

- Grab the hair on the right side of his head with your left hand and plunge the fingers of your right hand into his eyes.

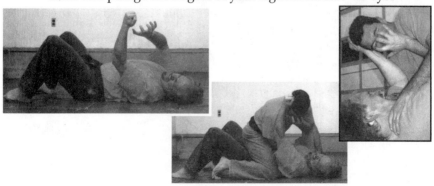

- Raise your hips sharply to buck him off in the direction of his collapsed left arm.

- Roll over and punch him, lock him up, or leap to your feet and flee.

Do 2 sets of 10 reps on both sides of all the listed solo grappling techniques.

There is no argument that training with a live partner is best for learning grappling, but when it's just you, your imagination, and an empty room, solo practice is a good way to train. But remember: Solo grappling will only be of value when you include every detail. Use that imagination of yours to conjure a life-like image of an opponent and see every detail of his attack and his response to your counter as you execute the movements. Do it right so that when you do have a live body you will execute the techniques as if you have been practicing with a real person all along. And in a way you have, albeit only in your vivid imagination.

Punch, kick and grapple the heavy bag

Workout
Tip

Up to this point you have been only grappling with your opponent. Now let's toss in the entire kitchen sink, and punch, kick, headbutt, elbow, knee and even scratch to get him off you. Let's also change your opponent from an imaginary one to a heavy punching bag, the heavier the better (no, your pillow won't work). It doesn't matter if it's canvas, leather or a slick vinyl. It does matter that it's heavy, bulky and hard to handle, just like a big, fat drunk guy. Expect to get a good aerobic workout, too.

TAKEDOWN

Let's look at ways to respond should you get forced to the floor, either by a tackle or a bear hug takedown.

Tackle takedown Lean the bag against your legs and assume your fighting stance.

• Fall backwards to the floor and deal with the tackler on your shins and knees.
    o Kick him off and scramble to your feet.
    o Kick him off and keep kicking him until you feel he is weakened enough for you to get up.
    o Kick him off and continue to kick and punch him. Get up when you think you have done sufficient damage to do so.
    o Kick him off and then dive on him. Hit him with punches, elbows and knees until you think you can get up safely.

o Kick him off and then grapple him into a pin or submission (yes, it's hard since the bag is missing a head and limbs. Use your imagination).
- Falling options when tackled
o Fall on your side and deal with the bag.
o Twist and fall on your stomach and deal with the bag.
o Land in a seated position and deal with the bag.

CHEST HUG TAKEDOWN

Begin by holding the bag to your chest as if your opponent has you in a bear hug.

- Fall backwards to the floor and deal with the attacker on your chest.
o Headbutt, punch its sides, drive your knees into it, and continue until you have weakened the stuffing-filled attacker and knocked him off. Get up.

    o Grapple it off you, mount it and pummel it with your fists.

    o Grapple it off you, scoot up so that you can hold the bag down and pummel it with knee strikes.

    o Throw it off you, leap to your feet and give it a "foot stomp party."

- Fall on your side and deal with the bag
- Twist and fall on your stomach and deal with the bag.
- Land in a seated position and deal with the bag.

OTHER ATTACKS

It's up to your imagination as to how you want your heavy bag to attack you.

- Sit on a chair holding a heavy bag and deal with it.
- Lie diagonally on stairs holding a heavy bag and deal with it (it's safer to practice on the bottom three steps than on the top three).
- Start out holding the bag against your chest as you stand in a crowded space. Fall to the floor and deal with the bag.

Use your imagination to come up with more variations to expand your experience and understanding of dealing with a ponderous weight. You will probably find a bag more difficult to handle than a real person, and that is okay, as it's better to sweat in practice than to bleed in the street. Speaking of sweat, unlike some real training partners, a bag doesn't forget to use deodorant.

14

16 Ways to Cheat Speed

Tremendous speed is impressive. Even after all these years of training, I'm still in awe of fighters who can move in the blink of an eye. Who isn't wowed every time they see that old black and white film footage of Bruce Lee's screen test? After sitting and talking for a long time, Lee stands to demonstrate a few moves. Wearing a business suit and without warming up, he throws several punches and kicks faster than most of us could even fantasize.

In my book *Speed Training*, I wrote about meeting a man who held 18 world titles in speed draw competition. On a given signal, he could draw his big ol' .45 pistol from his hip holster, pull the hammer back with his opposite hand, fire at a target, and hit it – all in a fraction of the time it takes a person to blink. And no, it wasn't a break-away holster. He pulled it all the way up and out. By the way, when I asked how often he practiced he said he did 3,500 reps a day of combined dry fire and live fire. His competitors did around 200 reps a day.

Speed is fun to watch and, if you had the right parents to give you lots of fast-twitch muscle fibers, it's fun to be fast. But what if you chose the wrong parents and you were born with a preponderance of slow-twitch muscles? Should you just resign to it and throw your face under a lawn mower? While that is always an option, it's better to save your face and look for ways to work around the slow twitchers.

In this section we are going to examine a few ways to train by yourself to cheat speed, that is, move in such a manner that your opponent will be convinced that he just got hit with a super-fast technique, even if you have all the slow-twitch fibers of a tortoise. Now, if you have been blessed with lots of fast-twitch muscle fibers, read on because the following techniques will make you seem even faster.

Sneaky backfist

Important

One of the most common errors when delivering the backfist strike is to draw the fist back before launching it forward. That is absolutely and without exception a big no-no. Except for now. With this method you're going to pre-chamber your attack, but the trick is to camouflage the movement so that your opponent doesn't know you're doing it.

SNEAKY BACKFIST WHEN SPARRING

Most experienced fighters know that when sparring in class or in a tournament it's important to keep the hands moving continuously. Well, that rule still stands. However, don't make the common error of moving your fists only in little circles or in an up and down motion as you stalk your opponent. What can happen is that every time you launch your backfist toward his face, he blocks it, and does so easily. This is because you have only conditioned his brain to seeing your hands making little circles or up and down movements. So when you launch your "surprise" backfist on a different track, on a straight line *toward* his face, he isn't surprised because he can detect the shift in direction.

This isn't a big error when you have extraordinary speed and explosiveness. But if you don't have it, you need to cheat speed by setting up the attack better.

• Condition your opponent to seeing your hand make little jerking motions toward his head.
• Then when you extend the motion into a backfist at his face, his mind won't perceive that your move is anything other than just another forward twitch.

It's even possible to condition his mind to seeing you retract your backfist a little in what is normally considered a chambering and telegraphing action. I'm in no way advocating telegraphing, but this is one way to do it and hide it for reasons of generating additional impact and seemingly great speed.

- The trick is to incorporate more retraction movements as you move about.
- Continuously circle your hands. Move your lead fist back toward your head, jerk it forward a little, and then move both hands up and down. Continue to do this as you spar.

- When you launch that backfist from one of the retractions, it not only snaps out with surprise but with greater power.

Do 2 or 3, 2-minute rounds in front of a mirror shuffling about in a sparring mode.

- Move your hands as just described and note how they look from your opponent's point of view.
- Does your backfist seem to come out of nowhere?
- If you can detect that it's about to be launched, so can a savvy opponent.
- Can you see an element of surprise when you jerk your lead hand forward a little, then jerk it back a little, then launch a completed backfist from that chambered position?

Sneaky Backfist on the Street

In a street confrontation, there is often a moment where each participant comments on the other's mother, lineage, and so on. It's all silliness, but silliness that leads to violence, blood and bruises. But here is a way to make the silliness come to an abrupt end with your backfist as the victor. It's a moment based on a pre-emptive strike (be sure you're legally justified).

- Stand in your I-don't-want-to-fight stance, hands up, palms toward the threat.
- Position yourself so that you're just outside of arm's reach when your hands are up and between the two of you.
- As he consciously or unconsciously measures the distance to your nose, his sense of space is partly construed by your open palms between the two of you.
- As he woofs like a junk yard dog, draw your hands back toward your chin in the universal sign of fear.
- Lean your upper body back 15 to 20 degrees as if fearful, and jerk your hands nervously as you tell him that you don't want to fight. It's all theatrics, but it's a good way to keep your hands in motion.
- **What he sees** He sees another victim of his bullying. He sees someone drawing his arms and body back from him. With your hands nearly against your upper body, he sees a person too far away to be a threat. But what he doesn't see is a person who is playing him for a sucker.

Important

- Launch your backfist, and follow a hair of a second later by a fast forward jerk of your body. In other words, your hand leads your body.

Your fist lands with a resounding *thunk!* against the bully's ear because he thought you were too far away to hit him. It was your false sense of distance that fooled him. He will get two things out of your backfist: pain and a respect for what must be your incredible speed.

Practice this illusion in front of the mirror and on the heavy bag. Check out your image to see that you look believable.

- Don't bend back so far that you can't move forward quickly or so far that he can knock you over with a quick forward charge.
  - o Find that happy place where you appear to be out of range, where your hand position looks natural, where your stance is mostly stable, and where you can explode forward and touch the mirror.

- Once you feel comfortable assuming the position, practice on a heavy bag.
- Practice shooting out your fist, jerking your body forward, and hitting the bag solidly. It's all about creating an illusion of distance and speed.

Do 3 sets of 10 reps on both sides in front of the mirror and another 3 sets of 10 reps on both sides against a heavy bag.

Scoop kick and finger jab

The premise here is the same as with "Sneaky backfist": To create an illusion of distance between you and your opponent, then hit him easily since you really aren't out of range. When he regains consciousness, he is convinced you have Bruce Lee-like speed.

SPARRING

This works better in the street than in school sparring because it's based on impact to your opponent's vulnerable knee to set him up for the finger jab. If your teacher allows light contact to the knees when sparring, you can get some idea of how the blow distracts from the eye poke. It works really well when you can slam your opponent's knee but it won't take long before no one will train with you. Best to use your imaginary opponent.

- Retract your on-guard hands back toward your body to create the illusion that you're farther away than you really are.

- Your lead leg stays out in front.

- As with the last technique, your opponent's eyes will determine the distance between the two of you by assessing the largest mass in his field of vision, your upper body. To underscore this, keep your upper body and hands in motion without moving your lead foot too much.

- When he closes on you – within range since your position has deceived him – ram the arch of your lead foot into his closest knee.

- There is no need to chamber your kick because it's already bent. All you have to do is straighten your leg in a snapping motion right into the target.

Note: I like to lean a little to my kicking leg side, as I feel it gives me more power. If I'm kicking with my left, I lean to my left. Experiment to see if it works for you, too.

STREET SELF-DEFENSE

The difference between a street confrontation and school sparring is that in the street you're more likely to lean back in your I-don't-want-to-fight stance, seemingly because you're intimidated by the bully. He falls for your intimidation act, measures the distance between you based on your upper body mass, and moves right into your scoop kick range, your field of fire. *Crack!* The arch of your foot slams against his knee, which will likely snap his head forward and right into your eye jab. He will swear that you move like grease lightening because you crossed the gap so quickly. The reality, of course, is that he crossed the gap right into range.

MIRROR AND BAG TRAINING

- Check yourself in the mirror to see if you're believable when leaning back and leaving your leg extended.
- It's a fine line between being awkward and looking silly, and being positioned just right so you can move aggressively and quickly. Practice repetitiously to find that right spot without looking in the mirror.
- If your heavy bag allows you to kick its bottom, great. If not, you will have to kick air and jab the heavy bag. Work on it so that the two hits go *"Bop, bop"* not *"Bop"* dead space *"Bop."*

Talk with your lead hand

The previous three techniques had you leaning back from your opponent to create an illusion of distance based on the position of your arms and your upper body mass. With this technique you're going to move your weapon virtually under his nose, but off to the side a little. The better you are at talking and gesturing realistically, the greater your chance of success with this one. This is a street technique only.

STREET SELF-DEFENSE: EYE RAKE

Say you have been confronted by a bully who is woofing in your face about how he is going to beat you to a pulp. He has made a couple of clear references about cutting you with his folder

Caution

(knife), which he is carrying attached to his belt in open view. You can't get away because you're cornered without even a small avenue of escape at your disposal. These are all critical elements that justify using a level of force that carries a connotation that is distasteful to many people, including the all-important jury: I'm talking again about eye gouging, eye raking and eye poking.

- You have your hands up in the I-don't-want-to-fight stance, but with a slight difference.
- Instead of your lead arm bent at, say, 90 degrees, you extend it slightly off to the side of the bully's line-of-sight with your palm down.
  o When your open palms are in front of you, you create, at least to the bully's eyes, a wall. But in this variation, your lead hand isn't as apparent because it's positioned slightly off to the left or right of bozo's face.
  o It would be a stretch to say that it's "out of sight out of mind," but almost since he is unconsciously measuring the distance between you based on where your body mass is, though your hand is about 12 inches from his face.

- When the moment is right, simply straighten your arm, lean forward if needed and scrape your fingers across his face.
  o You don't need to wind up your arm, inhale sharply, flex your muscles or do anything else to generate power because that isn't what the technique is about. It's about deception, quickness and one to five fingers raked across the threat's most valuable asset.

• You probably won't blind him unless you sink your fingers up to the second or third knuckles, which is impossible when raking.

o Your intent is to startle him and make him focus on his agony instead of you.

• Your "speed" will amaze him because he was judging your distance by where your body was, not your hand.

• After you have hurt his eyes, follow with kicks and punches, or push him aside to make your escape.

MIRROR, AIR AND BAG TRAINING

To practice solo, begin by checking your form in the mirror.

• Extend your lead arm while your rear palm faces forward and covers your chest area. The key to this working is that you don't look posed to attack.
• Make sure your face is neutral or even fearful, but don't ham it up.
• Use your face in the mirror as the target.
• Check to see in the mirror that your hand is positioned palm down on either side of your face.
• Check your distance. How far back can you stand and still reach the eyes when you extend your arm and lean forward a tad? Try bending your lead knee a little as you rock forward to get a few additional inches.

Do 3 sets of 10 reps of both sides in front of a mirror.

• When practicing in the air, position your hand next to an object you can see in the background, though it appears fuzzy to you. It might be a doorknob, a picture on a wall, a window. Then claw across it, simulating contact.

Do 3 sets of 10 reps on both sides in the air.

• Use a mannequin-type bag or use chalk to mark a set of eyes on a heavy bag. Assume your stance, check your distance, and strike. Remember, you don't have to smash the bag, only rake your fingers across it.

Do 3 sets of 10 reps on both sides.

VARIATIONS

Instead of targeting the eyes, shove or grab his face from the same starting position. Though you can strike his face from this range, you won't deliver much impact since your attack starts when your arm is nearly extended. Therefore, hit his nose to distract him with a dash of pain, providing you with an opportunity to follow with other techniques. Here are a few other ideas:

• Shove his face and hit him in an opening with your other hand.
• Shove his face and run past him.
• Grab his face as if you were catching a melon and hit with your other hand.
• Grab his face and push him onto his back.
• Palm-heel his nose (be careful not to telegraph by drawing your hand back) and hit him with your other hand.
• Palm-heel his chin and finger-flick his eyes with the same hand.

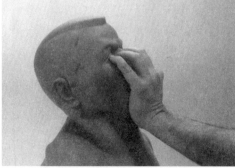

Do 3 sets of 10 reps on both sides of all of the above. Refer back to the mirror often to ensure your form is deceptive.

High/low

I've talked about this fantastic concept in other books but it's worth revisiting briefly because when done correctly it easily overwhelms your opponent with what he thinks is your great speed. Here is how it works. Jab your opponent in the face, follow with a scoop kick to his knee, a reverse punch to his neck, and a shin kick to his groin. You're hitting high, low, high, and middle in one continuous flow. Your opponent's mind first races to the high target, then down to the low one, maybe to the next high one, and who knows if it will make it to the middle one.

If you're really hitting him, say in a street situation, it's quite possible that his mind will stick on the second target, though it wants desperately to keep up. Pain has a way of slowing a person's thinking. If you're sparring in class and making only light contact, your opponent might have an easier time of keeping up, but still his brain and blocks are going to slow around the third attack, turn to molasses at number four, and should you toss in a fifth attack, his brain will go, "Aaaghhh!." The brain can only deal with so many attacks to opposite ends of its body before it throws in the towel. You don't have to be blindingly fast to make this work, but you do have to move smoothly, which is what you work toward when training by yourself.

MIRROR AND BAG TRAINING

Your solo high/low work should emphasize smooth delivery to a combination of targets. The idea isn't to memorize a sequence of blows but rather to enhance your skill at continuous hitting. Visualize an opponent as clearly as you can so that you're able to hit specific targets given your imaginary foe's openings.

I like to practice by making up a combination then do 1 or 2 sets of 10 reps on both sides. Then I forget about that combo and make up another, and do 1 or 2 sets of 10 reps on both sides. Then I forget about that one and do another. When I say "forget about them," I'm saying that the objective isn't to memorize techniques. That doesn't work in the real world. Instead, your objective is to develop sound coordination which allows you to respond to what-

Workout
Tip

ever is presented to you. Here are three examples:

- Left palm to the face, left front kick to the shin, right claw to the eyes, and right round kick to the closest thigh.
- Left sidekick to the shin, left backfist to the nose, right reverse punch into the upper thigh and left forearm into the throat.
- Left hand finger rake to the eyes, right lead roundhouse to the thigh, right reverse punch to the middle and right scoop kick to the knee.

Use the mirror to make sure you have good form, balance, and that your transition from blow to blow doesn't leave you vulnerable. Work your combinations on a hanging bag. If you have a short one, your low kicks will hit the air below it, and your middle and high blows will impact the bag. Strive for smoothness and good power in all the techniques. As mentioned, your objective isn't to memorize combinations, but rather teach your body to work in smooth coordination when hitting at different levels.

Once you feel that you're competent at this, train to throw high/low combinations using techniques that you devise instantaneously based on the targets you see in your imaginative mind. Don't stop to think up a combination, just do it spontaneously. Go slowly at first and build your speed as you gain confidence and ability.

Do it in front of a mirror and on a bag.

Free extra: Timing practice

As Wim Demeere and I discuss in *Timing in the Fighting Arts*, most experts agree that precise timing is even more important than speed. Actually, pin-point timing looks like speed. We might even say that good timing is like cheating speed.

Clearly the preferred way to improve your timing is with a live training partner but there are a few things you can do by yourself to help keep your timing razor sharp.

Audio stimulus revisited

I talked about this training concept earlier but it's worth using it again here. Think of your body as an Olympic athlete's: a swimmer bent and perched to explode out as far as possible into the pool on the sound of the starter pistol, or a track sprinter with powerfully-muscled legs chambered on the starter blocks ready to explode on the audible signal. Audio stimulus drills work marvelously to prime and ignite your reflexes into exploding on the designated trigger, sending your punch or kick into the target like a rocket. In class, your instructor might stand behind the students at the back of the room so he can bang two sticks together to make an audible stimulus for the group to launch a technique. When training solo, you have to seek out other devices.

- Choose a training place where you have access to a radio or television. Find a talk show and decide on two or three words to use as a trigger, such as "the," "a," "I."
  - Decide on a technique, say, a jab/cross combination.
  - You hear, "the." You hit.

The word "the" or whatever word you choose isn't the same as a sudden opening in your opponent's guard, but you're still benefiting from a sense of *Now!* so that you explode without thought, without going *Oh, there's the trigger. I better hit it soon.* Instead, you detonate the instant you hear the trigger: "The." *Bam!*

Try it with music. Hit every time you hear the horns, the cymbals, (the harp?) or best of all, every time you hear the pronounced beat. Use that sound, that beat – every other one if it's a fast song – to set off your combination as if it were a stick of dynamite.

Visual stimulus revisited

The concept here is the same as with audio stimulus: You use a trigger to condition your reflexes to react seemingly without conscious thought. This drill, coupled with the audio stimulus drill, will have your reflexes as jumpy as a cat on a windy day.

Your television offers the most consistent visual, though I've used objects such as a tree branch moving with each gust of wind past a designated point. I know of a fighter who can see the freeway from his window. He uses a color trigger, throwing a punch every time a blue car or a white truck passes a specific light post on the freeway.

Say you're standing in front of your television with a plan of hitting every time the scene changes. This requires you to imagine an opponent in front of you while at the same time being aware of what is happening on television. Programs for kids are good choices because the scene or camera angle changes frequently to keep the kids' attention. (I like to hit Sponge Bob.) Decide on what trigger you're going to use and assume your fighting stance. Your objective is to explode when you see the stimulus.

Workout Tip

There's your trigger! *Wham!*

No thinking. No hesitation. No wind up. Just *Wham!*

15

14 Combinations on a Mannequin Bag

It's my opinion that once you have about three months of consistent training under your belt you're ready to progress from throwing mostly single techniques to throwing mostly combinations. My theory on combination hitting is simple: If hitting him once hurts, hitting him several times really hurts. I love simply theories.

I like the mannequin-style bags because they help develop hitting accuracy. The big, swinging heavy bags are excellent for learning about distance, developing power and cardio fitness, but the mannequin bags give you that and specific targets to hit: eyes, ears, nose, neck, heart, solar plexus, and ribs. You want more neck to hit? Just lead with a palm thrust to his forehead so his head leans back to expose Mr. Adam Apple. Want to smack his ear with a straight punch without stepping to his side? Just lead with a palm to the side of his nose to turn his head enough, and there it is: one ear. Here is another of my simply theories: Getting hit hurts. Get hitting hit in a vulnerable target, such as any of those just mentioned, hurts more.

Workout Tip

As I've discussed before, practicing combinations doesn't mean memorizing combinations. Anything you try to memorize is likely to fall apart under the stress and fear that accompanies a real fight, not to mention that your opponent's openings might or might not appear in a way that allows you to use your precise, pre-set combination. It's far better to consistently practice combinations with a variety of techniques in your solo training and with a partner, to mentally and physically condition yourself to hitting multiple targets. It's important to practice combos:

- to learn how to hit multiple times fast, hard and without losing your balance.
- to ingrain in your mind that hitting multiple times is an option, as opposed to hitting just once.
- to open your eyes to the target-rich environment that exists when your opponent leaves himself open.
- because most often hitting once isn't enough.

Partners

When training with a live partner, you train your reflexes to react quickly to available openings, moments that are brief and ever changing. Training on combinations by yourself frees you from having to react reflexively, allowing you to focus on good body mechanics so that your multiple blows are executed with speed, power and solid balance. Working with and without a partner provides you with well-rounded training that will turn your combos into a devastating arsenal.

COMBINATION RULES

Important

The only rule when throwing combinations is that they are logical. How do you know if they are? If they aren't, they are awkward. A silly example would be for you to throw a left jab and then spin in place like a ballerina and then throw a reverse punch. That's awkward, though I've seen combos about as ridiculous. Here is what makes a combination logical:

- It's fluid.
- It's fast.
- It's smooth.
- Each blow follows the one before without a missed beat.
- Each blow follows the one before without awkward body shifting.
- Each blow in succession hits with power.

Keep your combinations simple and you won't have problems.

A few combinations   When kicking to the knees, thighs, and groin on a mannequin, you have to visualize the target in the area of the base.

• Snap roundhouse to the groin, lead-hand claw to the eyes and downward hammer to the side of the neck.

• Jab or palm-heel to the face, reverse punch to the solar plexus, then step off to your left and whip your right shin across his ribs.

• Pretend to block outward with your left arm, then drive a left hook into the side of your opponent's neck, followed by a right punch to his solar plus and a right round elbow into his ear. You're hitting two blows with your left arm and two with your right.

o Work to make the transitions smooth and without telegraphing.

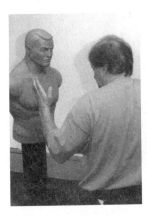

• Hit his groin with a lead-leg shin kick, followed by a lead-hand back fist to the side of the head and a rear-arm round elbow to the neck. You hit in all three ranges as you work your way in: long, middle and close range.

• Lead elbow to the face, right palm to the face and left roundhouse kick to the groin. You hit in all three ranges as you work your way out: close, middle and long range.

• Palm-heel his nose to drive his head back, and then step in to execute left and right hook punches into his ribs.

• Palm-heel his forehead to force his head back, then right punch his throat and right elbow the side of his neck.

o If this combination were used in a real fight it could be lethal. Be justified and know the laws on use of force where you live.

• As you clinch your opponent's neck, headbutt him twice in the nose followed by two right knee strikes to his ribs.

• Slap his ear with your left hand and return with a left backfist to his nose. Follow with a right elbow to the side of his neck and return with a right claw across his eyes.

o If this combination were used in a real fight it could be lethal. Be justified and know the laws on use of force where you live.

• Drive a lead front kick into his bladder (just below his belt), follow with a right shin kick into his lower ribs and finish with a left knee into his other ribs.

Do 2 or 3 sets of 10 reps of all combinations on both sides.

Don't just stand there

Each time you finish a combination scoot away and reassume your on-guard stance. Too many fighters practice a combination in the air or on heavy bag and then remain in place. That is a dangerous habit since your combo might not have hurt his hard head and drug-sopped brain.

Hit and move out of range. Make a habit of it.

Here are a few themes you can try once you're comfortable enough with combinations to create them on the spot. The first three develop a sense of hitting in all ranges so that you keep your opponent busy defending instead of hitting. Pay attention to good footwork as you progressively push for more speed and greater power.

• **Work from the outside in**   Example: Throw a kick to the knee, jab to the face, reverse punch to the solar plexus, and an elbow to the neck.

• **Work from the inside out**   Example: Execute a round knee strike to the ribs, a slap to the face, and a kick to the groin.

• **Work from the outside in and then from the inside out** This develops a good sense of flowing through the ranges, improves your coordination, and it works your cardiovascular system. Example: To get inside, throw a kick to the inner thigh, backfist to the ear, and knee to the groin. Then move away using an elbow to the nose, reverse punch to the neck and kick to the outside of the thigh.

• **Work for speed** – Use any of the first three concepts to work your combos at top speed. Do four techniques per combination to develop speed and anaerobic endurance.

The number of possible combinations is infinite. Practice for speed, power and flawless execution, but don't memorize them. With consistent practice in the air, on the bag, and with a live opponent, your spontaneous combinations will flow as if rehearsed.

16

10 Ways to Create Same-Arm Combinations

I like to think of a fight as consisting of beats of time, similar to music. *Bop,bop…bop…bop,bop…bop.* Your objective is to make every *bop* yours. But this doesn't always happen. For example, your opponent throws a punch at your face. You sweep block it with your left hand, pause for ¼ of second and then counter punch with your right, pause ¼ second and then follow with a left punch. So the beat looks like this: *Bop* (his punch), *bop* (your sweep block)… pause… *bop* (your right counter)… pause… *bop* (your left counter). So all together it's: *Bop, bop,* pause, *bop,* pause, *bop.*

This beat is common among newer fighters in the martial arts but too many veterans use it, too. The problem with pauses – which are most often brief moments when the fighter looks for a target or decides how to respond – is that they present opportunities for the opponent to hit. To prevent that from happening, you want to fill every beat of time with *your* blows. Make every *bop* your *bop.*

Let's look at how to fill beats of time with your blows, but let's get away from the standard way of hitting where a right punch is followed by a left punch that is followed by another right. Instead, let's look at how to execute multiple hits with one arm so that when you throw a punch with, say, your right, you hit at least two times before bringing it all the way back. Too easy? Okay, let's go for three hits.

Here is why training with one arm is a good thing.

- When you get proficient with one, a two-arm combination is easy.
- Should you hurt an arm in a real fight or in competition, you not only have the ability to defend yourself with one arm, you have an extraordinary ability to do it.
- Your arm muscles get a good workout since most of the blows are executed from multiple directions.
- You increase your awareness and ability to see multiple targets quickly.

Do the following combinations in the air and against a heavy bag or mannequin-style bag.

PUNCH HIS FACE, ELBOW HIS NECK, CLAW HIS EYES

This is a nice beginner one-armed combo that gives you a feel of the concept.

- Assume your fighting stance, left side forward.
- Launch a right reverse punch and hold it extended.

- Fold your arm by snapping your hand back to your chest as you snap your elbow forward on a horizontal plain. Step in as needed.

- Whip out your open, claw-like hand so that it rakes down his face (raking downwards is faster than raking across because it requires less body motion). Retract it to your beginning on-guard position and scoot out of range.

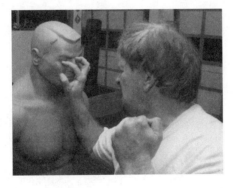

Do 3 sets of 10 reps on both sides.

Punch, Forearm Slam, Vertical Backfist

- Assume your fighting stance, left side forward.
- Drive a reverse punch into your imaginary opponent's chest.
- Fold your arm and drive your forearm up (in a rising block motion) into your opponent's neck and chin area. Step forward as needed.
- Draw your fist back toward your chin and, in a rolling, snapping motion, deliver a vertical backfist to your opponent's face.

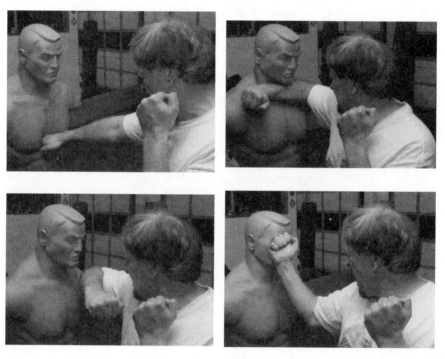

Do 3 sets of 10 reps on both sides.

EYE RAKE, BACKFIST, THROAT PUNCH

- Assume your fighting stance, left side forward.
- Whip your left claw from left to right across your imaginary opponent's face.
- Then immediately whip your left backfist so that the impact slices through your opponent's face.
- Just as it loops back, snap a punch into your opponent's throat.

Do 3 sets of 10 reps on both sides.

Try these variations

For the sake of your initial training, I've suggested that you begin each of these combination drills from your fighting stance. I've also said to do all the drills with the rear hand. Once you have done a few sessions of this and you're feeling comfortable with it, you should add two other variations. This will help you to be well-rounded and able to do these combinations from all common positions.

Workout
Tip

- Practice all the drills with your lead hand. While you lose some power because of less hip rotation, you're quicker because you're closer to the target.
- o Experiment with angling your body a little to increase your power, but be careful not to slow yourself down.

- Practice the drill from different stances.
o When both feet are parallel with each other.
o While rising out of a chair.
o While in the chair.
o When coming off a wall where you have been leaning

STRIKE THROAT, ELBOW CHIN, HAIR PULL TAKEDOWN

- Assume your fighting stance with your left side forward.
- Form your right hand into what is commonly called "tiger's mouth" and thrust it against your imaginary opponent's Adam's apple.
- Whip your right elbow into his chin. Move forward as needed.
- Snap your right hand forward and grab a handful of your opponent's hair and jerk his head down to the floor as you scoot back out of his way. (Unless your heavy bag or mannequin bag has hair, you're going to have to pantomime this portion.)

Do 3 sets of 10 reps on both sides.

ARMBAR, FOREARM STRIKE ELBOW, BACKFIST EAR, ELBOW TO NECK

- Assume your fighting stance left side forward.
- When your imaginary opponent tries to push you with his left hand, twist your body away from his reach and grab his wrist with your left hand.
- Rotate his wrist and apply pressure against his elbow (I prefer to press one inch above his elbow) with your palm or forearm. Pull up slightly on his wrist and push down on his elbow until he bends at the waist.
- Normally, you continue to spin him down to the floor, but let's say he begins to defeat the hold.
- Did I mention that he is gripping a knife? Let's say that he is to justify the force you are about to use.

- Disengage pressure from his forearm long enough to draw your arm back a little then slam your forearm against his elbow joint.
- Snap the fist of that same arm into his ear.
- Then drive your elbow into the back of his neck. Bend down as needed.

Do 3 sets of 10 reps on both sides.

BACKHAND BLOCK A PUNCH, SWEEP BLOCK A JAB, RISING BLOCK A ROUNDHOUSE PUNCH, EYE RAKE, AND BACKFIST TO GROIN

You don't always get to hit right away; sometimes you have to earn the right by blocking first. Practice this one in the air or on a bag. Block in the air first and then hit the bag with the counters. This combination works great on a wing chun dummy.

- Assume your fighting stance, left side forward.
- Imagine that your opponent launches a right reverse punch which you block with a quick, left backhand block.
- He follows immediately with a jab, which you sweep off track with your left.

- He follows with a right arcing hook punch to your head. You lean away slightly and stop it with a left, rising block.
- You whip your left claw-hand down across his face, stopping it at your belt.
- You whip your left backfist into his groin.

Do 3 sets of 10 reps on both sides.

JAB HIS THROAT, SWEEP BLOCK HIS JAB, BACKFIST HIS FACE,

HEAD-SHIELD BLOCK HIS PUNCH, PALM-HEEL HIS FACE

Too many times when we work combinations we assume that each blow is going to hurt and wither our opponent. The harsh reality is that those same blows that hurt our training partners when we accidentally connect too hard, don't always hurt a hyped up street thug. Sometimes our blows miss or, because the target moves a little, they don't hit as hard as we intended or as accurately.

Training Tip

When he isn't hurt, he hits back. Those need to be blocked, too. Then you got to hit him again. Busy, busy, busy.

- Assume your fighting stance left side forward.
- Snap out a left jab (fist or palm-heel) to your imaginary opponent's neck. He blocked, it missed, or it didn't hurt him
- He jabs at you, which you deflect with a left sweep block.
- You snap a left backfist at his face. He blocked, it missed, or it didn't hurt him

- He throws a right hook punch at the left side of your head.
- You execute a quick left head-shield block.
- You counter by snapping a left palm-heel strike down from your block and into his nose. (That one connected and stopped him.)

Do 3 sets of 10 reps on both sides.

ADDING YOUR OTHER ARM

Practice one-arm combinations often. Create your own combos and experiment with ways to angle and position your body to hit with your greatest power and speed. While you should never stop working one-arm combos, experiment to see where and how you can include your second arm. Let's use the first combo listed in this section to see how you can add your other arm to it. This is how you first practiced it.

REVERSE PUNCH HIS FACE, ELBOW HIS NECK, CLAW HIS EYES

Now let's add the underlined techniques so that it becomes:

Left jab his chest, right reverse punch his face, right elbow his neck, right claw his eyes, left slap his ear and left backfist his face

- Assume your fighting stance, left side forward.

- Launch a left jab. As it retracts, launch a right reverse punch.
- As soon as your right punch lands, fold your arm and whip a right elbow into his neck.
- As you begin to move back from your opponent, claw his face with your right hand and begin to rotate your upper body a little to the right.
- Taking advantage of that same subtle rotation, whip your left palm into his ear.
- Stop your upper body rotation to your right and snap it slightly back to your left as you whip a left backfist into his face.

Do 3 sets of 10 reps on both sides.

12 Ways to Increase Your Hitting Accuracy

If you have watched a street fight you probably saw lots of missed blows that only struck air, or hits intended for one target but landed on others less vulnerable. Most boxing matches, karate point matches, and mixed martial arts matches are full of missed blows. If you have been in a street fight you no doubt experienced the same thing. It's not unusual; in fact, it's inevitable when the stakes are high, such as in a real fight or in competition. Inevitable, yes, but that doesn't mean you can't take steps to reduce the number of missed punches and kicks.

Groin and legs

Let's begin by looking at your opponent's low targets, well, not really looking at them because the idea is to hit them while your eyes are gazing at the triangle formed by the person's chin and shoulders. Looking at the target before you strike is a dead giveaway to even the dumbest bully.

You know from training with live partners that in most cases, if not all, your standing opponent's legs are directly under him. In fact, you can see them vaguely in your peripheral vision. That is all you need to see. By using your peripheral vision and what you have learned in your training about hitting specific, vulnerable targets, your accuracy, your hit rate, will increase dramatically.

Free trick: Look at your opponent's knee for a second, then look up abruptly at his face and kick him in the knee without looking back at it. He probably won't fall for this two times in a row.

LIFE-LIKE DUMMIES AND WING CHUN POSTS

If you have one of those hanging bags with arms and legs, or a wing chun dummy with legs that correspond with a human's, you're fortunate because both provide you with a sense, physically and mentally, of working with a live person.

- Stand before whichever bag you have and gaze at the dummy's chin and shoulder area, while using your peripheral to see one of its knees.
- Execute a toe-out kick (your toes are turned out as you impact with your arch).
- o Every few reps, take a quick peek to ensure that you're on target.
- Execute an inside crescent to smack the target's groin. Don't look at the target but see it in your peripheral vision.
- Execute an angle roundhouse kick into the vulnerable peroneal nerve located on the outside of the thigh.

Practice all of these kicks from in-range, or begin outside of your kicking range and use any manner of footwork to close and strike the target.

Do 2 or 3 sets of 10 reps of all the kicks, each leg.

WALL SILHOUETTE MAN

Draw an outline of a human form on a wall so that the figure's feet and head correspond to yours. Mark little circles to indicate the location of the groin, knees, shin, and the inside and outside of the upper leg.

- Get into your fighting stance or the I-don't-want-to-fight stance and focus on the silhouette's chin/shoulder area.
- o Use your peripheral to see the circled targets and strike at them.
- Begin by using a low, snapping sidekick to the shin.

o If you are uncertain how accurate your kicks are, it's okay to take a quick peak but only *after* you have kicked. Then look right back up again. Don't make a habit of this. You want to learn to be accurate without giving away your intention by looking at the target before you hit it.

• After you do a few sets with each leg, practice snapping front kicks to the target's groin, and round kicks to the inside and outside of its legs.

Do 2 or 3 sets of 10 reps of all the kicks, each leg.

POST-IT MAN

This is a similar concept to Silhouette Man except you don't draw on your wall.

• Use your body as a reference and place Post-its at the same height and location as your chin, knees, shins, groin, and outer and inner thighs.

• Then as you focus your gaze on the Post-it representing the chin, practice kicking at the lower body targets just as you did in Silhouette man.

Do 2 or 3 sets of 10 reps of all the kicks, each leg.

USE YOUR IMAGINATION

Once you have developed accuracy with drills that use dummy and wall targets, you're better able to use your imagination to see the targets when practicing in the air.

• Get into your fighting stance or the I-don't-want-to-fight stance and "see" your opponent in front of you. Focus on his chin/shoulder area.

• See him standing in a neutral stance with both legs parallel with each other and directly under his shoulders.

- Start by kicking his groin. Look straight ahead and snap your lead shin up and into the imaginary target.
- As you execute the reps, don't allow your mind to wander, otherwise you're just doing reps in the air.
  o Don't think about the mechanics of your technique or which drill you're going to do next.
  o Focus on seeing the target in your peripheral vision each time you kick.
- Use the same format to kick his knee, thigh and shin with any kick you choose.

Do 2 to 3 sets of 10 reps per target and with both legs.

Upper body

Just as when striking at low targets, you don't want to give away your intention by looking at, say, your opponent's abdomen before you try to drive in a hard reverse punch. Still, you want to hit with precision. Here are a few drills to help:

USE YOUR POINTY FINGER

I got this from my sometimes co-author, Wim Demeere. When a student is having trouble hitting with accuracy, he has them point at what they want to hit.

- Stand before a hanging bag, a mannequin-type, or a wall, and choose a small target: a mark on the bag, the mannequin's eye, or a blemish on the wall.
- From your stance, point at the target.
  o Use all the body mechanics you normally employ when punching, including the rotation of your hand, but just point.

Weird? Yes. Does it work? Yes. You might improve after just a few reps, or you might have to do it for a few workouts. Try it with your jab, uppercut, hook, and backfist.

Do 2 or 3 sets of 10 reps with both arms.

Hit B.O.B.'s blemish

Look for a small blemish in the area of the upper chest on your mannequin bag or regular hanging heavy bag. If there isn't one, mark one with chalk. Hit the mark in any manner you choose, adding techniques as you improve until you have a combination of three or four. Hit the mark with:

- a lead-leg front kick for 10 reps.
- a lead-leg front kick followed by a right reverse punch for 10 reps.
- a lead-leg front kick followed by a right reverse punch, followed by a left straight punch for 10 reps.
- a lead-leg front kick followed by a right reverse punch, followed by a left straight punch, followed by a right elbow strike for 10 reps.

Do 2 or 3 sets on both sides.

Tennis ball man

This gives you immediate feedback as to your accuracy, or lack of it.

Drill a hole on opposite sides of a tennis ball, or baseball as pictured, and poke a small rope through it. String might break. Don't tie a permanent knot because you want to be able to adjust the ball to knee height, thigh, groin, solar plexus, neck and ear.

- Assume your stance and look straight ahead, as if gazing at the opponent's chin.
- See the ball in your peripheral and snap your lead round-house kick into it. After two or three sets with each leg, adjust the ball to another height, say neck or solar plexus.
- Keep adjusting the ball's height until you have worked the target's entire body.
- Remember, don't look at the target.

Do 1 to 3 sets of 10 reps, each leg at each level.

Parakeet Bellman

Get a little bell, like one of those you find in a birdcage and hang it by a small rope at head, chest, groin, and knee height. You can kick at an imaginary opponent in the air and tell yourself that you hit the target and you can kick a heavy bag or even a mannequin bag and tell yourself that you hit the kidney, spleen or knee cap. With a little bell as a target, however, you know you hit it when you hear the little tinkling reward. Hey, some people like tinkling bell rewards!

Training Tip

Kick s-l-o-w-l-y Do the following slowly and feel those leg muscles bunch and cramp and grow stronger. By going slowly, you also learn exactly which muscles are involved with each kick. That helps you to know which muscles to target with your supplemental weight and free-hand exercises.

- Hang the bell at, say, rib height.
- Pick a kick and slowly extend your foot at the bell.
- Touch the bell with the appropriate kicking surface and retract your leg.

Do 1 to 3 sets of 10 slow reps with front, round, side and back kicks.

Do 1 to 3 sets of 10 fast reps with front, round, side and back kicks.

Do 1 to 3 sets of 10 alternating reps – 1 rep slow, 1 rep fast – with front, round, side and back kicks.

Punch Through the Hole

In *Solo Training*, I suggested that you hang a pair of reading glasses, with the glass removed, from a string and practice thrusting your fingers through the openings. It's an excellent drill for developing accuracy with your eye techniques and I encourage you to include it in your training.

Here is a similar one, except with this you punch through a hole in a piece of cardboard hanging from the ceiling. The hole should be a little larger than your fist.

- Punch slowly at first and then pick up the speed as you improve.

- When you're ready, hang the cardboard where it's a little breezy, or aim a fan at it. This way you have to wait for an opportunity to hit through the opening or you have to move around to find it.

Do 2 or 3 sets of 10 reps with both arms.

Weapons

A champion shooter once told me that the difference between an average shooter and a champ is that the champ practices more. I love "simple" solutions like that. You practice shooting a lot and you get more accurate. What a concept! Although the same answer applies to martial arts weapons, too many martial artists spend their practice time on aspects other than hitting accuracy. Well, to state the obvious: you have to be able to hit the target or all the fancy moves are meaningless. Can you hit the head of a nail with your bo staff? With your sai? Can you swing the nunchaku at a mannequin-type bag and hit it square on the nose eight out of 10 times? If these are your weapons of choice and you can't hit with accurately with them, you need to take steps to correct this omission.

Here are a few accuracy exercises that I use for my weapons of choice, the arnis stick and knife. These are good for many other weapons, too.

THRUSTING

Since the blade is closely related to the arnis stick, here is a fun way to work on your accuracy with both. This also works well for other thrusting-type weapons of roughly the same diameter. All you need is a wire fence with hundreds of 2-inch by 2-inch squares in it and preferably located where there aren't any passersby. Let's use an arnis stick.

- Stand before the fence in your on-guard stance and focus on one square.
- Form a triangle in your mind: The end of your stick and your eyes serve as the base, with the point being the square in the fence.
- Concentrate, and slowly thrust the stick at the square.
- You missed. No big deal, just do it again. And again.

o Keep doing it until the triangle begins working for you.

• Increase your speed as you improve, but never go faster than your accuracy.

Do 1 or 2 sets of 10 reps.

Caution

When practicing with a knife, sai or some other metal weapon, wrap the end in tape, cloth, or make a cardboard sheath so it's not damaged by the metal fence.

War story: I was a shooting instructor for a while on the police department. I've never been interested in guns, but for a couple of years I was an FBI and NRA certified instructor.

We taught a course called Point Shooting where the shooter would imagine a triangle formed by the end of the gun barrel, the target, and his eyes. The technique worked so well that after 45 minutes of practice even the worst shooters could hit the center of the target without aiming. They would pull their weapons from their holsters, make an instantaneous triangulation, and fire.

I was always an average shooter, scoring somewhere between barely passing and expert. But after three months of teaching this course every day to a new batch of shooters, I could, in one fluid motion, quick draw, triangulate and shoot, and hit a dime lying several feet away on a dirt embankment.

STRIKING AND SLASHING

Here is a simple way to improve your striking and slashing accuracy with your knife, stick, bo, and sai. If you use a bell, protect the metal on your weapon as you did in the thrusting exercise. When using a ball, use a rubber knife or a wooden dowel so you don't cut it.

- Hang a ball at head height using sturdy cord or rope.
- Practice your strikes and slashes from right to left, left to right, diagonal, upward and downward.
- Go slowly and increase the speed as your accuracy improves.

Do 1 to 2 sets of 15 reps in all directions.

It's not that difficult to come up with an idea for a target, though too many martial artists are content on striking only the air with their weapon. Practicing in the air is good, but never hitting a tangible target isn't. When attacking an invisible one, it's easy to convince ourselves that our slashes and thrusts hit right where we wanted to hit. But the truth lies in hitting something real.

A COMMENT ON NEGATIVITY

Allow me to get on my soapbox for a moment. Always keep in mind that there are negative people in the martial arts just as there are in other areas of your life. Sure, every fighting style has elements that need to be fixed, just as every fighter has elements that need to be fixed. The real issue isn't that there are things that need fixing, but it's how you view them. Acknowledging problems and then setting out to correct them is what your study of the martial arts is all about. Fixing, improving and moving forward. It's also about staying positive - always positive. Never allow anyone or anything to bring you down and disrupt your path toward being the best martial artist you can be.

Okay, I'm off my box now.

6 Differences Between Practice and Real Fighting

Let's look at 6 differences between real fighting and practicing for fun or competition that you should consider when training by yourself. While most writers talk about the negatives of real fighting – "That technique would never work in the street." "What you practice isn't real fighting." "An assailant would never attack like that." - let's look at these aspects in a more positive light.

Anger

TRAINING/COMPETITION

Martial artists are taught not to lose their head, their temper, when sparring. Good advice, since totally loosing your head prevents you from thinking clearly and executing fine-motor skills. But is it okay to lose your head a little bit? Can you be just a little mad? Half mad? Most trainers in the martial arts, police work, and in the military agree that a little bit of anger sharpens your thinking and increases your strength and speed. To some extent, the same it true of fear.

Lt. Col. Dave Grossman and I talk about fear in our book *On Combat*, saying that it's hormonal induced physiological arousal. "A little bit of fear can manifest itself as Condition Red [a state in which you're performing physically and mentally at your optimum], and this can be a useful response. Intense fear, helplessness and horror is defined as Condition Black [a condition in which you cannot think or perform physically]. Researcher and author S. L. A. Marshall noted that fear in combat is ever present, "but it is uncontrolled fear that is the enemy."

The same is true of anger.

REAL FIGHT

I'm going to make a blanket statement: Fights in bars and at parties are often a result of hot tempers, whereas a confrontation on the street is more likely the result of a mugging or some kind of bullying. Since bar fights and party fights involve tempers and alcohol, the nature of the fights usually consist of two combatants crashing into furniture and rolling about on the floor, demonstrating all the skill of brainless cavemen. However, in the street where it's more likely that the nature of the fight is self-defense based, rather than temper-tantrum based, there is a greater chance that the trained defender will respond with some finesse. Yes, I know there are lots of exceptions.

THE SOLUTION

The best way to learn how to control yourself under stress is to train in realistic, stress-inducing scenarios. Of course you can't do this alone (well, you could knock over all the Harleys parked outside an outlaw motorcycle club and then as the bikers stream out the door, you taunt, "Helloooo boys. Here I ammmmm."). The only thing you can do alone is to practice certain aspects of your solo training with commitment and good visualization.

Commitment When you're committed to hard training, there isn't anything other than emergencies and illness that can stop you from your workout schedule. You train for personal enjoyment and growth, but you also train because there are human predators in the world training. I have two posters tacked to a wall in my school. One depicts a giant of a guy wearing sweat pants and a "state penitentiary" tank top as he squats with a barbell loaded with hundreds of pounds. The caption reads: "Missed a workout? This man hasn't." The other poster depicts a street-tough old con wearing a *gi* and a black belt. The caption says that the man has spent most of his life in prison for robbery, murder and others violent crimes – and he has just earned his 5th-degree black belt. It's knowing that there are people like that out in the world – lots of them – that should keep you focused. Hard committed training goes a long ways toward building a powerful mind-set and an iron-clad confidence that you're fit and good to go.

Visualization   With practice it's possible to conjure similar emotions – anxiety and tension – and similar physical reactions – increased heart rate, breathing, and perspiration - that you experience in a real street confrontation, though usually these reactions are less intense. Read Chapter 19, "4 Mental Techniques for Women" to learn how to conjure deep-seated emotions and incorporate them into your physical training.

• As you sit comfortably in your easy chair at home, see yourself in your mind's eye waiting for the bus on a dark, empty street; or walking across a dark parking lot late at night to your car; or going down the steps to catch the subway; or any other high-risk environment that you frequent.
• Imagine a street creep stepping out of the shadows and saying something threatening to you.
• See yourself take an I-don't-want–to-fight stance.
• Hear yourself respond to his threat with calm, well-chosen verbiage.
• See yourself move to a position where you can escape. See yourself block his grab or punch and see yourself respond with an appropriate counter.

Practicing in your mind ahead of time how to react calmly, speak coherently, and physically defend yourself against his attack serves as a dress rehearsal that helps you control your fear and anger, and respond with the right technique.

THERE ARE NO REFEREES ON THE STREET

This is an old song that everyone and their brother choruses as if they just made it up. Next time some sage utters this to you, say, "Really? I-did-not-know-that. I thought there were referees who had nothing else to do but follow me around."

Okay, enough sarcasm. Though the comment is cliché, it's a thought you still need to keep in the forefront of your mind so that your training doesn't become over reliant on the presence of a ref or an instructor to keep things under control.

PLAYING TO THE REF

Are you like a lot of competitors in that you have figured out how to play to the ref? When you hook kick your opponent, do you smack your opponent with the bottom of your foot instead of the heel so that the impact makes a louder noise to draw the referees' attention? If you notice two taekwondo refs on your right side and a Japanese traditionalist on your left, do you deliberately throw more kicks with your right leg? Have you designed certain techniques that should they miss you can step quickly out of bounds before your opponent counters? These and many other gimmicks are all part of the game of point karate and taekwondo competition, but they are gimmicks that will likely get you hurt in a real fight.

If your martial arts slant is competition first and self-defense second, that is okay – as long as you keep the difference in mind. When you practice self-defense, be sure you're not using competition-only tricks. As hard as it is - and some teachers would argue that it's impossible – you must separate the two genres in your mind.

STREET/COMPETITION

No ref in the street means no rules. You can do anything to survive. An eye gouge gets you disqualified in a tournament, but not in the street. Grab your training partner's groin in class and rip, and you get a reprimand from the instructor and harsh words from your partner (in a high-pitched voice), but not in the street. Stomp your opponent's forehead, chest and knee joints after you have taken him down in a tournament, and you get thrown out of the tournament. Do it in the street and you survive.

SOLUTION

If you train in a school that is primarily competition oriented, use your solo workouts to train to fight for survival in scenarios where there are no referees to pull you apart.

• Train in everything that is illegal in competition and disallowed in your school.
o One session concentrate on eye techniques, using a mannequin dummy or marks on a wall to represent eyes.
o The next session place a heavy bag on the floor and work on stomping an attacker after you have taken him down.

Use your imagination to see the attacker, his targets and the fierceness of your techniques.

A street fight isn't always evenly matched

TRAINING/COMPETITION

In training and competition, students and fighters are most often matched by rank and size. A white belt on his second day of training should never be pitted against a 3rd-degree black belt in all-out competition. While mismatches in physical size happen in tournaments, most instructors try to match students by size for drills and sparring unless there is a deliberate reason to do otherwise.

REAL FIGHT

In a street fight, you don't get a choice. Bullies pick on those they believe they can intimidate and defeat physically. Usually, this translates to the bully being bigger and stronger than his victim. If a bully is much smaller than you, he is either a masochist and enjoys getting hurt, he has something to prove to himself and others, or he is a superior fighter who is confident that he can defeat you.

SOLUTION

Partners

In class Train with a variety of partners in your school: big, small, advanced, new, young and old. Yes, even new students can be a challenge since their techniques are relatively crude and they don't always do what you expect. Older students can be difficult, too. I had a 70-year-old retired Marine who never backed up when sparring. No matter what his opponent did, he just kept coming and coming. Once a Marine always a Marine.

Marine drill sergeant: "What do you do when you're all alone, unarmed and surrounded by a thousand enemy troops, boy?"

Recruit: "Sir, kill 'em, sir."

Training solo When training alone there is a tendency to hit at the height of *your* knees, *your* groin, *your* midsection and *your* face. To get out of this same-height rut, you need to purposely imagine larger and smaller opponents.

• Adjust your mannequin dummy to its highest position so you have to punch and eye gouge at an upward angle.

- Adjust it so that you have to strike downward.
- Practice striking at the highest point on a heavy bag.
- When practicing in the air, imagine your opponent to be several inches taller than you and launch your techniques accordingly.

    o Pretend your attacker's head is as high as your shoulders so that you have to strike downward at his eyes and ears.

Conditioning: There are no rounds in a street fight

TRAINING/COMPETITION

Many point karate competitors gear their training toward two- or three-minute rounds with a minute rest between them. Full-contact fighters gear their training toward 3 to 15 rounds of 3-minute duration with one-minute rest sessions. It's a good way to train for competition format, but is it a good way to train for a street encounter? Only if you and an attacker can agree to have 1-minute rest sessions every 3 minutes.

REAL FIGHT

Although most of my fights as a street cop lasted one to three minutes, there were some that occurred in segments and lasted seemingly forever. For example, I would brawl with the guy to get him into handcuffs. Then I would wrestle him out of the bar, across the sidewalk and into the back seat of the police car. If he had to be interviewed by detectives, I had to fight him out of the car at the precinct (many prisoners don't want to get out of the police car after being forced into it), fight him down the hall to the elevator, into the elevator, fight him all the way to the 13th floor, fight him out of the elevator, down the hall and into a holding room. When the detectives were done with him, I had to fight him out of the room, down the hall, into the elevator, out of the elevator in the basement and into the receiving cage at the jail.

All of this took aerobic condition (and patience of Biblical proportions). However, most "beefs," to use police parlance, were of short duration, lasting a few seconds to two or three minutes. Even when I was in top condition, I was often winded after these bouts, sometimes coughing and wheezing for a couple hours. Eventually it dawned on me that the reason for this was that while I was training aerobically my real fights were intense, all-out efforts. They were anaerobic.

THE SOLUTION

Training Tip

Your training must consist of both aerobic and anaerobic exercise. Sparring at a slow to medium pace improves your heart and lungs, while going all-out for 30 to 45 seconds improves your anaerobic fitness. Let's say that for your solo workout today you want to do a 20-minute shadow sparring session. Here is a simple way to get in both types of exercise.

- Shadow spar at slow to medium speed.
- Every fourth minute, go as hard and as fast as you can for 30 to 45 seconds.
- Then resume shadow sparring at slow to medium rate.

Go for 20 minutes.

Here is how you can get in both types of exercise on the heavy bag.

- Punch and kick the bag for three minutes using light to medium impact.
- On the fourth minute go all-out hitting the bag hard and fast for 30 to 45 seconds.

- Don't rest, but resume hitting at light to medium impact.
- Repeat going back and forth for the entire session.

Go for 20 minutes.

If you find that going all-out every fourth minute is too easy (you animal), decrease the time to every third minute.

Training and competition environments are different

TRAINING/COMPETITION

Unless your teacher occasionally has you train in realistic environments, you have an expectation each workout of training in a debris-free space. Mixed martial arts fights are held in a canvas–covered ring with ropes or a wire screen that prevents the participants from falling over the edge. Point karate matches are typically held on a gymnasium floor within taped rings that are clean of debris.

REAL FIGHT

In my years as an MP in Vietnam and as a city cop for 25 years, I fought in just about every conceivable environment. I did battle in snow, ice, rain and blistering sun. I fought in wretchedly foul public restrooms, in flop houses amongst a dozen passed out drunks, and on blood-slippery floors. Some occurred in cluttered basements, in attics, on steep roofs, and on car hoods. On a couple of occasions I fought resisting suicidal people as I drug them over bridge railings to the safe side. I never ever had a fight in a canvas-covered ring or on a cushy mat, and I'm guessing you never will either.

THE SOLUTION

In *Solo Training* and in *Fighter's Fact Book* I discuss several ways to train by yourself in various environments, so I will just touch on it here. Your objective is to make your solo session as difficult as you can. The worse it is the better it is for you. It's all about learning what you can and can't do when it's difficult for you to step, kick and punch.

In your weight training area.

- Train in your weight room around the weights, benches, and cable machines.
    o Instead of resting between sets, practice your kicks, punches and foot work around the iron clutter.
    o You will occasionally stub your toe, so watch your language.

Wear clothing that you're apt to have on when trouble starts.

- Put on your heavy winter coat and your work boots.
- Now do 2 or 3 sets of your favorite combinations.

Back yourself into a tight corner.

- See which kicks you can and cannot throw from this awkward position.
    o Concentrate on the ones you can do and work them in sets and reps to feel comfortable and confident with them.
- See what punches you can and cannot throw from this position.
    o Concentrate on the ones you can do and work them in sets and reps.

Yes, the street and your training environment are two separate entities, but don't be like so many fighters and dwell on the negative aspects of this obvious fact. Instead, charge ahead positively and think and train so that you understand the differences and can use them to your advantage.

19

4 Mental Techniques
for Women

To be effective in self-defense, you need to know how to defend, and how to attack back. For a female, this is the ultimate reversal: You become the huntress, not the hunted; the predator not prey. You summon and unleash all your life forces – courage, will, wrath, cunning, physical powers – and use them like secret weapons. Nothing is out of bounds, nothing is unthinkable. There's little to compare this to: You dial up the creature within; you trade in your polite self for your animal-self; you issue the "sic" command and give that beautiful junkyard bitch within carte blanche permission to go for the throat.

---- Melissa Soalt from her essay "Fierce love: The heart of the female warrior" from the book Warriors: On Living with Courage, Discipline and Honor

Black belt Lisa Place uses her imagination combined with total commitment to unleash on a mannequin dumy.

If you've been in the fighting arts for a while and have slanted your training toward realism, you have probably looked at some of those self-defense articles in non-martial arts magazines, especially the so-called "women's magazines" and thought, "If these models try this stuff for real they're going to get killed." While the techniques might be viable – a kick to the assailant's knee, a house key thrust into his face, a purse upside his head – there is something not quite right in the photos. Is it that the models are, well, simply models, and as such are too pretty, too poised, with hair too perfect? Yes, that is part of it. But mostly it's about their intensity, or rather, their lack of it.

Okay, these magazines aren't martial arts magazines and the models probably aren't martial artists, but the articles and photos illustrate, in a way, how too many women train because, sadly, that is how their instructors teach them.

Why aren't more women outraged by this? Why is it even happening? Could it be:

- a belief that "the weaker sex" shouldn't train like a man?
- that some females have been conditioned to believe they can't train like males?
- a concern that hard, realistic training will drive off some female students?
- because female students often have a lesser status in the class than do males?

The answer is probably one or all of these because one or all of these exist in far too many schools. Who is at fault? For sure the instructor is to blame as are the male students for going along with it. So are the females just innocent victims?

No, it's their fault too.

Now, in defense of the instructor, he has legitimate concerns: injuries, lawsuits, and loss of paying female students. (These are the same concerns that result in poor fighters and ridiculously fast belt promotions.) In defense of the male students, they are simply going along with the guidelines set forth by the instructor and/or the organization (but this doesn't mean they can't file a protest), not to mention a lifetime of being conditioned to "take it easy" on the female gender.

As for the females they have no defense. The way in which the individual woman is trained is *her* responsibility. Of course there are a certain percentage of females who enter the martial arts with the same motivation as some males: They want a unique form of exercise, a friendly, club-like atmosphere, and the camaraderie of like-minded friends. If that is all a woman wants out of her training, fine. But if she wants killer-hard workouts, she doesn't mind eating a little hard contact, and she is okay with developing an aggressive personality with the ability to fight with the savagery of a highly-trained urban warrior, then it's her responsibility to ensure that that is what she is getting.

Martial arts instructor and author Martina Sprague, who trains every day like a gladiator readying herself to face the lions, says this: "Women would be more successful if they focused on building physical strength and mental confidence. In other words, they have to understand that they need to get off their lazy behinds and start training like men, which means getting sweaty and stinky, doing full-range pull-ups and full push-ups, instead of push-ups on their knees or other modified exercises. I have seen remarkable results in small and otherwise timid women who took their training seriously."

You have to seek the way

What do you do if you want to train with greater intensity, realism, and "like a man" (yes, it's an unfortunate term), but your teacher doesn't allow it? Simple, you switch to a school that does respect your needs. There are plenty out there that aren't going to short change a woman because of liability and all the other reasons mentioned.

Of course this can be a problem when you live in a community with few schools to choose from. If there is only one, you're stuck. You can either quit training and buy a Glock 9 mm, or stay with the school and make the best of it.

Let's look at how you can get optimum training both in the school, out of the school with a training partner, and in your solo training workout. We aren't going to talk about physical techniques but rather where you need to be in your head to train like a warrior. Specifically, you need to attack your training as Martina Sprague instills in her female students: with commitment, intensity, anger, and at times, as if crazed. You need to think about these things ahead of time and ingrain them into your mind so that they are always present in your training.

Commitment

In your school   Commitment is your pledge to yourself, your vow that you're going to do whatever it takes to get the kind of training you want.

- If the instructor insists that females be treated differently, you can still train with hardcore intent in your mind. Punch hard, kick hard and encourage (when the instructor isn't looking) your training partners to do the same back at you.
- If doing this could get you and your partner into trouble (especially typical of martial arts school in health clubs), consider asking one or more students to meet somewhere away from the school to train harder and more realistically.

When you're committed to training hard, you will find a way to do it.

In your solo training   Commit yourself to training hard in your solo workouts.

- Punch and kick the heavy bag all-out.
- Push yourself to do more and more reps in the air and on the bag.
- Commit yourself to having a warrior-like and savage-like mind-set every time you train alone.

Intensity

For our purposes, let's define intensity as the fighting spirit you put into everything you do in your training. Whether you're doing push-ups, crunches or round kicks into a heavy bag, you must do them with the mind-set that you're fighting for your life.

Workout Tip

- When doing push-ups - regular ones, not on your knees - imagine that you're thrusting yourself up to knock an attacker off your back.
- When you do crunches, clench your fists alongside your head and imagine that you're flexing your abs as you punch or kick.

• When you practice roundhouse kicks on a bag, imagine that each rep is the only one you get to stop the assailant.

Think of it this way: No matter how intense your training, fighting for your life or a family member's life is far more intense. Train for it.

TALK TO MYSELF?

Yes. Hey, you do it all the time anyway because your brain is going 24/7, even when you're copping Zs. It's happening right now. You're reading this; you're thinking it over; you're thinking about getting a snack. At any given time your brain is chatting up a storm, much more chat than you get from your school teacher, your martial arts instructor, your spouse, and your boss - combined. Your brain is chatting and you're listening, and that makes whatever you're talking about in your head powerful and influential – and that is why the input needs to be positive.

Negative self-talk has a powerful influence. You tell yourself you're going to lose, and you do. You tell yourself that you're going to be nervous in class, and you are. You tell yourself that you're going to fight poorly in the match, and you do.

Positive self-talk is equally powerful but it gets the results you want. Positive self-talk prepares you for a positive outcome, one in which you win, grow, improve and learn.

As long as all that self-talk is going on anyway, strive to make it positive and see how your training and your life changes for the better.

Self-Talk

- Arrive at your school 15 minutes early and tell yourself in your car that though the school tries to inhibit your full growth potential, you're going to do all that you can to get the most out of this training session.

o School policy and the instructor can control what you do and how they perceive a female, but they can't control what you think.

- When training solo, spend a few moments to self-talk yourself into a powerful, positive mind-set that guides you to getting exactly what you want out of the workout.

o Tell yourself that your training time is valuable, that life is short, and that you want every session to move you forward.

Anger

You need to tread softly here because anger in the extreme is debilitating, much the same as extreme fear is debilitating. The degrees of anger range from minor irritation – "Darn. I dropped my fork in the kitty litter box." – to uncontrollable rage – "That's the creep who stole my wallet!" The first makes you grip the fork better and the second can lead to a boiling surge of anger that dissipates your fine-motor control and reduces even the most highly trained fighter to nothing more than a crude mauler vulnerable to defeat.

Righteous indignation While it might be a matter of semantics, I prefer the term "righteous indignation." Someone is trying to hurt you or a family member. He wants to intimidate you, hurt you, make you fearful, and make you subservient to his brutality and dominance. He is actively discriminating against your right to be safe and free. That should fill you with a righteous indignation that fuels your adrenaline to sharpen your reflexes, increase your speed and power, and ignite your explosiveness.

The opposite of this optimal condition is that of unbridled rage, a condition that inhibits your performance and reduces your well-trained fighting techniques to junk. Have you ever listened to two enraged people bellowing at each other? Ever notice how incoherent they sound? How awkward their phrasing? How they curse because they can no longer think clearly enough to choose more effective verbiage. If their speech falls apart when they are angry, imagine what happens to their muscles, to their well-honed techniques. Executing junk isn't what you want when a threatening situation demands your martial arts skill.

Conjuring righteous indignation   Solo training is an ideal time to train to function within a state of righteous indignation. To create this state, as least to a small degree, you must use your creative imagination, your mental imagery. Take a few moments to meditate on a scenario that would spark this emotion.

• Imagine that you have found a burglar in your home, or you're being threatened by a bully, or someone is terrorizing a family member.
    o Feel the righteous indignation trigger an alarm that accelerates your breathing, and fills your arms, fists, legs and feet with a rush of adrenaline.
    o Feel it make you stronger, more energized and more pumped as you verge toward exploding like a rocket.

With practice you can conjure a mental state that approximates to some degree how you would feel in a real situation. Here is an example of how I used my mind to stir my fighting spirit. During my kata competition days, I would find a quiet place to work myself into a warrior mind-set, a state of mind in which I was a samurai preparing to defend a village against half a dozen bandits (hey, I don't laugh at your fantasies). Within minutes my breathing would accelerate, my eyes would burn with intensity, and my muscles would charge with adrenaline for battle. It was all I could do to hold myself back until they called my name to perform. I firmly believe that if I hadn't found this mental place, I wouldn't have won over 50 trophies.

Although the feeling I conjured was intense, it was not as extreme as it would have been if I had stirred up righteous indignation in me. If I were competing today, I would change the scenario so that I would be a samurai standing before the front door of his home in which his family huddled in fear of the approaching killers, rapists and thieves. That would make it personal. Who are these low-lifes to want to hurt my family and me?

Of course a tournament isn't the same as staring into the face of someone who wants to hurt you or a loved one. Some might argue that it's impossible to call up a powerful sense of feeling wronged and violated, but I believe the more you practice the closer you can come. Is it possible to move yourself to a place where you feel it totally? My first inclination is to say no, but then the mind is capable of incredible powers. A safer answer might be: maybe. What about those people who say that they don't carry anger within them? Don't believe it. It's definitely there, perhaps way down deep, but it's there. With work, they can bring it out.

Spend a few quiet moments alone before you begin training to reach into yourself to bring forth the powerful emotions of righteous indignation and anger. Will it be easy? For some. But even if it isn't easy for you, it's worth the effort because you will learn how to ignite it, control it, and use it.

GO BERSERK

My dictionary defines berserk as "out of control," "mad," and "crazy." During my years as a cop, I thrashed about with many people who had gone berserk, who had slipped "over the top" to a place mentally where their physical strength was that of two people, sometimes four. The berserkers I dealt with ranged in age from 14 to 75, and I must admit that the 14-year-old pregnant girl and the 75-year-old man were about as tough to handle as those barroom brawlers, loggers and, in one case, a 400-pound weight lifter who had been in the Olympic Games. The ability of a berserker to focus his strength can be extraordinary.

Workout Tip

For our purposes here, let's say that going berserk is a mental state that is beyond righteous indignation. You still have your mental facilities and control over your actions, though you're a thin line away from going over the top. You're able to throw quality techniques but any thought of strategy, conserving energy, and not getting hit are shoved into the back of your mind. Here is what Martina Sprague says about it.

"Berserk can be defined as working yourself into frenzy. When this happens, you don't feel pain, fear, or fatigue, and you don't think and analyze; you just act."

Let's look at how you can practice going berserk by yourself and, in the process, learn what you're capable of physically and learn a little about what is going on in your psyche. To get yourself into the right mind-set, you again have to rely on your power of mental imagery. I've had students tell me that they have trained using the influence of past incidents with bullies, ex-spouses, and road ragers. I once had a female student who had been raped. She would conjure that horrific event in her mind and then go berserk, not on a bag or an invisible opponent – but on me. And I allowed it. Her objective was to win this time, to block her attacker's punches, kicks, and bites. We repeated the session eight or nine times over two days, and in the end, she felt liberated and empowered because this time, by going completely berserk on her attacker, she won. I, however, felt beat to a pulp.

Martina says: "If you have a hard time working yourself into frenzy, spend a few minutes thinking about things that have really angered you in your life. When you're in a true frenzy, your only concern is to press forward. If you knew you would die doing it, it wouldn't stop you. If you don't have a mannequin dummy to practice on, you can use visualization techniques, but know it might upset you. Some of my students have said that they were unable to sleep if they practiced prior to going to bed."

Okay, let's do it.

- Conjure whatever image, experience or thought stirs your frenzy.
- Exaggerate it and add to it to make it horrific beyond your worse fears.
- Feel what it's doing to your body, your mind, your spirit.
- Feel *it* surge in you, feel *it* accelerate everything within you, higher and higher, driving you all the way to berserk.
- Now, attack your bag or imaginary air opponent with all that you have.
  o Punch, kick, claw, scream, smash, and crush.

Martina says: "I recommend setting a timer for 30 seconds, and then attack the dummy without letup, while screaming, growling, and foaming at the mouth. You can wear gloves if you're afraid of hurting your hands. For variation, attack with a stick. If you do it right, your face will turn red, your blood pressure will rise, and you might even feel dizzy and drained when it's over. But while you're doing it, you should not feel tired or in pain. If you do, you haven't really gone berserk."

- 30 to 45 seconds is long enough when going totally, absolutely, completely berserk.
- Afterwards you can shadow spar slowly for a minute or two and then repeat the 30- or 45-second berserk attack.
- Make this part of your anaerobic training, but keep in mind

that it's first and foremost about bringing forth a berserk state and then functioning in it.

Martina Sprague takes this a step further: "You can also find an object in the environment, such as a tree stump in the forest. Bring a stick or an axe and go berserk on it. This might be difficult because of what any onlookers might think, but I feel it is an invaluable experience to know that you are capable of being blinded by your own anger."

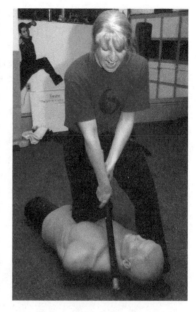

Include berserk training in your solo practice once or twice a month for 30- to 45-second intervals. Include as many intervals as you want or as your fitness level allows. There is no other way to answer the question: If you haven't practiced it how do you know what you're capable of?

Warning This training is so physically and mentally intense that should you have high blood pressure or in some other way be in poor health, it's recommended that you talk to your doctor about if first.

Caution

HOW TO RETURN TO NORMAL

Now that you have worked yourself into a berserk frenzy, you need to return to normal before your family comes home or before you go out into public. The best way to do that is through deep 4-count breathing.

• Stand with your feet a little wider than your shoulders with your hands open and along your sides.
• Lift your hands, palms up, slowly up the front of your body, as you inhale slowly to the count of four.
• Complete your inhalation by the time your hands are as high as your shoulders, pause and hold in your breath for a count

of four.

- Slowly push outward, palms forward, as you exhale to the count of four.
- Hold with your arms extended for a count of four
- Slowly draw your arms back as you inhale slowly to a count of four.
- Hold for a count of four and then slowly push outward again as you inhale to a count of four.
- Repeat this cycle three of four times so that on your last inhalation, you draw your hands back to your chest, hold for four seconds and then slowly lower them back to your sides as you exhale.

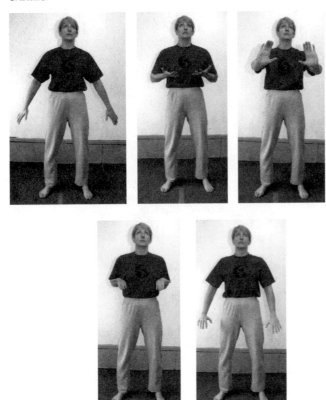

Now it's safe to be around others.

4 Things to Do the Day of the Tournament

You have trained hard and the day is finally here. You wish you would have slept better last night, but you didn't. Now it's time to go. So what's the big deal? Don't you just show up and do your thing? No. Not if you want to perform at your very best.

Whether you're going with your friends, family or other classmates, here are some ideas for you to do by yourself on tournament day.

Get there on time, even early

If you're consistently late for work, concerts, appointments and everything else, change your ways on the day of the tournament. You have trained hard, sacrificed, and prepared. Why jeopardize all that because you have trouble getting to places on time? Running behind time on the big day creates pressure and debilitating stress. While you want to compete with a level of stress that aids your performance, you don't want the kind that comes from frantic driving, blowing through red lights, careening around a parking lot looking for a parking space, and dashing from your car with your uniform belt dragging on the wet pavement, only to find yourself at the end of a long line at the door. If the tournament requires a weigh-in and your tardiness causes you to miss it, all your preparation was for naught.

To minimize bad stress, organize yourself to get to the tournament site an hour or more before it begins. This gives you plenty of time to mentally and physically prepare so that you're ready and willing to trash anyone unlucky enough to be your competitor. Here are some things to do when you show up early.

CHECK OUT THE VENUE

Stroll around the tournament site to get a sense of the space and a feel for the atmosphere.

- Examine the rings, the mats and other types of surfaces.
- Where are the out-of-bound marks?
- Where will the judges be positioned?
- How close will the fans be seated or standing?
- Do you recognize any of the refs?
  o Are there any who award more points for punches or more for kicks?
  o Do you see any judges who penalize for contact more than others?

This is all critical information for competing. Arrive late and you have to play catch-up as you dash into the ring.

SEE YOURSELF IN COMPETITION

Take a few moments to stand at the edge of the competition ring and imagine your fight or kata performance.

- Hear the crowd, see the judges, feel the intensity, and see your opponent.
  o You don't have to go into a deep trance. Simply spend three or four minutes using your imagination to get a feel for the event that will soon happen.

When you do get into the ring, it will feel as if you have already been there before, which gives you a sense of familiarity and comfort.

GREET OR AT LEAST NOTE THE COMPETITION

If you're an outgoing person, say hello to your competitors and wish them well (try to appear earnest). This helps you perceive how they are feeling and allows them to get a sense of how ready you are. When I competed, I always reminded my competitors of their past injuries and asked if they were still being hindered by them. "You know, those old injuries can come back to bite you when the heat is on." Take advantage of the moment and mess with their heads a little.

If you have never met the competitor but you recognize him from past competitions or the martial arts magazines, watch him from afar.

- Watch him move, watch him warm-up, and watch how he throws his techniques.
  - Determine how you will move against him.
  - Is he a show off?
    o If so, can you use that to your advantage?

FIND A QUIET PLACE

- A tournament is an all-day affair in a venue of noise and hustle that can drain your energy.
  o You might find that getting away for a while every couple of hours helps you relax mentally and stay fresh.
  o Find an empty hallway, room, or staircase and practice 4-count breathing.
  o Be sure to let someone know where you are and ask them to listen for the announcement of your event so they can come get you.

Should you arrive at the competition at the last moment, you don't get the opportunity to do any of these things.

Warm-up

Now isn't the time to do a new warm-up that you saw someone doing at the tournament. Do your usual routine so that your mind and muscles recognize it and the familiarity helps to prepare you.

GET YOUR HEAD INTO IT

Include in your warm-up a few combinations from your fight repertoire or a couple moves from your form to help your mind get into the battle. For example:

- Throw your favorite kick/punch combination.
  o See and feel it scoring
- Execute two of your kata movements with razor sharpness.
  o Feel your intensity in your mind and muscles.
- Feel energy surge through your body and feel the tingle of anticipation for the pending battle.

TIMING YOUR WARM-UP

Timing your warm-up isn't always easy at tournaments because events are frequently delayed or started earlier than you anticipated.

- Since you should do your warm-up just a few minutes before the event, you need to be cognizant of changes in scheduling.
- Too many competitors warm up an hour before the event, kicking full power on the shields and doing a dozen aerial somersaults.
  o This might impress novices but old-timers laugh at how much precious energy they are burning.

On-deck

They have called your event. It's time to put up or shut up. The competitors are gathering in the ring, an official is jotting down competitor's names, and eyes are darting about checking out the competition. Time to get your psyche boiling.

My trick was to step away from the others and turn my back on them. I'd close my eyes and begin to accelerate my breathing and open and close my fists. In my mind I was that Samurai I mentioned earlier, standing at the edge of a village awaiting a group of bandits coming around a turn in the dusty road. I'd feel the itch of the pending battle, feel the juices surge into my muscles, and feel the controlled rage rush throughout my body. (I'm a product of all those black and white Samurai movies of the '60s and '70s.) I'd even visualize Japan's Mt. Fuji in the background, with a little snow on the top.

Perhaps you like to stand away from the fray and do deep breathing to calm your agitated spirit and relax your tensing muscles. Or maybe you routinely get last minute instruction from your coach or instructor. All that matters is what works for you.

Although you have visualized accepting the trophy in your mental imagery practice, *now* is the time to think only about technique. Tell yourself that your sparring moves are fast and accurate and that you will overwhelm your opponent with your ferocity. Or tell yourself that your kata will be strong, fast, dynamic, and intense. Mentally talk to yourself continuously as you await your moment.

ELEMENTS YOU MUST HAVE IN PLACE

- Know your strengths and weaknesses.
  o Know how to maximize strengths and camouflage weaknesses.

- Knows the rules of this specific tournament.
  o Know what gets a warning and what gets a point.

- Be in top fighting condition: endurance, strength, polished techniques.
  o Be versatile on left and right sides.
  o Be able to move quickly and smoothly in all directions.
  o Be a master of distance.

- Be mentally primed: focused and warrior spirit activated.
  o You're in control of your emotions.
  o You can quickly change strategy depending on the circumstances.

The competition

All your training and preparation has led up to this moment.

BE IN THE MOMENT

It's all about right now. Tune out the crowd and all other distractions. When you're doing a form, nothing else matters but your battle with all those imaginary attackers. If you can see them, so will the crowd and, most importantly, the judges. When fighting, it's all about your opponent, or more accurately, it's all about what you're doing to him. Stay focused; stay in the moment.

Be a Warrior

Martial arts are about doing what needs to be done to succeed, to grow, and to be a warrior. There is no place for whining about a referee's call, stomping about angrily, and all the other shenanigans so often seen at tournaments.

- Keep a neutral face no matter how you feel.
- If your opponent nails you, accept that you erred and that you just learned something. Then walk back to the starting line and bow.
- If you nail him, walk back to the starting line and bow to him.

Judges love that, as does the crowd and other competitors. It's the right thing to do and it shows class. There is too little of that these days.

Important

Keep Your Mind on the Immediate Task

Just as you did when warming up, put the thought of winning a trophy on a back burner because right now your thoughts need to be on the task at hand.

- When doing a form:
  - o think about nailing the first jump.
  - o think about that complex stance change.
  - o think about the precision needed in the triple flip.
- When fighting, think about dominating the opening exchange of the match.
  - o Then think about controlling the next exchange.
  - o Then the next one.

What's the Score?

Get someone – your coach or a team-mate – to keep you informed of the score as you're fighting. If you're ahead by a point, don't attack unless an opportunity is ridiculously ripe.

COMBAT BREATHING

Important

Practice the 4-count breathing technique at every opportunity to help you stay calm and in control. If there is a pause, say, the refs need to discuss a rule, begin 4-count breathing though you probably won't have enough time to finish. That is okay because even a little of it is good for you.

BE A GOOD WINNER AND LOSER

This goes back to what was said in "Be a warrior." Few people are impressed when a winner pumps his fist in the air and bellows like an injured cow. Nor are people impressed when a loser curses loudly and refuses to bow or shake hands with the winner. Act like a true warrior: Acknowledge the win or the loss with a nod of the head and a bow to your opponent and judges. Be memorable to the judges, competitors and the audience because of your *correct attitude*, not because of idiotic behavior.

Section 3

15-, 20- and 35-minute
workouts

I've mentioned in other books that I like 20- and 30-minute workouts because they fit so well into a busy lifestyle. When I'm on a time crunch, an intense, short session fits the bill. If I have extra time, I go through one 20-minute session twice or I choose two different ones to do, sometimes three.

Consider these typical scenarios.

Scenario: You need a little workout but it's 12:30 p.m. and the movie starts at 2.

Solution: You have just enough time for a 30-minute session, a shower, and the drive to the theater.

Scenario: You had too much dinner and you feel like a fat pig. You had class last night and you have class tomorrow night so you don't want to train too hard. But you have to do something to kill some excess calories and burn off a little guilt.

Solution: A 20-minute session will satisfy both of these needs.

Scenario: Your back kick is so sloppy and inaccurate that you're afraid to throw it in class for fear of hitting an innocent bystander.

Solution: Do three 20-minute workouts a week practicing only on that kick. In two or three weeks you will be able to kick a buzzing fly.

Scenario: Lately your regular Monday and Wednesday martial arts classes have been so easy cardio-wise that now you get winded channel surfing with the TV remote.

Solution: A 20-minute high-rep, aerobic session on Tuesday and Thursday and a nonstop, 30-minute heavy bag session on Saturday will get you back into condition quickly, while simultaneously improving your martial arts techniques.

Scenario: You're so weak that you have to ask your grandmother to open a jar of peanut butter for you, and when you kick the heavy bag your foot lands as if a cotton ball had been thrown against it. You need to get stronger, but you don't have time for two-hour pump sessions at the gym.

Solution: Schedule two or three 20-minute workout sessions designed to increase your martial arts power.

WHEN YOU WANT A LONGER SESSION

Modify any of the following workouts to fit your needs.

Training Tip

- Go through any of the workouts twice.
- Increase the sets of only those exercises in a workout that target an area that needs improvement
- Choose a 20-minute workout followed by a 30-minute workout.
- Choose a workout for hands and one for kicks.
- Do the 35-minute boxer's workout followed by a 20 minute karate workout

Let's look at the workouts. Do them as laid out here, tweak them a little to fit your needs, or use their format to design workouts that target what you need.

35-minute workout: boxer workout

Here is a different workout for you, a little something from the sweet science. But you're a taekwondo or a karate person. Why would you want to do a boxer's workout?

- Since your style emphasizes kicks, this is a fun and productive way to focus only on your punching skills.
- Maybe you want an all-hand workout since you jammed your toe and can't kick.
- Maybe you just want to do something different to break up your routine while at the same time improving your aerobic fitness.

A boxer's workout serves all these purposes, and more.

This is fun workout that can be done at whatever intensity you desire. If your aerobic fitness is poor, proceed through the session at a moderate pace. As your fitness improves, increase the speed and intensity of all the techniques. You will know you're in good shape when you can go all-out for the entire time period. If you're already in top aerobic condition go as hard as you like.

Since this is a boxer's workout, it focuses on the basic punches: jab, cross, hook and uppercut, techniques often ignored in the martial arts or executed differently. Do this workout twice a week when you're not in your regular martial arts classes and be sure to get plenty of rest. Expect fantastic improvement in three or four weeks.

BAG OR AIR

Train on a heavy bag, a mannequin-type bag, or simply punch the air. Hitting a bag helps develop your power and gives you a feel for hitting something, while hitting the air is good for working on speed. If you want to mix the two within a 3-minute round, first do 90 seconds on the bag and then 90 seconds in the air.

HIT LIKE A BOXER

To make this fun and to underscore that it's a boxer's workout, execute the techniques as similar to boxer style as you can. If you have never boxed, watch a couple of matches on television to observe their footwork and punching style, then put on the theme to *Rocky* and have at it. Even if you don't look as good as Sylvester Stallone, you can still have fun with this workout. Who knows, you might find new ways to punch that you really like. After all, they have been working for boxers for decades. Do you want to tell Tyson his punches are ineffective?

Pick up a copy of *Boxing: The American Martial Art* by R. Michael Onello, published by Turtle Press. It contains all the basics in an easy-to-follow format that will have you boxing like a veteran in no time.

1-MINUTE RESTS

You get to rest for a minute after every 3-minute session. Granted, that isn't enough time to go out and get a latte, but it does allow you to catch your breath and think about your next 3 minutes. While taking a minute break between rounds is standard boxing training, should you occasionally want to push your lungs and heart to work overtime, skip the 1-minute breaks and do one, long boxing workout.

WARM-UP: JUMP ROPE

Workout Tip

Since this workout is all punching, you want to thoroughly warm up your wrists, elbows and shoulders as you usually do. To warm-up your legs, heart and lungs, do as boxers do and grab the jump rope.

• Keep your elbows tucked in and jump for 1 minute on the balls of both feet.
• Then do the boxer's shuffle for 2 minutes: the rope passes under one foot at a time, the left, the right, the left, as if jogging in place.

If you're new to jumping rope, keep at it and you will be a master in no time. It's a fast way to get your heart pumping and your blood racing through your veins. Sing about Lizzie Borden and her axe if it helps.

Go 3 minutes non stop and then rest 1 minute.

Okay, hang up the rope and let's get into the techniques. Since some martial arts styles don't have jabs, uppercuts and hooks, or if they do they don't do them as boxers do, I've provided a brief description as to how to throw them.

JAB

The jab is a boxing basic and for good reason: It's versatile, fast, harassing, good for creating distance, good for setting up a hard cross and, for some fighters, it packs knock-out power. Most boxers believe it's the most important punch in their arsenal and if they had to keep only one technique, the jab would be it.

- You can hit with your thumb side up, or twist your fist until your palm is facing downward. Many believe that a fast twist adds extra snap to the blow.
  o Always the politician, I turn my fist half way between thumb-side up and palm down. I find the position stronger and less likely to tweak my wrist should it land poorly.
- Keep your elbow under your arm as opposed to letting it flip out to the side.
- Feel your shoulder thrust with each punch.
- Never telegraph your intent by retracting your fist. Shoot it straight out from your on-guard position.
- Try jabbing different ways:
  o Sometimes pop out lightning-quick ones and other times step into the blows to generate more power.
  o Jab and leave your arm extended for 1 second (to cover your opponent's face so you can follow with a cross).
  o Shuffle into range and pop a quick jab and then shuffle out.
  o Move to your left delivering sharp jabs then scoot to your right jabbing.
  o Circle the heavy bag popping jabs.
- Be sure to change stances every few jabs to work both arms.

Go 3 minutes non stop and then rest 1 minute.

CROSS

The cross, or reverse punch as it's called in the martial arts, is a basic technique in most fighting styles. It's a tad slower than the jab since it's coming from a greater distance, but it delivers much more wallop because of the added hip rotation, the opposing action of the opposite hand, and the driving thrust of the rear leg.

As a boxer, your rear hand is positioned at the side of your chin. Don't telegraph by lowering your rear hand before punching, but rather launch it from your jaw line.

- Twist your hips and drive with that rear leg to incorporate as much body mass as possible into the blow.
- More and more martial arts styles are discovering the benefits of holding their arms higher in the on-guard position, similar to boxers and muay Thai fighters.

    o While this is a preferred position, it's easy to get sloppy and not retract the non punching arm. Remember, the simultaneous snap back of the non punching arm adds power and speed to the cross.

    o Although the distance of the snap-back is less in the high guard as opposed to the low guard position found in some traditional fighting arts, every little bit helps.

    o Even if you hold your fists on either side of your face, or even touching your face, you can still retract the non punching arm to some degree.

- Move about just as you did when jabbing.

    o Shuffle in and out as you land hard crosses each time you're in range.

    o Move to your left as you deliver powerful crosses, then scoot to your right as you punch.

    o Circle the heavy bag and punch.

- Change from left leg forward to right leg forward so that you throw crosses with a different arm every few hits.
- Sometimes snap your cross out and back, other times sink it deeply into the bag or the imagined target.
- A basic combination: Snap out a jab and, as it retracts, launch your cross. *Boom, boom!*

Go 3 minutes non stop and then rest 1 minute.

Hook punch, lead and rear

I'm guessing that the lead hook punch is found in more street-realistic fighting styles than in schools that emphasize tournament sparring. This is too bad, but understandable. Tournament points are usually garnered by attacks that travel a relatively long distance and are easily seen by corner judges. A lead hook doesn't fall into that category unless it's thrown wide and lands unchecked by the recipient. But in the street, the hook is an excellent weapon to get around an opponent's arms and hit him in the ear, neck and body.

Since most boxers are right handed and fight with their left side forward, lead hooks are delivered to their opponent's right side, specifically the ribs and the liver. Liver is not a popular dish at dinner time, but it's an extremely popular target in the boxing ring. The ribs never like to catch a hook punch, but the liver – located on the right side, just behind the ribs - especially hates it. If getting punched there with a big boxing glove churns the intestines, wobbles the legs, and envelops the recipient in a world of nausea and regret for having gotten out of bed that morning, imagine what a hard, bare fist would do to a street bully. More on this in a moment.

Note: A quick comment on precise form. If a boxer throws 50 hook punches in a match, maybe one or two of them are thrown with the same precise form as described here. In the heat of battle, when windows of opportunity are small, the hook is most often delivered less precisely, which is okay because it still delivers tremendous penetrating power. However, when practicing solo, I like to do it as close to perfection as possible. Then when throwing it against a live partner, I let the circumstances dictate how close I come to throwing it with precision.

Important

The lead hook Assume your left-side-forward fighting stance, arms close to your body and fists near your head, facing 12 o'clock.

- Move your upper body a little to the left toward 11 o'clock and over your lead, left leg. Lower your knees a little.
- Push off the ball of your left foot as you pivot back toward 12 o'clock.
- Raise your left elbow and execute the punch.
- Think 90, 90, 90. At the completion of the punch, your body should be turned almost 90 degrees to the right (when punching

with your left), your lead foot is turned 90 degrees to your right, and your punching arm is bent 90 degrees. All three 90s add up to a very powerful punch.

   • **Note:** When punching the liver, your arm is still bent 90 degrees, but your lead shoulder is dipped and your punch is angled at a 45-degree angle upward. This is because when you make contact with the liver on your opponent's right side, just below his ribs and above his hip bone, you want the angle of your force to travel diagonally toward his opposite shoulder. Hit with a digging motion, as if shoveling deep for the organ. Be cruel.

The rear hook   Assume your left-side-forward fighting stance, arms close to your body and fists near your head, facing 12 o'clock.

   • Turn your upper body slightly to the right to 1 o'clock so that your rear leg supports much of your weight. Bend your knees a little.

   • Push off with the ball of your rear foot and pivot back to 12 o'clock.
   • Pivot your right foot and leg about 45 degrees to your left as you launch your hook. Your lead foot remains straight ahead or pivots to the left a little.
   • Move about the heavy bag just as you did with the other punching techniques.
   o Shuffle in and out as you land a hard rear hook each time you're in range.
   o Since you want to hit with your two large knuckles, you need to be a tad closer to the target than does a boxer who hits with his padded little knuckles.

COMBINING THE TWO

Move about throwing both lead and rear hooks.

- Circle the heavy bag hitting at random.
- Change from left leg forward to right leg forward every few hits.
- Put your body into the blows by cranking hard into the 90-degree angles and sink your fist deeply into the bag or the imagined target in the air.
- Throw some hooks where your lead is less than 90, 90, 90 to see how it feels and to learn what your power capability is when your body is less than ideally aligned.

Go 3 minutes non stop and then rest 1 minute.

UPPERCUT, LEAD AND REAR

If you're ever attacked on a dark street by a thug who fights with his tongue sticking out between his teeth, hit him with an uppercut. It will be easy to pick him in a police line-up: Just ask each guy to say a sentence with words that have lots of S sounds.

The uppercut is a devastating blow that is most effective when thrown in close. When in a clinch or a near clinch, shoot your uppercut straight up your opponent's chest and into his jaw.

Note: Keep in mind we're talking about a boxer's workout here, a fighting art that uses big gloves. A bear-knuckled uppercut to the jaw in the street will likely damage your fist. When practicing the uppercut for self-defense, hit with your palm.

Since many styles don't use this technique, here is a brief description.

LEAD UPPERCUT

- To launch a left, lead-hand uppercut, assume your fighting stance and look straight ahead to 12 o'clock.
- Rotate your upper body to about 11 o'clock, and bend your knees a little more as you lean slightly to your left.
- Snap your upper body back to 12 o'clock, as you drive off the ball of your left foot. Rise up a little as you uppercut.

Rear uppercut

- To launch a right, rear-hand uppercut, assume your fighting stance and hold your rear arm close to your body.
- Rotate your right hip forward as you launch the punch and lift your body slightly.
- Some fighters straighten their rear leg with a snap while others don't because they feel it compromises their stability. If you don't like straightening it, keep the knee slightly bent as you uppercut. Experiment to see what works best for you.
- The palm side of your fist is toward you upon impact.

Combining the two

- Shuffle around an uppercut bag slamming with both your lead and rear hands.
- If you don't have such a bag, punch the air to establish good form and speed.
- Change from left leg forward to right leg forward every few hits so that both arms get a chance at throwing lead-hand and rear-hand punches.

Go 3 minutes non stop and then rest 1 minute.

Good body targets

Workout Tip

When hitting the heavy bag or punching the air, see your imaginary opponent's vital targets: liver (right side of his body just below the ribs and above the pelvic bone), solar plexus (just below and between his pecs), and heart. Learn to hit these targets with power, speed, finesse, and with either hand.

THE THROW-EVERYTHING ROUND

In this 3-minute block, you're going to throw jabs, crosses, uppercuts and hooks non-stop as you move about. Be cognizant of good form and footwork as you land your combinations and singles on the heavy bag, or on an imaginary air opponent. Move from right to left, left to right, and forward and back. Stay loose, move fast and hit hard.

Go 3 minutes non stop and then rest 1 minute.

ALWAYS BE ABLE TO THROW ONE MORE

No matter how you're positioned at any given moment when executing a combination, you should be able to throw one more punch without losing your balance. It's all about being aware of your stability.

When throwing a right cross, you should be able to follow with a left hook or uppercut. When you throw a lead hook, you should be in position to launch a right cross. If you ever throw a punch with, say, the right hand, and you aren't in position to throw another with the left without having to take a recovery step of some kind, you threw that punch incorrectly.

BOB AND WEAVE ROUND

You're going to throw everything as you just did in the last round and add some bobbing and weaving, too. For example:

- Imagine a punch coming at your head and lean away from it as you deliver a strong counter cross.
- Duck that next punch and drive in two jabs to the body before straightening up.
- Shuffle to the side and hook punch. Lean back to avoid his counter and return with a hard uppercut.

If your energy starts to drag at, say, the 2-minute point, don't stop. Simply slow down a little and keep on going. Stay tough.

Go 3 minutes non stop and then rest 1 minute.

30-SECOND SPEED ROUNDS

There is good news and there is good news concerning this round: The first good news is that it's a hard session which is good for you. The other good news is that you get a break every 30 seconds. There is no bad news, unless you just had a lunch of chili and fries.

- Attack the bag or your invisible foe with all the ferocity and speed you can muster for 30 seconds.
  o There is no holding back, as now is the time to push your body and test your warrior spirit.
- Pause for 30 seconds.
  o Make the most of your rest by taking in slow, deep breaths and relaxing your body.
- Go nuts for another 30 seconds throwing jabs, crosses, uppercuts and hooks, intermingled with bobbing, ducking, weaving, shuffling, sidestepping and lunging in and out.
- Pause for 30 seconds.
- Explode for one more 30-second bout.
- Aaaaand stop.

COOL DOWN

But don't really stop. The best way to recover and to cool down is to do a little slow shadow boxing. Stay loose as you throw out easy and slow versions of the hard and fast ones you have been doing. Don't let your form deteriorate, but do let your breathing and your heart rate return to normal. Do this for about 5 minutes.

Now stretch and hit the showers. *Pleeease*, take a shower.

PUTTING IT ALL TOGETHER

Here is the boxer workout in one neat package

Warm-up: jump rope	3 minutes
Jab	3 minutes
Rest	1 minute
Cross	3 minutes
Rest	1 minute
Lead and rear hook	3 minutes
Rest	1 minute
Lead and rear uppercut	3 minutes
Rest	1 minute
Throw everything	3 minutes
Rest	1 minute
Bob and weave	3 minutes
Rest	1 minute
30-second speed rounds	30 on 30 off for 3 minutes
Cool down	5 minutes

WHY DO ONLY ONE SPECIFIC PUNCH PER ROUND?

Why not just shadow box, you ask. Well, you're getting 9 minutes of shadow boxing with this session when you do the "Throw everything round," "Bob and weave round," and the "30-second speed rounds." You can certainly add more of these if you want. But the purpose of this workout is to isolate basic techniques so that you get in plenty of reps of each one.

Important

When you just shadow box, you might do only six or seven uppercuts or lead hooks in a round. When done as presented here, you do an entire 3-minute round of each technique – perhaps 100 or more – as well as however many you do in the three shadow sparring rounds.

Give this boxer's workout a try. It's different, it's fun and it doesn't take long to look and feel like a boxer. Watch a few boxing matches on television and do you best to mimic them. Not only does this workout give a respite from your regular training, you just might discover some good techniques you can incorporate into your regular training.

20-minute workout: I-don't-want-to-fight stance

(See Chapter 11)

If you want an aerobic exercise do the following drills nonstop. If you complete the session at, say, the 15-minute mark, repeat any part of it you want to get in an additional 5 minutes. If you don't want an aerobic session, take breaks, pause to analyze something, repeat a drill, or add something to a drill.

Begin by assuming the I-don't-want-to-fight stance, either The Classic or The Wall. As you proceed, fluctuate from one to the other. For example, if you're doing two sets of each drill, do one from The Classic position and one from The Wall.

PALM-HEEL STRIKE

Lead-hand jab   2 to 3 sets of 10 reps with each arm
Rear-hand straight thrust   2 to 3 sets of 10 reps with each arm
Lead-hand, rear-hand combination   2 sets of 10 reps from
    both sides

PUNCH WITH FIST

Lead-hand jab   2 to 3 sets of 10 reps with each arm
Rear-hand straight thrust   2 to 3 sets of 10 reps with each arm
Lead-hand, rear-hand combination   2 sets of 10 reps from
    both sides

SLAP WITH OPEN HAND

Lead-hand slap   2 to 3 sets of 10 reps with each arm
Rear-hand slap   2 to 3 sets of 10 reps with each arm
Lead-hand, rear-hand slap combination   2 sets of 10 reps
    from both sides

EYE ATTACKS

Lead-hand fingers strike   2 to 3 sets of 10 reps with each arm
Rear-hand fingers strike   2 to 3 sets of 10 reps with each arm
Lead-hand fingers strike, rear-hand fingers strike
    combination   2 sets of 10 reps from both sides
Lead-hand outside rake, rear-hand inside rake combination
    2 sets of 10 reps from both sides

BLOCKS AND COUNTER WITH YOUR CHOICE OF HITS

Sweep block followed by a lead-hand hit and a
rear-hand hit 2 sets, 15 reps
Back-hand block followed by a lead-hand strike and
rear-hand strike 2 sets of 15 reps
Head-shield blocks followed by lead-hand hit and
rear-hand hit 2 sets of 15 reps
Kick blocks: block and counter as you normally do 2 sets
of 10 reps of each kick, front, round, side, back, crescent

KICKS

From the I-don't-want-to-fight hand position, deliver your
kicks with explosiveness and without telegraphing.

Lead-leg front kick 2 sets of 10 reps with each leg
Lead-leg round kick 2 sets of 10 reps with each leg
Lead-leg sidekick 2 sets of 10 reps with each leg
Lead-hand palm-heel strike, front kick combination
2 sets of 10 reps both sides
Lead-hand fingers jab, lead-leg round kick combination
2 set of 10 reps both sides
Lead-hand punch, lead-leg side-kick combination
2 sets of 10 reps both sides

21-minute workout: cheating speed

(See Chapter 14)

If you want an aerobic exercise do the following drills non-stop. If you complete the session at, say, the 15-minute mark, repeat any part of it you want to get in an additional 6 minutes. If you don't want an aerobic session, take breaks, pause to analyze something, repeat a drill, or add something to a drill.

The body mechanics involved in creating an illusion of speed are subtle and critically important. Review Chapter 14 to ensure that you're doing the moves correctly.

SNEAKY BACKFIST

Shadow sparring   Do 1, 3-minute round of the sneaky backfist in the air.

Heavy bag   Do 1, 3-minute round of the sneaky fist on the heavy bag.

SCOOP KICK AND FINGERS JAB

Shadow sparring   Do 1, 3-minute round of scoop kicks and fingers jab in the air.

Heavy bag   Do 1, 3-minute round of scoop kicks and fingers jab on a heavy bag.

HIGH/LOW

Shadow sparring 1.   Do 1, 3-minute round of left palm to the face, left front kick to the shin, right claw to the eyes, and right round kick to the closest thigh.

Shadow sparring 2.   Do 1, 3-minute round of left sidekick to the shin, left backfist to the nose, right reverse punch into the upper thigh and left forearm into the throat.

Shadow sparring 3.   Do 1, 3-minute round of left finger rake to the eyes, right lead roundhouse kick to the thigh.

25-minute workout: up-and-down kicking drill

(See Chapter 12)

If you want an aerobic exercise do the following drills non-stop. If you complete the session at, say, the 15-minute mark, repeat any part of it you want to get in an additional 10 minutes. If you don't want an aerobic session, take breaks, pause to analyze something, repeat a drill, or add something to a drill.

A backfist to the head doesn't burn as many calories as does a roundhouse kick to the head. Since your legs and rear contain the largest muscles in your body, they burn the most calories when you put them through a systematic and rigorous kicking regimen. So, to drop a few pounds, do lots of kicking.

Training Tip

Similarly, standing and lying on the floor consume very few calories, but getting up and down does. Since kicking burns lots of calories as does getting up and down from the floor, combine the two whenever you need to drop a few excess pounds.

Work on the following four fighting positions to improve your cardiovascular system, burn calories at an accelerated rate, and to improve your fighting ability.

Warning: This drill is quite stressful on your knees so be sure to do a thorough warm-up first. If you have chronic knee problems, approach this one cautiously or consider not doing it at all.

SQUATTING ON YOUR HEELS

• Drop onto your left side and do a right front kick. Stand up quickly then squat back down and do one on your right side.
  o Do 10 reps on each side for a total of 20 reps.
• Drop onto your left side and do a right roundhouse kick. Stand up quickly then squat back down and do one on your right side.
  o Do 10 reps on each side for a total of 20 reps.
• Drop onto your left side and do a right sidekick. Stand up quickly then squat back down and do one on your right side.
  o Do 10 reps on each side for a total of 20 reps.

Hey, come back here. You can't hit the showers yet. You got

more positions to do. You still have to do the same three kicks for 10 reps each on both sides in:

- Squatting with your upper legs parallel with the floor.
- With both knees on the floor.
- With your left knee on the floor.
- With your right knee on the floor.

So it looks like this:

Squat with butt on heels
Left and right front kick – 20 total reps
Left and right roundhouse kick – 20 total reps
Left and right sidekick – 20 total reps

Squat with upper legs parallel with the floor
Left and right front kick – 20 total reps
Left and right roundhouse kick – 20 total reps
Left and right sidekick – 20 total reps

Kneel on both knees
Left and right front kick – 20 total reps
Left and right roundhouse kick – 20 total reps
Left and right sidekick – 20 total reps

Kneel on left knee
Left and right front kick – 20 total reps
Left and right roundhouse kick – 20 total reps
Left and right sidekick – 20 total reps

Kneel on right knee
Left and right front kick – 20 total reps
Left and right roundhouse kick – 20 total reps
Left and right sidekick – 20 total reps

Ha! That's only 300 kicks, you scoff. True, but remember that you have to get up after each rep and then squat or kneel back down again for the next one. Combined, you have a heck of a calorie-burning workout. Did I mention the huffing and puffing? Do this non-stop at a pace between medium and fast and you also get an outstanding aerobic workout.

20-minute workout: core grappling cardio
(See Chapter 4)

Here is a great way to work your cardiovascular system as you work your core grappling muscles. Exclude neck bridges from this routine since they are too small too have an effect on your breathing. You can always do them after you have completed this drill. Do the four bag exercises in a circuit, each one for 3 minutes with 1 minute rest in between. Then finish the session with a repeat of any of the four exercises for 4 minutes. It looks like this.

- Clean and Press for 3 minutes, and then rest 1 minute.
- Lift, Rotate and Put Down for 3 minutes, and then rest 1 minute.
- Hug and Lunge for 3 minutes, and then rest 1 minute.
- Hug and lift for 3 minutes, and then rest 1 minute.
- Option round. Do one 4-minute round of any of the above.

This gives you a 20-minute aerobic workout (counting the rest minutes), though it might feel like an hour at first. Once you're in shape and feel like having a killer session, go through the four exercises twice, with 1-minute rest round between each. Tough? Oh yes. But will your grappling muscles and heart and lungs be in top condition? Definitely.

15-minutes workout: weights

This 15-minute workout works best when there is a convenient weight gym where you work, where you go to school or, best of all, in your home.

Say that for the next three weeks your life is going to be so hectic that it will be impossible for you to do your usual one-hour, weight training sessions three times a week at your health club. Don't fret; there is a solution. The following three exercises attack all of your basic muscle groups, as well as the smaller ones. Besides keeping you in shape, these three work all the muscles applicable for martial arts. Actually, there is a good chance you will increase your strength in these lifts since you will be focusing all of your energy on just the three. Not a bad deal for 15 minutes of your time.

- Bench press: builds punching, pushing and grappling muscles.
- Dumbbell one-arm rowing: builds pulling, punch-retraction, and various grappling muscles.
- Squats: builds kicking and grappling muscles.

Do each set followed by a 30-second rest break. Or do all three exercises one after the other without rest, then rest 30 seconds before you do another circuit. Do 3 to 4 sets, 10 reps each, 1 to 3 times a week.

20-minute workout: free-hand power builder

(Chapters 1, 2, and 3)

The good news about this empty-hand workout is that it attacks your major upper body muscles groups – triceps, shoulders, back, abdomen, and chest – and it attacks your legs – the quadriceps on the front and the ones you sit on, your glutes. The bad news is that there is nothing for your biceps and the muscles on the back of your legs. Therefore, it's not one that you would do for several months in a row. I use it as a way to shock my body for three or four weeks, specifically targeting those muscles that add power and explosiveness to all my basic techniques.

For the upper body muscles, you will be doing push-ups, lots of them, but never the same exercise twice. For the abs you're going in hard and fast with a new exercise each set. And for the legs, you guessed it: hard reps and a new exercise each set.

You need a Swiss ball.

SUPER-SET 1:

Uneven push-ups   1 set of reps to near failure with your right arm on a block and 1 set of reps to near failure with your left arm on a block.
Rolling jackknifes   1 set of 10 reps
Hindu Squats   1 set of 50 reps

SUPER-SET 2:

Side-to-side push-ups   1 set of reps to near failure with your body over your right hand and 1 set of reps to near failure with your body over your left hand.
Praying Mantis   1 set of 10 reps.
One-legged plyometric squat jumps   1 set of 10 reps.

SUPER-SET 3:

Bullet push-ups Choose one variation from Chapter 1. Do 1 set of reps to near failure.

Backfist crunches   Since your arms are fatigued from all of the push-ups, you don't have to do the backfists hard. Strike at a slow pace but contract your abs hard.) 1 set of 15 reps with each arm.

Sumo squats If your legs are trashed after the first two leg exercises, do these without weights. 1 set of 25 reps. However, if you have the strength and energy to hold a heavy dumbbell, great. Do 1 set of 10 reps.

20 Minutes: Combinations on a Mannequin

(See Chapter 15)

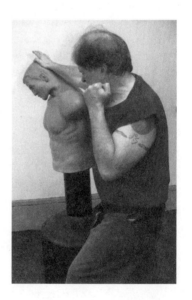

If you want an aerobic exercise do the following drills non-stop. If you complete the session at, say, the 15-minute mark, repeat any part of it you want to get in an additional 5 minutes. If you don't want an aerobic session, take breaks, pause to analyze something, repeat a drill, or add something to a drill.

This is a good, well-rounded session that works your entire body as you combine all your weapons into devastating attacks that hit with pinpoint accuracy. Readeeee GO!

DOUBLE COMBO

• Lead backfist ear, rear-hand hook punch ribs   3 sets, 10 reps both sides

- Lead palm-heel face, rear-arm round elbow to neck 3 sets, 10 reps both sides
- Lead roundhouse kick groin, reverse punch solar plexus 3 sets, 10 reps both sides

TRIPLE COMBO

- Lead roundhouse groin, lead-hand claw to the eyes and rear-hand downward hammer to the side of the neck   2 sets, 15 reps both sides
- Lead palm-heel to the nose to drive his head back, then step in and execute right and left hook punches to the ribs 2 sets, 15 reps both sides
- Pretend to block outward with your left arm, then drive a left hook into the side of the neck, followed by a right reverse punch to the solar plexus and a right round elbow into the ear 2 sets, 15 reps both sides

QUADRUPLE COMBO

- As you the clinch the neck, headbutt the nose twice, followed by two right knee strikes to the ribs 2 sets, 10 reps, both sides
- Lead-hand slap to the ear then come right back with a left backfist to the nose. Follow with a right elbow to the side of the neck and come right back with a right claw across the eyes 2 sets, 10 reps both sides
- Front kick into the bladder (just below his belt), followed with a right shin kick into the lower ribs, clinch neck, and finish with two left knees into the other set of ribs 2 sets, 10 reps on both sides

Notice that the sets and reps decrease as the combinations grow longer. If you're in top physical condition now, you might not have to reduce the sets and reps. But if you're not in the best shape, follow the sets and reps as described and add to them as your fitness level improves.

Training Tip

Unless your mannequin dummy in anatomically correct, you will have to throw the low kicks near the base where the targets would be.

20-minute workout for women: mental commitment

(See Chapter 19)

If you want an aerobic exercise do the following drills non-stop. If you complete the session at, say, the 15-minute mark, repeat any part of it you want to get in an additional 5 minutes. If you don't want an aerobic session, take breaks, pause to analyze something, repeat a drill, or add something to a drill.

This is a tough workout designed to bring out the warrior spirit, especially in those females who train at a martial arts school where they are seen as the "gentler sex" and are discouraged from or simply not allowed to train all-out. Please reread "Four Mental Techniques for Women," Chapter 19 and keep in the forefront of your mind that the warrior spirit *is* within you. Workouts such as this will help bring it out.

As you change into your workout attire, self-talk yourself into a kick-butt mind-set. Tell yourself that your training time is valuable, life is short, and you're going to progress during this workout by pushing yourself physically and mentally to bring out your warrior within.

Warm-up and get ready to rumble.

ADDITIONAL WARM-UP WITH COMBAT PUSH-UPS AND CRUNCHES

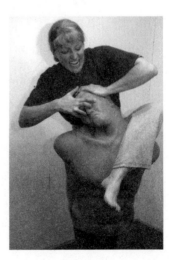

Push-ups hit virtually every muscle in your body and crunches target your midsection and core area. Think of them as a device to jump-start your thinking into a warrior mind-set. When you think of these movements as described below, they will link together your mind and body, and ready you for the fight that follows.

Push-ups

Do regular ones; don't do them on your knees. Imagine that you're thrusting yourself up to knock an attacker off your back. Growl, grunt or yell on each rep.

Do 1 set of 2 to 10 reps.

Ab crunches   Clench your fists and hold them alongside your head. Contract your abs hard and imagine that you're pushing against someone holding you down. Growl, grunt or yell on each rep.

Do 1 set of 25 reps.

Warmed up now? Good. Now let's fight.

Righteous indignation

A scum-sucking low life just pushed a member of your family into the dirt and is now swaggering toward you, laughing at what he just did and saying he is going to do the same to you.

Ain't going to happen. Preemptive strike him - Now! Yell, scream and grunt as you:

In the air
• Backfist his ear and reverse punch his solar plexus.
Do 2 sets of 10 reps both sides.

• Lead-hand claw to his eyes and angle round kick his groin.
Do 2 sets of 10 reps both sides.

• Lead-hand palm-heel to his face and rear-arm elbow strike his neck.
Do 2 sets of 10 reps, both sides.

• Ab crunches This set of crunches keeps your fighting spirit up while giving your arms, shoulders and legs a breather.
o Groan, scream or yell as you come up on each rep.
o Imagine that you're raising up against someone trying to hold you down
Do 1 set of 25 reps.

ON THE BAG

- Lead-hand palm-heel to face, rear-hand palm-heel to face

Do 2 sets of 10 reps both sides.

- Double roundhouse kick.
o Kick, then bounce your foot off the floor into another roundhouse kick. Both should land with equal intensity.

Do 2 sets of 10 reps both sides.

- Backfist to the ear and rear-hand hammer fist to the side of the neck.

Do 2 sets of 10 reps both sides.

GO BERSERK

Use the ab reps as a way to transition your mind into the violence that follows.

- Ab crunches
o Imagine that scum-sucking, bottom feeder doing something even worse than knocking you down. Conjure whatever horrific image stirs your frenzy, perhaps something that has really happened to you. Feel your righteous indignation and your absolute need to strike out surge through your body, your mind and your spirit. Feel it accelerate everything within you, driving you, enraging you.

Do 1 set of 25 reps at medium speed to allow your adrenaline to build

SHADOW SPARRING

(two levels of intensity)

- Shadow spar for 60 seconds at medium speed
o Perform your kicks, punches and blocks at medium speed, allowing your adrenaline to build.
o Contort your face into a rage, curl your lips like a pit bull, glare with your eyes until they water, deliberately accelerate your breathing, and fight to restrain your techniques from exploding all-out.
o 58 seconds, 59, aaaand 60! *Unleash your might fury!*

- Go berserk for 30 to 45 seconds
o Punch, kick, claw, scream, smash, and crush!
o Don't hold anything back - go as hard and fast and fero-cious as you can - thinking only thoughts of mayhem and destruc-tion.
o This is an anaerobic session that will have you sucking for air like a drowning victim.

Alternate for 7 to 8 minutes as follows:

60 seconds medium speed
30 to 45 seconds all-out berserk speed
60 seconds medium speed
30 to 45 seconds all-out berserk speed
60 seconds medium speed
30 to 45 seconds all-out berserk speed
60 seconds medium speed
30 to 45 seconds all-out berserk speed
60 seconds medium speed

Want to go longer? Keep alternating from all-out berserk to medium speed for as many more sets as you like.

Variation: Since this workout is as much about your mind and spirit as it is about your physical side, you might want to use a weapon instead of punching and kicking. Grab an arnis stick, nunchaku, or staff and pummel a heavy bag for 60 seconds at me-dium speed, and then 30 to 45 seconds at all-out berserk speed.

Warning: If you have health problems check with your doctor first before doing this routine. You shouldn't do it more than once a week even if you are completely healthy and in good condition.

Caution

Conclusion

Random thoughts to ponder

I am sure that not numbers or strength bring victory in war; but whichever army goes into battle stronger in soul, their enemies generally cannot withstand them.

Greek General Xenophon, 4th century B.C.
Anabis

I'd like to leave you with a few thoughts to mull over when you're alone in your car, having a sleepless night, or when you're sitting in your easy chair watching the rain splatter against a window. I believe these are weighty issues that every martial artist – sports oriented and street oriented - needs to consider.

We are living in dangerous times with war ever present and street crime ever more brutal. I'm glad to see so many martial arts schools striving to make their material street oriented. While some are doing a better job of it than others, what is important is that teachers and students are thinking about real fighting, about real self-defense. More and more discerning martial artists are asking: What would I do if...

Asking questions and seeking answers is what learning and growth is all about. Your teachers ask questions and you answer. You ask question and your teacher answers.

Well, here are a few important questions you need to ask yourself, and answer.

Considering the times, never have the answers been more important.

Sheep, wolves and sheepdogs

The concept of sheep, wolves and sheepdogs is one taught by Lt. Col. Dave Grossman in his lectures. The Colonel and I wrote about it in the books *On Combat: The Psychology and Physiology of Deadly Conflict in War and in Peace* and in *Warriors: On Living With Courage, Discipline and Honor*. The concept is taught primarily to soldiers and law enforcement officers, people who live and work in the warrior community, laying their lives on the line for others every day. I believe that martial artists – people who train to function in violence for self-protection and to protect others – also need to think about the concept and understand the roles it presents.

The world consists of sheep, wolves and sheepdogs. Those who are sheep are generally kind, gentle and productive creatures who can only hurt one another by accident. It's not meant to be an insult to call them sheep; it's just what they are.

Then there are the wolves who feed on the sheep, and do so without mercy. Those who don't believe there are evil, salivating wolves in the world are sheep, sheep in denial, and denial isn't a safe place to be.

Then there are the sheepdogs. They live to protect the flock and confront the wolf. They train for it, they dedicate themselves to it, and sometimes they give their lives to it.

Think of the concept this way: Those who have no capacity for violence are healthy, productive people: sheep. Those who have a capacity for violence, but no empathy for others, are aggressive sociopaths: wolves. But those who have a capacity for violence and a love for others, they are the sheepdogs, the warriors.

Which one are you?

Denial

Sheep are in denial. "Nothing will ever happen to me," they say. "I'll never run into problems. No one will ever hurt me."

The problem is that denial hurts twice: The first time it hurts is at the moment of truth when the sheep aren't physically prepared to face the wolf. Then denial hurts a second time because of what violence can do psychologically to the one who sees the world through rose-colored glasses. The shock of this sudden reality can cause debilitating fear, helplessness, horror and shame at the moment of truth.

Gavin de Becker wrote this in his bestselling book *Fear Less*: "...denial can be seductive, but it has an insidious side effect. For all the peace of mind deniers think they get by saying it isn't so, the fall they take when faced with new violence is all the more unsettling. Denial is a save-now-pay-later scheme, a contract written entirely in small print, for in the long run, the denying person knows the truth on some level."

A martial artist can't be in denial. He must know that there are wolves out there and he must prepare himself to be ready to face them down.

Think about it.

Keep fighting no matter what

I was at a tournament recently watching two brown belts compete. One guy caught my eye because he was strutting, posing and really full of himself. Then his opponent smacked him in the nose. Not a hard whack, just an accidental grazing shot. But you would have thought the guy had just learned that his entire family went down with the Titanic.

He was hurt, yes, since even a mild shot to the nose is unpleasant. But this guy was shocked and stunned that he had actually been hit. He staggered back clutching his nose with a look of disbelief on his face. "You hit me!" his expression conveyed. "You hit me! Why? Why would you do such a thing?"

To me, this guy conveyed the mind-set of far too many martial artists. Yes, it was just a tournament match and yes you're not supposed to hit each other hard in point fighting, but would this guy have reacted differently in a real fight? I'm betting no.

Clearly he didn't have a warrior's mind-set, one that drove him to continue fighting in spite of the hard contact and violation of the rules, a mind-set not based on revenge, but one based on a need to get the job done (and let the judges do theirs). Do you have such a mind-set?

Spend time contemplating this critical question. Possessing the mind-set to continue fighting no matter how hurt you are, no matter how grave the situation, is a powerful tool that law enforcement officers and combat soldiers are encouraged to develop. Consider this police officer's mind-set. It's a quote from *On Combat* and I've cleaned up the language a little. Still, the man's powerful mind comes through loud and clear.

"In my mind, I'm never going to die in no ghetto. Absolutely never. If a man tries to punch me in the head, the fight is on. If he cuts me, the fight is on. If I'm shot, the fight is on. I'm not losing no fight to no scumbag out there in no ghetto. Period. That's it. No #&*%!! out there is going to get me. The only way he gets me is to cut my head off, and I mean that. I'll fight you until I got a breath left in me. I don't think any of those animals in that street can beat me. I've gone that way for 18 years of street service, street duty, and that's the way I'm going to keep on going. You don't lose the fight."

If your primary concentration is tournament fighting, you're in a great position to toughen your mind for the street. Should your opponent land a hard one, eat it and keep fighting. Don't be one of those competitors who hams it up hoping the judges will penalize his opponent. Tell yourself right now that you're going to eat the pain and keep fighting until the judges call for a break.

If you train primarily for the street, use your contemplative moments to give yourself powerful and positive input to keep fighting no matter how hurt you are in a real situation. Use the above officer's statement as a basis if you need help and modify it to fit your personality. Use powerful words that have significance for you. If swear words do it for you, then swear. If another language speaks more clearly to you, use it. If you're more articulate when you write, then write out your thoughts.

Think about it, talk to yourself about it, or write about it. Use your contemplative time to develop a powerful mind-set *that you will survive.*

If you had no other choice, could you kill?

Here is a topic you probably won't be discussing with your grandmother, but it's one that you must think about. What if you were in a struggle with an assailant who by his words or actions has made it clear that he wants to kill you or a loved one? You can't run away, you can't call the police, you have tried knocking him out, and you have even apologized. This guy is determined to kill you. When you have no other choice, could you kill him?

This is a dead serious question that you need to think about and do so without machismo and swagger. The reality of such a life and death battle isn't like anything you have seen on television or any scenario you have enacted in your training. To use your hands or a weapon to beat someone to the extent that he is lying at your feet with his life ebbing out of his body is a reality like nothing you have ever experienced.

Could you do it?

When defending your life or someone else's, you cannot fight with limitations and you cannot hold back with compassion, whether it's for religious reasons, fear of going to prison, or fear of being sued. If you believe that there are situations in which you would use deadly force (not everyone does), then you need to look into yourself to see what you must do to bring out your killer instinct. If you're absolutely convinced that you're fighting for your life, you owe it yourself and your family to use whatever personal psychological ploy you need to get the job done. If that means you have to view the assailant as a rabid, junkyard dog, so be it.

When you're attacked with viciousness, you must fight back with viciousness. Why would you do anything less? When you or an innocent loved one in your presence is attacked with deadly intent, you must fight back with ferocity of mind, spirit and physical technique. Look inside yourself. Know yourself. Know what you need to do to bring out that killer instinct.

If you're convinced you could never do it, think about the consequences.

It will never happen, you say. Reread the earlier segment called "Denial."

Don't die in training

You throw a fast roundhouse kick at your opponent but he blocks it easily and counters you once, twice, three times. *Man, that would have killed me,* you think.

Your opponent slashes at you with a rubber knife. You knock it aside but he comes right back and "slices" your neck, then circles around to "stab" your chest. *I'm so dead,* you think.

You notice that the new student's black belt is worn and tattered and his knuckles are huge and calloused. There is a dangerous intensity about the guy: his piercing eyes, the way his face looks too tight for his skull, and the way his over-developed muscles threaten to rip through his uniform. Then the instructor calls out your name to spar him. *I'm so dead,* you think.

Wrong! You're not dead in any of these training scenarios, and you should never, ever think that way. In police and military training there are scenarios in which if the student errs he is shot with blanks or Simunition rounds (similar to paint ball rounds but more painful) and declared dead by the instructor, his peers and himself. This is wrong and more and more trainers are recognizing that this is the wrong way to think in training.

Why would you train to die?

When your training partner blocks and counters you multiple times, you're not dead. Yes, he hit you – a lot - but you're not dead. So keep fighting.

When your training partner cuts your neck with that rubber knife, your instructor should bark at you, "You're not dead! I don't give you permission to die! Keep fighting!"

When you get called out to face that frightening black belt, you're not going to die. You don't have permission. You're commanded to keep fighting.

In my years as a cop, I saw people continue to fight when shot multiple times. I was involved in two separate incidents where gunshot victims had been hit five times in the head - and they were still fighting! In two others incidents the victims continued to fight for a minute after they had been shot in the heart. I once fought a guy who had been shot in the spine and would eventually be paralyzed. I saw a man continue to fight after he had had his ear sliced completely off.

If you're an instructor, never kill your students in training. They come to you to learn how to defend themselves so that they will survive, so that they will live. Not die. Teach them to keep fighting no matter what.

Your opponent hit you multiple times to your one hit; you got a cut across your throat; and the intense black belt is using you for the dojo mop. What do you do? You keep fighting. It's the only answer.

You're not dead until you're really dead – and that is how you train.

Never admit defeat, even if you have been wounded. The good soldier's painful wounds spur him to gather his strength .
Dutch theologian Desiderius Erasmus
Enchiridion Militus

As I put the finishing touches on this book, I'm nearing my 40th year in the martial arts. It's been an incredible journey that helped me to survive 29 years of law enforcement, kept me physically fit, been there when other parts of my life were falling apart, and has led to friendships with fantastic people.

While the martial arts have taken me around the globe, my solo training has taken me to that place inside myself where I must continuously battle such villains as pride, laziness, self-satisfaction, smugness, procrastination, and a host of others. These battles will never end, as they are a constant enemy of the human condition. But that is okay, because I like the challenge. I like the battles. And I especially like to fight them alone in a quiet place.

I hope this book will help you like your battles, too.

Train hard,
Loren Christensen

ABOUT THE AUTHOR

Loren W. Christensen began studying the martial arts in 1965. Over the years he has earned 10 black belts, seven in karate, two in jujitsu and one in arnis. He used his training as a military policeman in Saigon, Vietnam, a police officer for 25 years in Portland, Oregon, and as a karate tournament competitor, capturing over 50 wins.

As a free-lance writer, Loren has authored 30 books (over half on the martial arts), dozens of magazine articles, and edited a newspaper for nearly eight years. He has recently starred in five instructional martial arts videos.

Retired from police work, Loren now writes full time, teaches martial arts to a small group of students, and gives seminars on the fighting arts, police defensive tactics, and verbal judo.

To contact Loren, visit his website LWC Books at www. lwcbooks.com

Index

Also Available from Turtle Press:

Timing for Martial Arts
Complete Kickboxing
Ultimate Flexibility
Boxing: A 12 Week Course
The Fighter's Body: An Owner's Manual
The Science of Takedowns, Throws and Grappling for Self-defense
Fighting Science
Martial Arts Instructor's Desk Reference
Guide to Martial Arts Injury Care and Prevention
Solo Training
Solo Training 2
Fighter's Fact Book
Conceptual Self-defense
Martial Arts After 40
Warrior Speed
The Martial Arts Training Diary
The Martial Arts Training Diary for Kids
TeachingMartial Arts
Combat Strategy
The Art of Harmony
Total MindBody Training
1,001 Ways to Motivate Yourself and Others
Ultimate Fitness through Martial Arts
Taekwondo Kyorugi: Olympic Style Sparring

For more information:
Turtle Press
PO Box 290206
Wethersfield CT 06129-206
1-800-77-TURTL
e-mail: sales@turtlepress.com

http://www.turtlepress.com